Qualitative Inquiry Outside the Academy

INTERNATIONAL CONGRESS OF QUALITATIVE INQUIRY

The International Congress of Qualitative Inquiry has been hosted each May since 2005 by the International Center for Qualitative Inquiry at the University of Illinois, Urbana-Champaign. This volume, as well as preceding ones, are products of plenary sessions from these international congresses. All of these volumes are edited by Norman K. Denzin and Michael D. Giardina and are available from Left Coast Press, Inc. Series volumes include

For more information on these publications, or to order, go to www.LCoastPress.com

Qualitative Inquiry Outside the Academy

Norman K. Denzin
Michael D. Giardina
Editors

Walnut Creek
California

LEFT COAST PRESS, INC.
1630 North Main Street, #400
Walnut Creek, CA 94596
http://www.LCoastPress.com

ISBN 978-1-61132-895-0 hardcover
ISBN 978-1-61132-896-7 paperback
ISBN 978-1-61132-897-4 institutional eBook
ISBN 978-1-61132-898-1 consumer eBook

green press
INITIATIVE

Library of Congress Cataloging-in-Publication Data

Qualitative inquiry outside the academy / Norman K Denzin, Michael D Giardina, editors.
    International Congress of Qualitative Inquiry (9th : 2013 : University of Illinois, Urbana-Champaign)
        pages cm
    Summary: "This volume of plenary addresses and other key presentations from the 2013 International Congress of Qualitative Inquiry shows how scholars convert inquiry into spaces of advocacy in the outside world. The original chapters engage in debate on how qualitative research can be best used to advance the causes of social justice while addressing racial, ethnic, gender, and environmental disparities in education, welfare, and health care. Twenty contributors from six countries and multiple academic disciplines present models, cases, and experiences to show how qualitative research can be used as an effective instrument for social change. Sponsored by the International Congress of Qualitative Inquiry"—Provided by publisher.
    Includes bibliographical references and index.
    ISBN 978-1-61132-895-0 (hardback)—ISBN 978-1-61132-896-7 (paperback)—ISBN 978-1-61132-897-4 (institutional ebook)—ISBN 978-1-61132-898-1 (consumer eBook)

    1. Qualitative research. 2. Inquiry (Theory of knowledge) 3. Social advocacy. I. Denzin, Norman K. II. Giardina, Michael D., 1976- III. Title.
    H62.I657 2013
    001.4'2—dc23
                                    2014007951

Printed in the United States of America

♾™ The paper used in this publication meets the minimum requirements of American National Standard for Information Sciences—Permanence of Paper for Printed Library Materials, ANSI/NISO Z39.48–1992.

Contents

Acknowledgments

We thank our publisher of all publishers, Mitch Allen, for his continued support and guidance throughout the years. We also thank Michael Jennings for expert copyediting, Hannah Jennings for superlative production design, and Katie Flanagan for assistance in gathering the index. Many of the chapters contained in this book were presented as plenary or keynote addresses at the Ninth International Congress of Qualitative Inquiry, held at the University of Illinois, Urbana-Champaign, in May 2013. We thank the Institute of Communications Research, the College of Media, and the International Institute for Qualitative Inquiry for continued support of the Congress as well as those campus units that contributed time, fund, and/or volunteers to the effort.

The Congress, and by extension this book, would not have materialized without the tireless efforts of Mary Blair, Katia Curbelo, Ted Faust, Bryce Henson, Shantel Martinez, Robin Price, Nathalie Tiberghien, and James Salvo (the glue who continues to hold the whole thing together). For information on future Congresses, please visit www.icqi.org.

Norman K. Denzin
Michael D. Giardina
December 2013

Introduction

Qualitative Inquiry 'Outside' the Academy

Norman K. Denzin and Michael D. Giardina

Though questions regarding whether the university should serve strictly public rather than private interests no longer carry the weight of forceful criticism they did in the past, such questions are still crucial in addressing the purpose of higher education and what it might mean to imagine the university's full participation in public life as the protector and promoter of democratic values.

— Henry A. Giroux (2012)

I never think of myself as a researcher; I think of myself as a philosopher and a humanities person.

— Maxine Greene (n.d.)

Proem

This book was written primarily during the latter half of 2013, at a time in which public debates centered around such pressing topics in the United States as: the implementation of the Affordable Care Act; the Supreme Court decision overturning the Defense of Marriage Act, a decision which served as a major turning point in

Qualitative Inquiry Outside the Academy edited by Norman K. Denzin and Michael D. Giardina, 9–31. © 2014 Left Coast Press, Inc. All rights reserved.

favor of equal rights for gays and lesbians; the release of classified documents by former U.S. National Security Agency contractor Edward Snowden; the racial politics of the George Zimmerman trial;[1] the Boston Marathon bombing; the existential crisis posed by Chronic Traumatic Encephalopathy (CTE) on contact sports; ever-growing levels of economic inequality; and the increasingly evident effects of global warming. Looking beyond U.S. borders, we also witnessed debates concerning: the death of former South African president Nelson Mandela, and his place in history; the election of Pope Francis, and the economic and social justice messages he has preached;[2] the civil war in Syria; and the (mainly but not exclusively) economic protests in Brazil.

Yet, too often in these debates are the voices of critically engaged scholars absent from the public discourse, whether as expert commentators in traditional media outlets or as someone who is "*translating* and *shortening* scholarly knowledge for *lay* persons outside of the research specialty" (Kalleberg, 2012, p. 46, emphases in original)—the latter definition of which we might generally associate with someone who acts as a public intellectual. By public, of course, we mean to invoke the word in opposition to the notion of a *private* intellectual, or someone who writes or directs his or her energies to the cloistered academy alone, and who through his or her very acts as a scholar contributes to "sustaining a knowledge economy that rewards its participants when they invest in burying and restricting knowledge" (Burton, 2009, para. 7).

Drawing in part from Grant Jarvie (2007), we have thus framed our volume to, in different ways, consider (at least) the following three questions:

• What is the capacity of qualitative inquiry to produce social change?
• What is the role of the public intellectual?
• What do we see as a way forward toward such ends, thinking 'outside' the academy? Or, put differently, what might a new public intellectualism look like in light of neoliberal assaults on education?[3]

Consider the following:

In a highly influential presidential address to the American Sociological Association's annual conference in 2004, Michael

Buroway (2005) made a forceful call to arms in favor of a public sociology. As part of his since-updated argument (Buroway, 2008), he characterized the field of sociology—though we believe it fair to speak to higher education more broadly—as increasingly being "a hyper-professionalized sociology that fetishized its separation from society, a self-referential community that organized and policed the exchange of papers and ideas, remote from the world it studied, a community that inducted its graduate students as though they were entering a secret society" (p. 191). Or, as Todd Gitlin (2006) framed it, that we have over the last two decades experienced an explosion of "not-so-public intellectuals—obscure writers and not-so-big thinkers who were content to train specialists"; in other words, academics who were "committed to professional advancement through hyperspecialization and technical proficiency and who were (therefore, it seemed) inhospitable to both broad-gauged social thought and clear, generally accessible writing" (p. 123). C. Wright Mills (1959) goes back even farther, as Gitlin rightly points out, identifying a similar turn in *The Sociological Imagination*, when he referred to the professionalization of the social sciences as an agglomeration governed by "a set of bureaucratic techniques which inhibit social inquiry by 'methodological pretensions', which congest such work by obscurantist conceptions, or which trivialize it by concern with minor problems unconnected with publicly relevant issues" (p. 20; also quoted in Gitlin, p. 126).

To this end, it would behoove us to resist the pressures for a single "gold standard" of research quality and excellence, even as we endorse conversations about evidence, inquiry, and empirically warranted conclusions (see Cannella & Lincoln, 2011). We cannot let one group define the key terms in the conversation. To do otherwise is to allow the rigid disciplinarity of the scientifically based research community define the moral and epistemological terrain on which we stand, for neither they, nor the government (nor grant funding agencies, promotion and tenure committees, etc.) own the word 'science' (nor 'quality,' 'impact,' or 'excellence'). Jürgen Habermas (1972) anticipated this nearly 40 years ago:

> The link between empiricism, positivism and the global audit culture is not accidental and it is more than just technical. Such technical approaches deflect attention away from the deeper

issues of value and purpose. They make radical critiques much more difficult to mount … and they render largely invisible partisan approaches to research under the politically useful pretense that judgments are about objective quality only. In the process, human needs and human rights are trampled upon and democracy as we need it is destroyed. (p. 122; 2006, p. 193; see also Smith & Hodkinson, 2005, p. 930)[4]

To give but one example of this professionalization in practice, Patricia Leavy (2012) quite rightly points out that "the existing tenure and promotion system continues to enforce disciplinarity" (para. 4).[5] She continues:

Academics have clear incentives to design small-scale projects that can be completed and published quickly. Moreover, sole authorship is favored over co-authorship and collaboration. Further, peer-reviewed articles and/or monographs are required for tenure and promotion at most, if not all, institutions. By requiring research that produces such limited outcomes, researchers' hands are tied. It is also clear that journal articles are highly unlikely to reach the public so by privileging this form the entire academic structure discourages scholarship that is truly of value to the public. (para. 4)

Although we may not agree with Leavy's broader argument completely, we do concur that the context she contests is one that clearly promotes the professionalization of the professoriate—that promotes positivist social sciences as currently practiced and taught in U.S. higher education. It is a context that the radical historian, Howard Zinn (1997), cogently outlined in his essay, "The Uses of Scholarship," in which he noted the five rules that "sustain the wasting of knowledge" (pp. 502–507):

1. Carry on "disinterested scholarship."
2. Be objective.
3. Stick to your discipline.
4. To be "scientific" requires neutrality.
5. Scholars must, in order to be "rational," avoid "emotionalism."

Put differently, what Zinn is talking about is "intellectual professionalism" of the kind challenged by Edward Said (1996), who defined it as:

Thinking of your work as an intellectual as something you do for a living, between the hours of nine and five with one eye on the clock, and another cocked at what is considered to be proper, professional behavior—not rocking the boat, not straying outside the accepted paradigms or limits, making yourself marketable and above all presentable, hence uncontroversial and unpolitical and "objective." (p. 55)[6]

Taking this line of thought to its natural end, Michael Silk, Anthony Bush, and David L. Andrews (2010) contend that such "*proper* professional behavior—and in our present moment we have to equate *proper* with that which holds the centre, the *gold standard*, EBR [Evidence-Based Research]—represents a threat to our *critical sense*, our ability to be prepared to be self-reflexive to relations of power" (p. 120, emphases in original).[7]

What we are seeing in the present tense then, at least in some regard, is the result of the increasing politics of research and evidence governing higher education. We have previously chronicled this dynamic in detail in other venues (see, e.g., Denzin & Giardina, 2013; Giardina & Laurendeau, 2013; Giardina & Newman, in press), but suffice to say, it can be summarized as follows: the increasing demands of the neoliberal university (one governed by the market-relations of intellectual products, the publish or perish mantra, and shrinking state and federal funding for higher education), coupled with a wide-spread economic crisis, increasing political and administrative emphases placed on the STEM disciplines (science, technology, engineering, and mathematics) and the job-market utility of such careers, and a decreasing public engagement with and support for the arts and sciences, have led not only to a the popular "embrace of a type of rabid individualism, anti-intellectualism, and political illiteracy" in the general public but also, and equally dangerously, have led to "intellectual and critical thought [becoming] transformed into a commodity to be sold to the highest bidder" (Giroux, 2010, paras. 4, 7).

This latter point speaks especially to our location in academia as critical scholars, and one of the primary reasons we titled our volume *Qualitative Inquiry* Outside *the Academy*; that is, *outside of the new normal ways of doing business as teachers and researchers in the university*:

> The unseen struggle we face is over the commodification of knowledge (see Giroux, 2013) and the marketization of science (i.e., engaging in research solely on the condition of its appeal to funding agencies and external dollars), what Finklestein (2002) argues results in us—*public* intellectuals—becoming nothing more than purveyors of "McKnowledge." ... For what does it look like to realize the above, to operate in, to be rewarded in, to "get ahead" in, such an environment—one that increasingly (if not explicitly) favors what Maxwell (2004) calls a reemergent scientism borne out of a positivist, so-called evidence-based epistemology (i.e., "scientifically-based research," or SBR) in which researchers are encouraged (if not outright directed) to employ "rigorous, systematic, and objective methodology to obtain reliable and valid knowledge" (Ryan & Hood, 2006). (Giardina & Laurendeau, 2013, p. 245)

Joe Sartelle (1992) thus raises a key question for us when he writes: "What is fundamentally at stake here is a question of accountability—to whom are we, as professional academics, finally responsible?" (para. 5). In the contemporary moment in general and in the halls of the neoliberal university in specific, Sartelle outlines, the answer to this question more often than not is: "academics must be accountable to their professional colleagues" (and, we would assume, the bureaucratic dictates of that profession following his line of thinking, in order to gain promotion and tenure, external grants, and other professional benefits). But, as Sartelle continues, we "need to start seeing ourselves as primarily accountable not to our fellow academics, but to a larger public—however that may be defined" (para. 11).

And why?

Because, as Patricia Hill Collins (2013) reminds us, we "must remember that, when it comes to our ability to claim the power of ideas, *we are the fortunate ones*. For our parents, friends, relatives, and neighbors who lack literacy, work long hours, and/or consume seemingly endless doses of so-called reality television, the excitement of hearing new ideas that challenge social inequalities can be risky" (pp. 38–39, emphasis ours). Because of this, and following Said (1996), it is our *responsibility*, as the fortunate ones, to act as "someone whose whole being is staked on a critical sense, a sense of being unwilling to accept easy formulas, or ready-made clichés, or the smooth, ever-so-accommodating confirmations of what the powerful or conventional have to say, and what they do. Not just passively unwillingly, but actively willing to say so in public" (p. 13). Said's point is similar to the position taken by Noam Chomsky (1968), who offered the following manifesto in the *New York Review of Books* at the height of the Vietnam War:

> Intellectuals are in a position to expose the lies of governments, to analyze actions according to their causes and motives and often hidden intentions. In the Western world, at least, they have the power that comes from political liberty, from access to information and freedom of expression. For a privileged minority, Western democracy provides the leisure, the facilities, and the training to seek the truth lying hidden behind the veil of distortion and misrepresentation, ideology and class interest, through which the events of current history are presented to us. The responsibilities of intellectuals, then, are much deeper than what [Dwight] Macdonald calls the "responsibility of people," given the unique privileges that intellectuals enjoy. (para. 2)

Yet it is important to acknowledge that operating outside the academy is not as straightforward as making a simple declarative statement in the affirmative toward such an end (nor, we would caution, is it about forsaking publishing in scholarly journals or the like). George Ritzer (2006), the esteemed American sociologist, notes that even though his most famous book—*The McDonaldization of Society*—has sold more than 200,000 copies and been translated into at least 15 languages, this has "not made me a public sociologist" (p. 211). He continues, explaining that books published by academic presses "are highly unlikely to attract much public attention or even be stocked by many book stores" (in contrast to books published by trade presses, such as Simon & Schuster) (p. 211). Importantly, Ritzer asks a key follow-up question, one that is deeply embedded in the market relations of ideas:

> Why, you might ask, have I not published with a trade press? The answer: They are not interested in publishing my work! I have tried, on many occasions, but neither publishers, nor literary agents who are a necessary conduit to the trade publishers,

have shown any interest. Sociology has a bad odour among people in the trade publishing business and that is another important reason why there is so little public sociology. (p. 212)

(As, we would add, is true for all critical arts and sciences in the present moment.) Ritzer's conclusion, then, is that the changes necessary to make one's scholarship accessible to the mainstream (potentially) forfeits its nuanced criticality, or is watered down for public consumption as "McKnowledge."

Although we agree with Ritzer on his overarching point about audience matters (to borrow a phrase from Laurel Richardson [this volume]), we would disagree that speaking only and/or directly to the lay public constitutes public sociology or public intellectualism. Suffice to say, while CNN or *The Today Show* or Simon & Schuster may not be interested in hearing or publishing Ritzer's insights on globalization (most assuredly a loss on their respective parts), that does not mean one must foreclose on speaking to and with the public, or engaging with various publics, outside of the academy (or, to be sure, thinking about how we act as scholars outside the strictures of "the Academy," a point we address below). Consider the growing numbers of high-volume readership academic collectives or blogs. *The Feminist Wire*, for example, claims a weekly total of 50,000–70,000 unique visitors and over one million unique visitors per year. Edited by esteemed scholars Monica J. Casper, Tamura A. Lomax, and Darnell L. Moore, its mission is "to provide socio-political and cultural critique of anti-feminist, racist, and imperialist politics pervasive in all forms and spaces of private and public lives of individuals globally" and "seeks to valorize and sustain pro-feminist representations and create alternative frameworks to build a just and equitable society" (Mission/Vision statement of *The Feminist Wire*, 2014). Or *The Society Pages*, an "online, multidisciplinary social science project" edited by sociologists Douglas Hartmann and Chris Uggen, supported by the W. W. Norton & Company. The site features the *Sociological Images* resource, as well as hosts *Contexts* magazine (the public engagement journal of the American Sociological Association) and the Scholars Strategy Network, directed by political scientist Theda Skocpol of Harvard University. Or *The Public Intellectuals Project*, which is supported by the Social Sciences and Humanities

Research Council of Canada and organized by Henry Giroux; the Project's mission is "to provide a forum for academics, students, activists, artists, cultural workers, and the broader community to communicate ideas, engage in dialogue, and support higher education and other cultural spheres as vital places to think and act collectively in the face of a growing crisis of shared public values and meaningful democratic participation" (Mission statement of *The Public Intellectuals Project*, 2014). Yet how often have we written something for or otherwise contributed to sites such as the ones listed above?[8]

At the same time, we should not be caught up in the idea of speaking only (or just directly) to 'the public' as a means of understanding working or directing our attention outside the academy. Nor should we, as Martyn Hammersley (2005) cautions, "allow the close encounters promised by the notion of evidence-based policymaking, or even 'public social science', to seduce us into illusions about ourselves and our work" (p. 5). Giroux (2001) makes this point abundantly clear in his essay on cultural studies as performative politics:

> Rather than reducing the notion of the public intellectual to an academic fashion plate ready for instant consumption by *The New York Times* and *Lingua Franca*, a number of critical theorists have reconstituted themselves within the ambivalencies and contradictions of their own distinct personal histories while simultaneously recognizing and presenting themselves through their role as social critics.... As public intellectuals, these cultural workers not only refuse to support the academic professionalization of social criticism, they also take seriously their role as critical educators and the potentially oppositional space of all pedagogical sites, including (but not restricted to) the academy. (p. 14)

It is our belief, then, that qualitative inquiry (and the qualitative inquiry community) can and should contribute to this discussion, in both acts and deeds.[9] Critical scholars are committed to showing how the practices of critical, interpretive qualitative research can help change the world in positive ways. They are committed to creating new ways of making the practices of critical qualitative inquiry central to the workings of a free democratic society. They can show, for example, how battered wives interpret the shelters, hotlines, and public services that are made available to them by social welfare agencies. Through the use of personal experience narratives the perspectives of women and workers can be compared and contrasted, with some tangible end in sight (see, e.g., Flick, this volume). Likewise, the assumptions, often belied by the facts of experience, that are held by various interested parties—policy makers, clients, welfare workers, online professionals—can be located, evaluated, deconstructed, shown to be correct, or incorrect (see Becker, 1967). And, to wit, strategic points of intervention into social situations can be identified. In such ways, the services of an agency and a program can be improved and evaluated. And, importantly, it is possible to suggest "alternative moral points of view from which the problem," the policy, and the program can be interpreted and assessed (see Becker, 1967, pp. 239–240). Because of its emphasis on experience and its meanings, the interpretive method suggests that programs must always be judged by and from the point of view of the persons most directly affected. Its emphasis on the uniqueness of each life holds up the individual case as the measure of the effectiveness of all applied programs.

As critical scholars, our task is to make history present, to make the future present, to undo the past (Smith, 2004, p. xvi). In *The Sociological Imagination*, Mills challenged us to work from biography to history. He asked us to begin with lived experience but to anchor experience in its historical moment. He invited us to see ourselves as 'universal singulars,' as persons who universalize, in our particular lives, this concrete historical moment (see Denzin, 2010, p. 115). *We hope this volume serves to renew his challenge to us all.*

The Chapters

Qualitative Inquiry Outside the Academy is organized into four parts: Public, With, Outside, and Beyond. Henry A. Giroux ("Public Intellectuals Against the Neoliberal University") opens our volume with a critical analysis of (North American) higher education under the throes of neoliberalism. He documents the need to reclaim our public institutions from private demands—demands that have turned universities into shopping malls, critical thought into market relations, and cast civic education and democratic values off to the side. In so doing, he advocates for academics to once again take up the mantel of public intellectualism, rejecting "market-driven pedagogy" in favor of what Edward Said referred to as a "pedagogy of mindfulness" that combines "rigor and clarity, on the one hand, with civic courage and political commitment, on the other" (Giroux, this volume).

Laurel Richardson's chapter ("Audience Matters") follows, illustrating what it is like to be an engaged public intellectual in the sense that Giroux introduces, and the politics of research that create obstacles for existing as such. Recalling instances from her career in which the public (i.e., mainstream, lay, non-academic) served as her primary audience, as well as instances in which orienting her scholarship in such a manner brushed up against the expectations of her home department, Richardson both delivers a forceful critique of scholarly life and presents a way forward toward realizing a productive public intellectualism.

Part II presents varied looks at working *with*, rather than conducting research *on*, communities, especially those of an Indigenous or Global South context. Maria Mayan and Christine Daum ("Politics and Public Policy, Social Justice, and Qualitative Research") open the section with their discussion of the intersection of public policy as it relates to community-based participatory research (CBPR) in the service of social justice aims. Which is to say, research derived from and driven by the community in question (e.g., First Nations, refugee group, etc.). To this end, Mayan and Daum write of the ways such change-oriented CBPR draws attention to neglected issues, invites debate, decenters academic authority, and dissuades the "us versus them" dichotomy often found in research acts. As such, they advocate for an approach to research that challenges us to expose our values and politics, work with (rather than against) those in power; levies productive critique rather than criticizes without regard to the sensitivity or realities of the historical present; and openly challenges our own system of doing things (both research and otherwise).

In a similar vein, Margaret Kovach ("Thinking *Through* Theory: Contemplating Indigenous Situated Research and Policy") makes the forceful case that if the "Indigenous voice is not being heard in the research theory that shapes Indigenous policy development, whose voice, then, is being relied upon? How trustworthy is this voice in offering an accounting of Indigenous people's lives?" She turns to policy debates within Indigenous education as a clear example of the theory/research/policy dynamic in action. She concludes by positing how, more often than not, outsider theorizing in research and policy has diminished rather than upheld Indigenous peoples.

Keeping our attention on the complex relationships forged between research and policy, politics and scholarship, C. Darius Stonebanks ("Confronting Old Habits Overseas: An Analysis of Reciprocity between Malawian Stakeholders and a Canadian University") chronicles the initial development process of working collaboratively with community members in the growth of an Experiential Learning Project (ELP) between a Canadian university and a community in the rural region of Kasungu, Malawi. Stonebanks acknowledges that while praxis was "an essential guiding concept" to the project, and that with it one of the main educational goals was to "demystify theory through application while at the same time embracing humility in one's endeavors and the complexity of the pursuit towards a common good," actualizing such goals was fraught with productive struggles between all parties involved. In revealing and analyzing such struggles, Stonebanks offers a practical research-based road map of both the development and the implementation of a reciprocal ELP-based education model in a developing country that can serve as a guide for others in similar positions.

Staying on the African continent, Beth Blue Swadener and Bekiszwe S. Ndimande ("Global Reform Policies Meet Local Communities: Critical Inquiry on the Children's Act in South Africa") focus on human rights policies, practices and attitudes in South Africa, and especially on the Children's Act of 2007, which covers a range of children's rights issues, including protection, provision, and participation. More specifically, they draw from interviews with parents and professionals regarding the implementation of the Children's Act in South Africa and how it is understood and interpreted within communities, particularly Indigenous communities. They conclude by showing the "limitations of policies constructed within Western perspectives and implemented in an African country with less attention to the local cultural values as they relate to children."

Moving to a Māori context, Russell Bishop ("Freeing Ourselves: An Indigenous Response to Neo-Colonial Dominance in Research, Classrooms, Schools, and Education Systems") "demonstrates how theorizing and practice that has grown from within Māori epistemologies has been applied in a number of settings as counter-narratives to the dominant discourses in New Zealand." He does so by elaborating Kaupapa Māori research examples, such as the "centrality of the process of establishing extended family-like relationships, understood in Māori as *whanaungatanga*," and how such research was then translated to classroom settings in mainstream schools. He then discusses how 'scaling-up' Indigenous-based education reform may hold the promise for "freeing public schools and the education system that supports them from neo-colonial dominance."

César Cisneros Puebla ("Indigenous Researchers and Epistemic Violence") brings the section to a close with an impassioned call for a "sociology of our own practices as researchers, as scientists, as persons of flesh and blood." Grounding himself in the modernity of his colonial past as a Latin American scholar, Cisneros Puebla argues that knowing more about ourselves in "historical, geopolitical, and epistemological views" is a major challenge, true, but that knowing more about ourselves is also a matter of "ethics and responsibilities." As such, he delves into discussions concerning core and peripheries in the 'knowledge divide'; specifically, the "historical consequence of the global dynamics of capitalism" that has divided the world into the core and the peripheries—including *researchers*. He then draws from a Mexican example that illustrates this "division of scientific labor in the context of globalized knowledge"; that of so-called "cover-science," or universalizing the local knowledge of 'great authors' of the Global North (in other words, the copying, drawing from, or otherwise importing of particular theoretical perspectives or traditions into another context; something, we might say, U.S. scholars did with British cultural studies in the 1990s). He concludes by arguing that "developing autochthonous research methods is decisive to overcome the epistemic...violence," as well as to "enrich our practices as researchers by getting into new ways of experiencing relationships and human interactions."

Part III shifts our focus to interventionist research related to health care practices and marginalized community relations. Uwe Flick and Gundula Röhnsch ("Episodic and Expert Interviews beyond Academia: Health Service Research in the Context of Migration") address problems faced by scholars in health services research who wish to conduct expert interviews and interviews in different languages. More specifically, they report on both of these instances with respect to the episodic interview. As such, they outline the use-value of expert interviews for analyzing the professionals' views on health problems, for the clients who have these problems and use (or do not use) professional services, and for analyzing institutional routines. Additionally, they combine small-scale narratives and question/answer approaches for analyzing clients' experiences in the health system (in this case, Russian-speaking migrants).

Donna M. Mertens ("Ethical Issues of Interviewing Members of Marginalized Communities Outside Academic Contexts") continues the discussion of interviewing, this time from the perspective of interviews conducted with members of marginalized communities. To this end, she details examples drawn from her research and involvement with the Deaf community, including "the identification of community members, inclusion/exclusion criteria, diversity within communities, appropriate invitational strategies, support in terms of communication and other logistical issues, strategies for addressing power inequities to insure accuracy and comprehensive representation, and responsiveness to cultural issues in terms of confidentiality and protection or revelation of identity."

Janice Morse, Kim Martz, Lory Maddox, and Terrie Vann-Ward ("Closing the Qualitative Practice/Application Gaps in Health Care Research: The Role of Qualitative Inquiry") discuss the use of qualitative research in health care, for qualitative health research that fills existing gaps in health care. To do this, they present three case study examples of such research in practice in which practitioners may come to a better or more holistic understanding of: 1) chronic and disabling conditions, such as Parkinson's disease and the lifestyle lived by those with it; 2) so-called 'work-arounds' by nurses who deal with bar-code medication administration

(BCMA) technology; and 3) new healthcare environments, such as assisted-living facilities (ALFs), and the ways in which 'consumers' of said environments come to understand them in their daily lives.

Part IV endeavors to move the discussion into the realm of the performative, and the promise such performance holds for translating research across the public-private divides. Virginie Magnat ("Performance Ethnography: Decolonizing Research and Pedagogy") opens the section by looking at performance ethnography in the context of indigenous epistemologies. Drawing from the work of Meyer, Tuhiwai Smith, Wilson, and Absolon, she argues that "decolonizing performance ethnography necessarily entails scrutinizing Euro-American conceptions of research and pedagogy" and suggests that engaging with "Indigenous epistemologies and methodologies can foster new embodied engagements and experiential solidarities.

Cynthia Dillard ("(Re)Membering the Grandmothers: Theorizing Poetry to (Re)Think the Purposes of Black Education and Research") draws on Black world women's poetry to theorize and reconceptualize theory, purpose, and practices in Black education. She foregrounds her discussion by specifically engaging with the works/words of Audre Lorde, and then moves forward to highlight the work of poets such as Abena P. A. Busia, Meiling Jin, Maud Sulter, Marita Golden, and Maya Angelou. From such endarkened feminist frameworks, Dillard argues, it is possible to engage new metaphors, texts, and representations of the cultural and spiritual knowledge of Black people worldwide.

Jane Speedy ("Ghosts, Traces, Sediments, and Accomplices in Psychotherapeutic Dialogue with Sue and Gracie") turns the discussion back to a clinical setting, and shows the promise of qualitative inquiry for engaging in those spaces. Specifically, she discusses narrative therapists "who are encouraged to listen to and share the stories from their own lives and the lives of others that have been evoked by clients' stories, believing that the powerful evocations that one person's stories can evoke in another are often sufficiently therapeutic events." To this end, Speedy writes through a performative lens how in her own work as a narrative therapist she often finds herself "accompanied by the voices and stories of accomplices who are dead, or imagined, or literary figures, as well as members of [her] own family and the lives of previous clients."

Brian Rusted ("Stampedagogy") next reflects on the value that art, nostalgia, and heritage play in the cultural pedagogy of the Calgary Stampede (an annual rodeo, exhibition, and festival held in Calgary, Alberta, Canada). His chapter thus explores the visual practices of this cultural performance and the social shaping of discursive performances of taste. Rather than offer a close or closed reading of the Calgary Stampede as a visual text, Rusted troubles the intersection of visual culture and performance as a way to begin a conversation about what the Stampede teaches and the possibilities for a sensory, embodied pedagogy.

Mirka Koro-Ljungberg and Fred Boateng ("A Marxist Methodology for Critical Collaborative Inquiry") bring the section—and the volume—to a close, as they experiment with representation of the pamphlet. They argue that "visual materials can serve as effective tools to break free from grand narratives by questioning the connections between seeing and knowing." Moreover, they aim to promote dialogue and engagement with those both inside and outside academia who are interested in methodological concepts and the practice of critical collaborative inquiry.

By Way of a Conclusion

So at the end of the first decade of the 21st century it is time to move forward. It is time to open up new spaces, time to explore new discourses. We need to find new ways of connecting people, and their personal troubles, with social justice methodologies. We need to become better accomplished in linking these interventions to those institutional sites where troubles are turned into public issues, and public issues transformed into social policy.

In their essay on the politics of research, Giardina and Newman (pp. 716–717) offer a series of practical and programmatic recommendations toward such an end, which we believe can serve as concrete starting points:[10]

1. *We must acknowledge that we are not innocent actors in academia.* How often do we agree to or volunteer to serve on grant award committees? Institutional Review Boards? Promotion and tenure committees? Are we standing for elected office in scholarly associations? Serving on editorial boards or as editors of journals in our field/s? Joining our faculty union, as

members if not as office holders? Engaging with research that takes as its primary goal social justice and social change rather than solely contributing to lines on a CV?

2. *We should take every opportunity to broadly communicate our research beyond just the traditional academic journal.* How often do we endeavor to publish critical essays outside of the scholarly journal, whether in the traditional press (e.g., in the *Atlantic Monthly*, the *New York Times*, the *Nation*, *Harpers*) or on public sociology and cultural criticism websites like the ones discussed earlier in this introduction? How often do we engage in open-access publishing, art exhibitions (see Rusted, this volume), or performance theater (see Magnat, this volume)? Although not necessarily a viable option for some, especially the untenured in departments that may frown on anything that does not have an Impact Factor attached to it, what are the rest of us waiting for? Moreover, how often do we advocate in our departments or colleges for such work to 'count,' whether for merit bonuses or in the promotion and tenure process?

3. *We must mentor our doctoral students to be cognizant of the politics of research and the context of research into which they are stepping.* On this point, the late Bud Goodall said it best: "How well do we train generations of writers in the practicalities of being a writer? About getting a literary agent? Writing literary inquiry? Putting together a blog? Putting together a website? These are things that should be part and parcel of the enterprise that we call academic preparation for the future. Because unless we give our students those tools, unless we cultivate that, it's like throwing someone into a very competitive ... market without any ... skill other than that they can write and they want to have a voice, and in this day and age *that's just not quite enough*. So what do we do? We nurture the young" (Ellis et al., 2008, pp. 330–331, emphasis ours).

4. *We must engage with our undergraduate students and programs lest they fall victim to the dictates of the corporate university.* The more influence and importance that is placed on graduate credit hours and graduate teaching, the more our undergraduate programs become targets (especially in the humanities). Targets to be leftover crumbs to be taught by (well-meaning,

for sure) doctoral students, grossly underpaid adjunct lec-
turers, or disinterested faculty members who would prefer
to work with graduate students. Targets to be shunted into
"online-only" course offerings that, while bringing in higher
differential tuition dollars and technology fees, erase face-to-
face contact and the building of community in the classroom,
erase dialogue and disagreement between students in a shared
environment.

5. *We must engage with and continue to build a community of
qualitative researchers.* We need to support and invigo-
rate discussion and debate about the state of our fields/
profession at major conferences (such as the International
Congress of Qualitative Inquiry, Association for Cultural
Studies, National Communication Association, American
Sociological Association, American Educational Research
Association, and so forth).

To these five points raised by Giardina and Newman, we would
add the following two:

6. *We should endeavor to make connections with and generate dialogue across disciplines, especially disciplines we often critique as
being part of the problem, such as those in schools of business or the
medical sciences.* As Newman writes (2013): "Remaking our
work in conversation with the *technes* of natural, 'exact science', by using fabrications the political public most readily
knows to be 'research', we can become better public peda-
gogues; we can become better advocates, better citizens of the
humanistic and democratic traditions" (p. 397). Would we
be willing to trade methodological purity for a language that
local city councils will actually listen to? As Denzin (2010)
reminds us: "We all want social justice. Most of us want to
influence social policy. All of us—positivists, postpositivists,
poststructuralists, posthumanists, feminists, queer theorists,
social workers, nurses, sociologists, educators, anthropologists—share this common concern" (p. 42). *How* we get there,
then, is perhaps less important than *actually getting there.* This
must be done with great care, of course, but there is potential
in entertaining such an idea.

7. *We must get beyond the notion that we are* private *intellectuals.* As Gideon Burton (2009) writes, "A scholar is doomed to a life of private intellectual inquiry and expression" if he or she only defines him or herself as a "scholar" in the traditional sense of the term—as someone dedicated only to developing and perpetuating "disciplinary knowledge" (para. 4). Too much is at stake to situate ourselves within such constricting language. Thus do we need to move outside and beyond what Arundhati Roy (2001) calls "the old Brahminical instinct: colonize knowledge, build four walls around it, and use it to your advantage" (para. 19), seeking instead to "de-professionalize the public debate on matters that vitally affect the lives of ordinary people" (para. 17). This does not mean abandoning our critical faculties, of course; rather, it means we should move beyond what Said (1996) termed "intellectual professionalism" to embrace a disruptive public intellectualism that is an inherent part of our jobs. To this end, we must contest the growing scale and scope of the audit culture within the university, for, as Bronwyn Davies and Eva B. Peterson (2005) argue, "These managerial techniques [governing intellectual professionalism] individualize performance. They require individuals to negotiate annual recognizable accounts of themselves as appropriate subjects, and to stage a performance of themselves as appropriate(d) subjects. The academic accomplishes him or herself, for the moment of that performance at least, *as* a neo-liberal subject" (p. 81, emphasis in original; also cited in Sparkes, 2013, p. 5).

We leave you with the words of Howard Zinn (2008), that great American writer of critical history:

> To be a public intellectual is the most satisfying of endeavors. It is a proper role for someone who loves ideas and the transmission of ideas, but who does not want to be isolated in the library or the classroom while the cities burn and people go homeless and the violence of war ravages whole continents. (p. 491)

Notes

1 George Zimmerman killed 16-year-old Trayvon Martin; he was acquitted on charges of second-degree murder and of manslaughter charges under the argument that Zimmerman had acted in self-defense.

2 See the 2013 apostolic exhortation of Pope Francis, *Evangelii Gaudium*, in which the Pope referred to unfettered capitalism as "a new tyranny."

3 Of course there is a long history, in many different disciplines—social work, public health, nursing, anthropology, sociology, psychology, education— of critical inquiry done outside the academy. This includes participatory action research (PAR), critical collaborative inquiry, public anthropology, clinical/ community psychology, and a range of other praxis-based practices that include social work and public health interventions. This is collaborative work. It privileges issues of equity and social justice. It addresses community defined needs, seeking a voice that is inclusive and responsive to the language of the people. Critical public inquiry aims to respond to the realities of the world today, with the intent of always working for the public good, however personally defined.

4 Pierre Bourdieu elaborates (1998) on Habermas's point, stating, "The dominants, technocrats, and empiricists of the right and the left are hand in glove with reason and the universal. … More and more rational, scientific technical justifications, always in the name of objectivity, are relied upon. In this way the audit culture perpetuates itself" (p. 90). Most assuredly, there is more than one version of disciplined, rigorous inquiry—counter-science, little science, unruly science, practical science—and such inquiry need not go by the name of science. We must have a model of disciplined, rigorous, thoughtful, reflective inquiry, a "postinterpretivism that seeks meaning but less innocently, that seeks liberation but less naively, and that … reaches toward understanding, transformation and justice" (Preissle, 2006, p. 692) . It does not need to be called a science, contested or otherwise, as some have proposed (St. Pierre & Rouleston, 2006; Eisenhart, 2006; Preissle, 2006).

5 This paragraph, and the one that follows it, is drawn directly from Giardina & Newman, in press.

6 See also our arguments along these lines in Denzin & Giardina, 2012, especially pp. 19–22.

7 As Denzin stated in reflecting on the state of tenure vis-à-vis qualitative inquiry: "I'm aware of three tenure cases this year where people are being turned back for tenure by campus committees and deans, promotions committees, because they're doing first-person narratives and autoethnography. And they're being turned back by people who don't have a clue about this work and who are passing judgments on this work" (in Ellis et al., 2008, p. 332). The impetus, then, is on us to make sure this doesn't happen.

8 In the spirit of full disclosure, we have both contributed in some form to *The Society Pages* (Giardina, in the form of an hour-long podcast about a recent book as part of the site's Office Hours series, see thesocietypages.org/office-hours/2013/01/07/) and *The Public Intellectual Project* (Denzin, an interview about qualitative inquiry, cooperwhite.com/denzin.html).

9 This paragraph re-works material in Denzin (2001, pp. 1–7).

10 The remaining paragraphs in this section are drawn directly from Giardina & Denzin, 2013.

References

Becker, H. S. (1967). Whose side are we on? *Social Problems, 14*(3), 239–247.

Buroway, M. (2005). 2004 Presidential address: For public sociology. *American Sociological Review, 70*(1), 1–28.

Buroway, M. (2008). Public sociology in the age of Obama. *Innovation: The European Journal of Social Science Research, 22*(2), 189–199.

Burton, G. (2009). A scholar or an intellectual? *Academic Evolution.* www.academicevolution.com/2009/04/scholar-or-public-intellectual.html (accessed January 3, 2014).

Cannella, G. S., & Lincoln, Y. S. (2011). Ethics, research regulations, and critical social science. In N. K. Denzin & Y. S. Lincoln (Eds.), *The SAGE handbook of qualitative research* (4th ed., pp. 81–90). Thousand Oaks, CA: Sage.

Chomsky, N. (February 23, 1968). The responsibility of intellectuals. *The New York Review of Books* (Special Supplement). www.nybooks.com/articles/archives/1967/feb/23/a-special-supplement-the-responsibility-of-intelle/ (accessed December 3, 2013).

Collins, P. H. (2013). Truth-telling and intellectual activism. *Contexts, 12*(1), 36–39.

Davies, B., & Peterson, E. B. (2005). Neoliberal discourse in the academy: The forestalling of collective resistance. *Learning and Teaching in the Social Sciences, 2*(1), 77–98.

Denzin, N. K. (2010). *The qualitative manifesto: A call to arms.* Walnut Creek, CA: Left Coast Press, Inc.

Denzin, N. K., & Giardina, M. D. (2013). *Qualitative inquiry and global crises.* Walnut Creek, CA: Left Coast Press, Inc..

Ellis, C., Bochner, A. P., Denzin, N. K., Goodall, H. L., Jr., Pelias, R., & Richardson, L. (2008). Let's get personal: First-generation autoethnographers reflect on writing personal narratives. In N. K. Denzin & M. D. Giardina (Eds.), *Qualitative inquiry and the politics of evidence* (pp. 309–334). Walnut Creek, CA: Left Coast Press, Inc.

Evangelii Gaudium. (2013). Apostolic exhortation *Evangelii Gaudium* of the Holy Father Francis to the bishops, clergy, consecrated persons and the lay faithful on the proclamation of the Gospel in today's world. The Vatican. www.vatican.va/holy_father/francesco/apost_exhortations/documents/ papa-francesco_esortazione-ap_20131124_evangelii-gaudium_en.html (accessed December 30, 2013).

The feminist wire. (2013). Mission/Vision statement. Retrieved February 5, 2014, from thefeministwire.com/about-us/mission-vision/

Finklestein, J. (2002). Novelty and crisis in the world of McKnowledge. In D. Hayes & R. Wynward (Eds.), *The McDonaldization of higher education* (pp. 180–189). Westport, CT: Bergin and Garvey.

Giardina, M. D., & Newman, J. I. (in press). The politics of research. In P. Leavy (Ed.), *The Oxford Handbook of Qualitative Research* (pp. 699–723). New York: Oxford University Press.

Giardina, M. D., & Laurendeau, J. (2013). Truth untold? Evidence, knowledge, and research practice(s). *Sociology of Sport Journal, 30*(4), 237–255.

Giroux, H. A. (2001). Cultural studies as performative politics. *Cultural Studies ↔ Critical Methodologies, 1*(1), 5–23.

Giroux, H. A. (2010). The disappearing intellectual in the age of economic Darwinism. *Truthout.* www.truth-out.org/archive/item/90639:henry-a-giroux-the-disappearing-intellectual-in-the-age-of-economic-darwinism (accessed December 29, 2013).

Gitlin, T. (2006). The necessity of public intellectuals. *Raritan: A Quarterly Review, 26*(1), 123–136.

Habermas, J. (1972). *Knowledge and human interests, 2ⁿᵈ ed.* London: Heinemann.

Hammersley, M. (2005). Close encounters of a political kind: The threat from the evidence-based policy-making and practice movement. *Qualitative Researcher, 1*(1), 2–4.

Jarvie, G. (2007). Sport, social change, and the public intellectual. *International Review for the Sociology of Sport, 42*(4), 411–424.

Kalleberg, R. (2012). Sociologists as public intellectuals and experts. *Journal of Applied Social Science, 6*(1), 43–52.

Leavy, P. (2012). Making research matter: The academy versus real-world problems. *The Huffington Post.* www.huffingtonpost.com/patricia-leavy-phd/making-research-matter-th_b_1854022.html (accessed December 12, 2013).

Maxwell, J. (2004). Reemergent scientism, postmodernism, and dialogue across the disciplines. *Qualitative Inquiry, 10*(1), 35–41.

Mills, C. W. (1959). *The sociological imagination.* Oxford, UK: Oxford University Press.

Newman, J. I. (2013). Arousing a [post-]Enlightenment active body praxis. *Sociology of Sport Journal, 30*(4), 380–407.

The public intellectuals project. (2014). Mission statement. Retrieved February 5, 2014, from publicintellectualsproject.mcmaster.ca/about/

Ritzer, G. (2006). Who's a public intellectual? *The British Journal of Sociology, 57*(2), 209–213.

Roy, A. (February 15, 2001). *The ladies have feelings, so...shall we leave it to the experts.* Public lecture given at Hampshire College, Amherst, MA.

Ryan, K. E., & Hood, L. K. (2006). Guarding the castle and opening the gates. In N. K. Denzin & M. D. Giardina (Eds.), *Qualitative inquiry and the conservative challenge: Confronting methodological fundamentalism* (pp. 57–78). Walnut Creek, CA: Left Coast Press, Inc.

Said, E. (1996). *Representations of the intellectual: The 1993 Reith lectures.* New York: Vintage.

Sartelle, J. (1992). Public intellectuals. *Bad Subjects.* bad.eserver.org/issues/1992/03/sartelle.html (accessed January 2, 2014).

Silk, M. L., Bush, A., & Andrews, D. L. (2010). Contingent intellectual amateurism, or, the problem with evidence-based research. *Journal of Sport & Social Issues, 34*(1), 105–128.

Smith, A. D. (2004). *House arrest and piano.* New York: Anchor.

Smith, J. K., & Hodkinson, P. (2005). Relativism, criteria, and politics. In N. K. Denzin & Y. S. Lincoln (Eds.), *Handbook of qualitative research* (3rd ed., pp. 915–932). Thousand Oaks, CA: Sage.

Sparkes, A. (2013). Qualitative research in sport, exercise and health in the era of neoliberalism, audit, and New Public Management: Understanding the conditions for the (im)possibilities of a new paradigm dialogue. *Qualitative Research in Sport, Exercise and Health, 5*(3), 440–459.

Zinn, H. (1997). The uses of scholarship. In H. Zinn (Ed.), *The Zinn reader: Writings on disobedience and democracy* (pp. 499–508). New York: Seven Stories Press.

Part I
Public

Chapter 1

Public Intellectuals Against the Neoliberal University

Henry A. Giroux

I want to begin with the words of the late African-American poet, Audre Lorde, who was in her time a formidable writer, educator, feminist, gay rights activist, and public intellectual who displayed a relentless courage in addressing the injustices she witnessed all around her. She writes:

> Poetry is not a luxury. It is a vital necessity of our existence. It forms the quality of the light within which we predicate our hopes and dreams toward survival and change, first made into language, then into idea, then into more tangible action. Poetry is the way we help give name to the nameless so it can be thought. The farthest horizons of our hopes and fears are cobbled by our poems, carved from the rock experiences of our daily lives. (Lorde, 1984, p. 38)

And while Lorde refers to poetry here, I think a strong case can be made that the attributes she ascribes to poetry can also be attributed to higher education—a genuine higher education.[1] In this case, an education that includes history, philosophy, all of the arts and humanities, the criticality of the social sciences, the world of discovery made manifest by science, and the transformations in health and in law wrought by the professions which are at the heart of what it means to know something about the human condition. Lorde's defense of poetry as a mode of education is especially crucial for those of us who believe that the university is nothing if it is not a public trust and social good; that is, a critical institution infused with the promise of cultivating intellectual insight, the imagination, inquisitiveness, risk-taking, social responsibility, and the struggle for justice. At best, universities should be at the "heart of intense public discourse, passionate learning, and vocal citizen involvement in the issues of the times" (Scott, 2012). It is in the spirit of such an ideal that I first want to address those larger economic, social, and cultural interests that threaten this notion of education, especially higher education.

Across the globe, the forces of casino capitalism are on the march. With the return of the Gilded Age and its dream worlds of consumption, privatization, and deregulation, not only are democratic values and social protections at risk, but the civic and formative cultures that make such values and protections crucial to democratic life are in danger of disappearing altogether. As public spheres, once enlivened by broad engagements with common concerns and multiple voices, are being transformed into spectacular spaces of consumption, the flight from mutual obligations and social responsibilities intensifies and has resulted in what Tony Judt identifies as a "loss of faith in the culture of open democracy" (quoted in Foley, 2010, para. 2). This loss of faith in the power of public dialogue and dissent is not unrelated to the diminished belief in higher education as central to producing critical citizens and a crucial democratic public sphere in its own right. At stake here is not only the meaning and purpose of higher education, but also civil society, politics, and the fate of democracy itself. Thomas Frank (2012) is on target when he argues that "over the course of the past few decades, the power of concentrated money has subverted professions, destroyed small investors, wrecked the regulatory state, corrupted legislators en masse and repeatedly put the economy through the wringer. Now it has come for our democracy itself." And, yet, the only questions being asked about knowledge production, the purpose of education, the nature of politics, and our understanding of the future are determined largely by market forces.

The mantras of neoliberalism are now well known: government is the problem; society is a fiction; sovereignty is market-driven; deregulation and commodification are vehicles for freedom; and higher education should serve corporate interests rather than the public good. In addition, the yardstick of profit has become the only viable measure of the good life, while civic engagement and public spheres devoted to the common good are viewed by many politicians and their publics as either a hindrance to the goals of a market-driven society or alibis for government inefficiency and waste.

In a market-driven system in which economic and political decisions are removed from social costs, the flight of critical thought and social responsibility is further accentuated by what Zygmunt Bauman calls "ethical tranquillization" (McCarthy, 2007). One result is a form of depoliticization that works its way through the social order, removing social relations from the configurations of power that shape them, substituting what Wendy Brown (2006, p. 16) calls "emotional and personal vocabularies for political ones in formulating solutions to political problems." Consequently, it becomes difficult for young people too often bereft of a critical education to translate private troubles into public concerns. As private interests trump the public good, public spaces are corroded and short-term personal advantage replaces any larger notion of civic engagement and social responsibility.

Under such circumstances, to cite C. Wright Mills (2008, p. 200), we are witnessing the breakdown of democracy, the disappearance of critical intellectuals, and "the collapse of those public spheres which offer a sense of critical agency and social imagination." Mills's prescient comments amplify what has become a tragic reality. Missing from neoliberal market societies are those public spheres—from public and higher education to the mainstream media and digital screen culture—where people can develop what might be called the civic imagination. For example, in the last few decades, we have seen market mentalities attempt to strip education of its public values, critical content, and civic responsibilities as part of its broader goal of creating new subjects wedded to consumerism, risk-free relationships, and the disappearance of the social state in the name of individual, expanded choice. Tied largely to instrumental ideologies and measurable paradigms, many institutions of higher education are now committed almost exclusively to economic goals, such as preparing students for the workforce—all done as part of an appeal to rationality, one that eschews matters of inequality, power, and the ethical grammars of suffering (Wilderson III, 2012, p. 2). Many universities have not only strayed from their democratic mission, they also seem immune to the plight of students who face a harsh new world of high unemployment, the prospect of downward mobility, and debilitating debt.

The question of what kind of education is needed for students to be informed and active citizens in a world that increasingly ignores their needs, if not their future, is rarely asked (Aronowitz, 2008, p. xii). In the absence of a democratic vision of schooling, it is not surprising that some colleges and universities are increasingly opening their classrooms to corporate interests, standardizing the curriculum, instituting top-down governing structures, and generating courses that promote entrepreneurial values unfettered by social concerns or ethical consequences. For example, one university is offering a Master's degree to students who, in order to fulfill their academic requirements, have to commit to starting a high-tech company. Another university allows career officers to teach capstone research seminars in the humanities. In one of these classes, the students were asked to "develop a 30-second commercial on their 'personal brand'" (Zernike, 2009). This is not an argument against career counselling or research in humanities seminars, but the confusion in collapsing the two.

Central to this neoliberal view of higher education in the United States and United Kingdom is a market-driven paradigm that seeks to eliminate tenure, turn the humanities into a job preparation service, and transform most faculty into an army of temporary subaltern labor. For instance, in the United States out of 1.5 million faculty members, 1 million are "adjuncts who are earning, on average, $20K a year gross, with no benefits or healthcare, no unemployment insurance when they are out of work" (Scott, 2012). The indentured service status of such faculty is put on full display as some colleges have resorted to using "temporary service agencies to do their formal hiring" (Jaschik, 2010).

There is little talk in this view of higher education about the history and value of shared governance between faculty and administrators, nor of educating students as critical citizens rather than potential employees of Walmart. There are few attempts to affirm faculty as scholars and public intellectuals who have a measure of both autonomy and power. Instead, faculty members are increasingly defined less as intellectuals than as technicians and grant writers. Students fare no better in this debased form of education and are treated as either clients or as restless children in need of high-energy entertainment— as was made clear in the 2012 Penn State University scandal. Such modes of education do not foster a sense of organized responsibility fundamental to a democracy. Instead, they encourage what might be called a sense of organized irresponsibility—a practice that underlies the economic Darwinism and civic corruption at the heart of a debased politics.

Higher Education and the Crisis of Legitimacy

In the United States and, increasingly, in Canada, many of the problems in higher education can be linked to diminished funding, the domination of universities by market mechanisms, the rise of for-profit colleges, the intrusion of the national security state, and the diminished role of faculty in governing the university, all of which both contradict the culture and democratic value of higher education and make a mockery of the very meaning and mission of the university as a democratic public sphere. Decreased financial support for higher education stands in sharp contrast to increased support for tax benefits for the rich, big banks, the military, and mega corporations. Rather than enlarge the moral imagination and critical capacities of students, too many universities are now encouraged to produce would-be hedge fund managers, depoliticized students, and modes of education that promote a "technically trained docility" (Nussbaum, 2010, p. 142). Increasingly, pedagogy is reduced to learning reified methods, a hollow mechanistic enterprise divorced from understanding teaching as a moral and intellectual practice central to the creation of critical and engaged citizens. This reductionist notion of pedagogy works well with a funding crisis that is now used by conservatives as an ideological weapon to defund certain disciplines, such as history, English, sociology, anthropology, minority studies, gender studies, and language programs. While there has never been a golden age when higher education was truly liberal and democratic, the current attack on higher education by religious fundamentalists, corporate power, and the apostles of neoliberal capitalism appears unprecedented in terms of both its scope and its intensity.[2]

Universities are losing their sense of public mission, just as leadership in higher education is being stripped of any viable democratic vision. In the United States, college presidents are now called CEOs and move without apology between interlocking corporate and academic boards. With few exceptions, they are praised as fundraisers but rarely acknowledged for the quality of their ideas. It gets worse. As Adam Bessie (2013) points out,

> the discourse of higher education now resembles what you might hear at a board meeting at a No.2 pencil-factory, [with its emphasis on]: productivity, efficiency, metrics, data-driven value, [all of] which places utter, near-religious faith in this highly technical, market-based view of education [which] like all human enterprises, can (and must) be quantified and evaluated numerically, to identify the 'one best way,' which can then be 'scaled up,' or mass-produced across the nation, be it No. 2 pencils, appendectomies, or military drones.

In this new Gilded Age of money and profit, academic subjects gain stature almost exclusively through their exchange value on the market. Pharmaceutical companies determine what is researched in labs and determine whether research critical of their products should be published. Corporate gifts flood into universities, making more and more demands regarding what should be taught. Boards of trustees now hire business leaders to reform universities in the image of the marketplace. For-profit universities offer up a future image of the new model of higher education, characterized by huge salaries for management, a mere "17.4 per cent of their annual revenue spent on teaching, while 20 per cent was distributed as profit (the proportion spent on marketing [is] even higher)" (Collini, 2013). Large numbers of students from many of these for-profit institutions—offering subprime degrees and devoid of any sense of civic purpose—never finish their degree programs and are saddled with enormous debts. As Stefan Collini (2013) observes, at the University of Phoenix, owned by the Apollo Group,

> 60 percent ... of their students dropped out within two years, while of those who completed their courses, 21 per cent defaulted on paying back their loans within three years of finishing. [Moreover], 89 per cent of Apollo's revenue comes from federal student loans and [Apollo] spends twice as much on marketing as on teaching.

What happens to education when it is treated like a corporation? What are we to make of the integrity of a university when it accepts a monetary gift from powerful corporate interests or a rich patron demanding as part of the agreement the power to specify what is to be taught in a course or how a curriculum should be shaped? Some corporations and universities now believe that what is taught in a course is not an academic decision but a market consideration. In addition, many disciplines are now valued almost exclusively with how closely they align with what might be euphemistically called a business culture. One egregious example of this neoliberal approach to higher education is on full display in Florida where Governor Rick Scott's task force on education is attempting to implement a policy that would lower tuition for degrees friendly to corporate interests in order to "steer students toward majors that are in demand in the job market" (Alvarez, 2012, para. 3). Scott's utterly instrumental and anti-intellectual message is clear: "Give us engineers, scientists, health care specialists and technology experts. Do not worry so much about historians, philosophers, anthropologists and English majors" (Alvarez, 2012).

Not only does neoliberalism undermine both civic education and public values and confuse education with training, it also wages a war on what might be called the radical imagination. For instance, thousands of students in both the United States and Canada are now saddled with debts that will profoundly impact their lives and their futures, likely forcing them away from public service jobs because the pay is too low to pay off their educational loans. Students find themselves in a world in which heightened expectations have been replaced by dashed hopes and a world of onerous debt.[3] For those struggling to merely survive, the debt crisis represents a massive assault on the imagination by leaving little or no room to think otherwise in order to act otherwise. David Graeber is right in insisting that the student loan crisis is part of a war on the imagination. He writes:

> Student loans are destroying the imagination of youth. If there's a way of a society committing mass suicide, what better way than to take all the youngest, most energetic, creative, joyous people in your society and saddle them with $50,000 of debt so they have to be slaves? There goes your music. There goes your culture. … And in a way, this is what's happened to our society. We're a society that has lost any ability to incorporate the interesting, creative and eccentric people. (Kelly, 2013)

Questions regarding how education might enable students to develop a keen sense of prophetic justice, utilize critical analytical skills, and cultivate an ethical sensibility through which they learn to respect the rights of others are becoming increasingly irrelevant in a market-driven university in which the quality of education is so dumbed down that too few students on campus are really learning how to think critically, engage in thoughtful dialogue, push at the frontiers of their imagination, employ historical analyses, and move beyond the dreadful, mind-numbing forms of instrumental rationality being pushed by billionaires such as Bill Gates, Amazon's Jeff Bezos, Facebook's Mark Zuckerberg, and Netflix's Reed Hastings. In this world, "all human problems are essentially technical in nature and can be solved through technical means" (Bessie, 2013). As the humanities and liberal arts are downsized, privatized, and commodified, higher education finds itself caught in the paradox of claiming to invest in the future of young people while offering them few intellectual, civic, and moral supports (Nussbaum, 2010).

Higher education has a responsibility not only to search for the truth regardless of where it may lead, but also to educate students to be capable of holding authority and power accountable while at the same time sustaining "the idea and hope of a public culture" (Scialabba, 2009, p. 4). Though questions regarding whether the university should serve *strictly* public rather than private interests no longer carry the weight of forceful criticism as they did in the past, such questions are still crucial in addressing the purpose of higher education and what it might mean to imagine the university's full participation in public life as the protector and promoter of democratic values. Toni Morrison (2001, p. 278) is instructive in her comment:

> If the university does not take seriously and rigorously its role as a guardian of wider civic freedoms, as interrogator of more and more complex ethical problems, as servant and preserver of deeper democratic practices, then some other regime or ménage of regimes will do it for us, in spite of us, and without us.

What needs to be understood is that higher education may be one of the few public spheres left where knowledge, values, and learning offer a glimpse of the promise of education for nurturing public values, critical hope, and what my late friend Paulo Freire called "the practice of freedom." It may be the case that everyday life is increasingly organized around market principles, but confusing a market-determined society with democracy hollows out the legacy of higher education, whose deepest roots are philosophical, not commercial. This is a particularly important insight in a society where the free circulation of ideas is not only being replaced by mass mediated ideas but where critical ideas are increasingly viewed or dismissed as liberal, radical, or even seditious.

In addition, the educational force of the wider culture, dominated by the glorification of celebrity life-styles and a hyper-consumer society, perpetuates a powerful form of mass illiteracy and manufactured idiocy, witness the support for Ted Cruz and Michelle Bachmann in American politics, if not the racist, reactionary, and anti-intellectual Tea Party. This manufactured stupidity does more than depoliticize the public. To paraphrase Hannah Arendt, it represents an assault on the very possibility of thinking itself. Not surprisingly, intellectuals who engage in dissent and "keep the idea and hope of a public culture alive" (Scialabba, 2009, p. 4) are often dismissed as irrelevant, extremist, elitist, or un-American. As a result, we now live in a world in which the politics of disimagination dominates; public discourses that bears witness to a critical and alternative sense of the world are often dismissed because they do not advance economic interests.

In a dystopian society, utopian thought becomes sterile and, paraphrasing Theodor Adorno, thinking becomes an act of utter stupidity. Anti-public intellectuals now define the larger cultural landscape, all too willing to flaunt co-option and reap the rewards of venting insults at their assigned opponents while being reduced to the status of paid servants of powerful economic interests. But the problem is not simply with the rise of a right-wing cultural apparatus dedicated to preserving the power and wealth of the rich and corporate elite. As Stuart Hall recently remarked, the state of progressive thought is also in jeopardy in that, as he puts it, "the left is in trouble. It's not got any ideas, it's not got any independent analysis of its own, and therefore it's got no vision. It just takes the temperature. ... It has no sense of politics being educative, of politics changing the way people see things" (Williams, 2012). Of course, Hall is not suggesting the left has no ideas to speak of. He is suggesting that such ideas are removed from the larger issue of what it means to address education and the production and reception of meaningful ideas as a mode of pedagogy that is central to politics itself.

The issue of politics being educative, of recognizing that matters of pedagogy, subjectivity, and consciousness are at the heart of political and moral concerns, should not be lost on academics. Nor should the relevance of education being at the heart of politics be lost on those of us concerned about inviting the public back into higher education and rethinking the purpose and meaning of higher education itself. Democracy places civic demands upon its citizens, and such demands point to the necessity of an education that is broad-based, critical, and supportive of meaningful civic values, participation in self-governance, and democratic leadership. Only through such a formative and critical educational culture can students learn how to become individual and social agents, rather than disengaged spectators or uncritical consumers, able both to think otherwise and to act upon civic commitments that "necessitate a reordering of basic power arrangements" (Wolin, 2010, p. 43) fundamental to promoting the common good and producing a strong democracy. This is not a matter of imposing values on education and in our classrooms. The university and the classroom are already defined through power-laden discourses and a myriad of values that are often part of the hidden curriculum of educational politics and pedagogy. A more accurate position would be, as Toni Morrison (2001, p. 276) points out, to take up our responsibility "as citizen/scholars in the university [and] to accept the consequences of our own value-redolent roles." She continues, "Like it or not, we are paradigms of our own values, advertisements of our own ethics—especially noticeable when we presume to foster ethics-free, value-lite education."

Dreaming the Impossible

Reclaiming higher education as a democratic public sphere begins with the crucial recognition that education is not solely about job training and the production of ethically challenged entrepreneurial subjects, but also about matters of civic engagement, critical thinking, civic literacy, and the capacity for democratic agency, action, and change. It is also inextricably connected to the related issues of power, inclusion, and social responsibility.[4] For example, Martin Luther King, Jr. (1967/1991, p. 644), recognized clearly that when matters of social responsibility are removed from matters of agency and politics, democracy itself is diminished.

> When an individual is no longer a true participant, when he no longer feels a sense of responsibility to his society, the content of democracy is emptied. When culture is degraded and vulgarity enthroned, when the social system does not build security but induces peril, inexorably the individual is impelled to pull away from a soulless society.

If young people are to develop a deep respect for others, a keen sense of social responsibility, as well as an informed notion of civic engagement, pedagogy must be viewed as the cultural, political, and moral force that provides the knowledge, values, and social relations to make such democratic practices possible. Central to such a challenge is the need to position intellectual practice "as part of an intricate web of morality, rigor and responsibility" that enables academics to speak with conviction, enter the public sphere to address important social problems, and demonstrate alternative models for bridging the gap between higher education and the broader society (Roy, 2001, p. 1). Connective ties are crucial in that it is essential to develop intellectual practices that are collegial rather than competitive, refuse the instrumentality and privileged isolation of the academy, link critical thought to a profound impatience with the status quo, and connect human agency to the idea of social responsibility and the politics of possibility.

Increasingly, as universities are shaped by an audit culture, the call to be objective and impartial, whatever one's intentions, can easily echo what George Orwell called the 'official truth' or the establishment point of view. Lacking a self-consciously democratic political focus, teachers are often reduced, or reduce themselves, to the role of a technician or functionary engaged in formalistic rituals, unconcerned with the disturbing and urgent problems that confront the larger society or the consequences of one's pedagogical practices and research undertakings. Hiding behind appeals to balance and objectivity, too many scholars refuse to recognize that being committed to something does not cancel out what C. Wright Mills once called 'hard thinking.' Teaching needs to be rigorous, self-reflective, and committed not to the dead zone of instrumental rationality but to the practice of freedom, to a critical sensibility capable of advancing the parameters of knowledge, addressing crucial social issues, and connecting private troubles and public issues.

In opposition to the instrumental model of teaching, with its conceit of political neutrality and its fetishization of measurement, I argue that academics should combine the mutually interdependent roles of critical educator and active citizen. This requires finding ways to connect the practice of classroom teaching with important social problems and the operation of power in the larger society while providing the conditions for students to view themselves as critical agents capable of making those who exercise authority and power answerable for their actions.

Higher education cannot be decoupled from what Jacques Derrida calls a 'democracy to come,' that is, a democracy that must always "be open to the possibility of being contested, of contesting itself, of criticizing and indefinitely improving itself" (Boradorri, 2004, p. 121). Within this project of possibility and impossibility, critical pedagogy must be understood as a deliberately informed and purposeful political and moral practice, as opposed to one that is either doctrinaire or instrumentalized, or both. Moreover, a critical pedagogy should also gain part of its momentum in higher education among students who will go back to the schools, churches, synagogues, and workplaces in order to produce new ideas, concepts, and critical ways of understanding the world in which young people and adults live. This is a notion of intellectual practice and responsibility that refuses the professional neutrality and privileged isolation of the academy. It also affirms a broader vision of learning that links knowledge to the power of self-definition and to the capacities of students to expand the scope of democratic freedoms, particularly those that address the crisis of education, politics, and the social as part and parcel of the crisis of democracy itself.

In order for critical pedagogy, dialogue, and thought to have real effects, they must advocate that all citizens, old and young, are equally entitled, if not equally empowered, to shape the society in which they live. This is a commitment we heard articulated by the brave students who fought against tuition hikes and the destruction of civil liberties and social provisions in Quebec and to a lesser degree in the Occupy Wall Street movement. If educators are to function as public intellectuals, they need to listen to young people who are producing a new language in order to talk about inequality and power relations, attempting to create alternative democratic public spaces, rethinking the very nature of politics, and asking serious questions about what democracy is and why it no longer exists in many neoliberal societies. These young people who are protesting against the 'one percent' recognize that they have been written out of the discourses of justice, equality, and democracy and are not only resisting how neoliberalism has made them expendable, they are also arguing for a collective future very different from the one that is on display in the current political and economic systems in which they feel trapped. These brave youth are insisting that the relationship between knowledge and power can be emancipatory, that their histories and experiences matter, and that what they say and do counts in their struggle to unlearn dominating privileges, productively reconstruct their relations with others, and transform, when necessary, the world around them.

Although there are still a number of academics, such as Noam Chomsky, Angela Davis, John Rawlston Saul, Bill McKibben, Germaine Greer, and Cornel West, who function as public intellectuals, they are often shut out of the mainstream media or characterized as marginal, unintelligible, and sometimes as unpatriotic figures. At the same time, many academics find themselves laboring under horrendous working conditions that either don't allow for them to write in a theoretically rigorous and accessible manner for the public because they do not have time—given the often intensive teaching demands of part-time academics and increasingly of full-time, non-tenured academics as well. Or they retreat into a kind of theoreticism in which theory becomes lifeless, detached from any larger project or the realm of worldly issues. In this instance, the notion of theory as a resource, if not theoretical rigor itself, is transformed into a badge of academic cleverness shorn of the possibility of advancing thought within the academy or reaching a larger audience outside of academic disciplines.

Consequently, such intellectuals often exist in hermetic academic bubbles cut off from both the larger public and the important issues that impact society. To no small degree, they have been complicit in the transformation of the university into an adjunct of corporate power. Such academics run the risk of not only becoming incapable of defending higher education as a vital public sphere, but also of having any say over the conditions of their own intellectual labor. Without their intervention as public intellectuals, the university defaults on its role as a democratic public sphere willing to produce an informed public, enact and sustain a culture of questioning, and enable a critical formative culture capable of producing citizens "who are critical thinkers capable of putting existing institutions into question so that democracy again becomes society's movement" (Castoriadis, 1997, p. 10).

Before his untimely death, Edward Said, himself an exemplary public intellectual, urged his colleagues in the academy to confront directly those social hardships that disfigure contemporary society and pose a serious threat to the promise of democracy.[5] He urged them to assume the role of public intellectuals, wakeful and mindful of their responsibilities to bear testimony to human suffering and the pedagogical possibilities at work in educating students to be autonomous, self-reflective, and socially responsible. Said rejected the notion of a market-driven pedagogy that, lacking a democratic project, was steeped in the discourse of instrumental rationality and fixated on measurement. He insisted that when pedagogy is taken up as a mechanistic undertaking, it loses any understanding of what it means for students to "be thoughtful, layered, complex, critical thinker[s]" (Cunningham-Cook, 2013). For Said, such methodological reification was antithetical to a pedagogy rooted in the practice of freedom and attentive to the need to construct critical agents, democratic values, and modes of critical inquiry. On the contrary, he viewed it as a mode of training more suitable to creating cheerful robots and legitimating organized recklessness and legalized illegalities.

The famed economist, William Black, goes so far as to argue that such stripped down pedagogies are responsible for creating what he calls 'criminogenic cultures,' especially in business schools and economics departments at a number of Ivy League universities. An indication of this crowning disgrace can be found in the Oscar winning documentary, *Inside Job*, which showed how Wall Street bought off high profile economists from Harvard, Yale, MIT, and Columbia University. For instance, Glenn Hubbard, Dean of Columbia Business School, and Martin Feldstein of Harvard got huge payoffs from a number of financial firms and wrote academic papers or opinion pieces favoring deregulation, while refusing to declare that they were on the payroll of Met Life, Goldman Sachs, or Merrill Lynch.[6]

In opposition to such a debased view of educational engagement, Said argued for what he called a 'pedagogy of wakefulness.' In defining and expanding on Said's pedagogy of wakefulness, and how it shaped his important consideration of academics as public intellectuals, I begin with a passage that I think offers tremendous insight on the ethical and political force of much of his writing. This selection is taken from his memoir, *Out of Place*, which describes the last few months of his mother's life in a New York hospital and the difficult time she had falling asleep because of the cancer that was ravaging her body. Recalling this traumatic and pivotal life experience, Said's meditation moves between the existential and the insurgent, between private pain and worldly commitment, between the seductions of a "solid self" and the reality of a contradictory, questioning, restless, and at times, uneasy sense of identity. He writes:

'Help me to sleep, Edward,' she once said to me with a piteous trembling in her voice that I can still hear as I write. But then the disease spread into her brain—and for the last six weeks she slept all the time—my own inability to sleep may be her last legacy to me, a counter to her struggle for sleep. For me sleep is something to be gotten over as quickly as possible. I can only go to bed very late, but I am literally up at dawn. Like her I don't possess the secret of long sleep, though unlike her I have reached the point where I do not want it. For me, sleep is death, as is any diminishment in awareness... Sleeplessness for me is a cherished state to be desired at almost any cost; there is nothing for me as invigorating as immediately shedding the shadowy half-consciousness of a night's loss than the early morning, reacquainting myself with or resuming what I might have lost completely a few hours earlier. I occasionally experience myself as a cluster of flowing currents. I prefer this to the idea of a solid self, the identity to which so many attach so much significance. These currents, like the themes of one's life, flow along during the waking hours, and at their best, they require no reconciling, no harmonizing. They are 'off' and may be out of place, but at least they are always in motion, in time, in place, in the form of all kinds of strange combinations moving about, not necessarily forward, sometimes against each other, contrapuntally yet without one central theme. A form of freedom, I like to think, even if I am far from being totally convinced that it is. That skepticism too is one of the themes I particularly want to hold on to. With so many dissonances in my life I have learned actually to prefer being not quite right and out of place. (Said, 2000, pp. 294–299)

Said posits here an antidote to the seductions of conformity and the lure of corporate money that insures, as Irving Howe (1990, p. 27) once pointed out caustically, "an honored place for the intellectuals." For Said, it is a sense of being awake, displaced, caught in a combination of contradictory circumstances that suggests a pedagogy that is cosmopolitan and imaginative—a public affirming pedagogy that demands a critical and engaged interaction with the world we live in mediated by a responsibility for challenging structures of domination and for alleviating human suffering. This is a pedagogy that addresses the needs of multiple publics. As an ethical and political practice, a public pedagogy of wakefulness rejects modes of education removed from political or social concerns, divorced from history and matters of injury and injustice. Said's notion of a pedagogy of wakefulness includes "lifting complex ideas into the public space," recognizing human injury inside and outside of the academy, and using theory as a form of criticism to change things (Said, 2000, p. 7). This is a pedagogy in which academics are neither afraid of controversy nor the willingness to make connections between private issues and broader elements of society's problems that are otherwise hidden.

For Said, being awake becomes a central metaphor for defining the role of academics as public intellectuals, defending the university as a crucial public sphere, engaging how culture deploys power, and taking seriously the idea of human interdependence, while always living on the border—one foot in and one foot out, an exile and an insider for whom home was always a form of homelessness. As a relentless border crosser, Said embraced the idea of the "traveler" as an important metaphor for engaged intellectuals. As Stephen Howe, referencing Said, points out, "It was an image which depended not on power, but on motion, on daring to go into different worlds, use different languages, and 'understand a multiplicity of disguises, masks, and rhetorics. Travelers must suspend the claim of customary routine in order to live in new rhythms and rituals ... the traveler crosses over, traverses territory, and abandons fixed positions all the time'" (Howe, 2003). And as a border intellectual and traveler, Said embodied the notion of always "being quite not right," evident by his principled critique of all forms of certainties and dogmas and his refusal to be silent in the face of human suffering at home and abroad.

Being awake meant refusing the now popular sport of academic bashing or embracing a crude call for action at the expense of rigorous intellectual and theoretical work. On the contrary, it meant combining rigor and clarity, on the one hand, and civic courage and political commitment, on the other. A pedagogy of wakefulness meant using theoretical archives as resources, recognizing the worldly space of criticism as the democratic underpinning of publicness, defining critical literacy not merely as a competency, but as an act of interpretation linked to the possibility of intervention in the world. It pointed to a kind of border literacy in the plural in which people learned to read and write from multiple positions of agency; it also was indebted to the recognition forcibly stated by Hannah Arendt (1977, p. 149) that "without a politically guaranteed public realm, freedom lacks the worldly space to make its appearance."

I believe that Said was right in insisting that intellectuals have a responsibility to unsettle power, trouble consensus, and challenge common sense. The very notion of being an engaged public intellectual is neither foreign to nor a violation of what it means to be an academic scholar, but central to its very definition. According to Said (2001, p. 504), academics have a duty to enter into the public sphere unafraid to take positions and generate controversy, functioning as moral witnesses, raising political awareness, making connections to those elements of power and politics often hidden from public view, and reminding "the audience of the moral questions that may be hidden in the clamor and din of the public debate." Said (2004, p. 70) also criticized those academics that retreat into a new dogmatism of the disinterested specialist that separates them "not only from the public sphere but from other professionals who don't use the same jargon." This was especially unsettling to him at a time when complex language and critical thought remain under assault in the larger society by all manner of anti-democratic and anti-intellectual forces. But there is more at stake here than a retreat into discourses that turn theory into a mechanical act of academic referencing, there is also the retreat of intellectuals from being able to defend the public values and democratic mission of higher education. Or, as Irving Howe (1990, p. 36) put it, "Intellectuals have, by and large, shown a painful lack of militancy in defending the rights which are a precondition of their existence."

The view of higher education as a democratic public sphere committed to producing capable young people willing to expand and deepen their sense of themselves, to think the "world" critically, "to imagine something other than their own well-being," to serve the public good, take risks, and struggle for a substantive democracy has been in a state of acute crisis for the last thirty years.[7] When faculty assume, in this context, their civic responsibility to educate students to think critically, act with conviction, and connect what they learn in classrooms to important social issues in the larger society, they are hounded by those who demand "measurable student outcomes," as if deep learning breaks down into such discrete and quantifiable units. What do the liberal arts and humanities amount to if they do not teach the practice of freedom, especially at a time when training is substituted for education? Gayatri Spivak (2010, p. 8) provides a context for this question with her comment: "Can one insist on the importance of training in [higher education] in [a] time of legitimized violence?"

In a society that remains troublingly resistant to or incapable of questioning itself, one that celebrates the consumer over the citizen, and all too willingly endorses the narrow values and interests of corporate power, the importance of the university as a place of critical learning, dialogue, and social justice advocacy becomes all the more imperative. Moreover, the distinctive role that faculty play in this ongoing pedagogical project of shaping the critical rationalities through which agency is defined and civic literacy and culture produced, along with support for the institutional conditions and relations of power that make them possible, must be defended as part of a broader discourse of excellence, equity, and democracy.

Higher education represents one of the most important sites over which the battle for democracy is being waged. It is the site where the promise of a better future emerges out of those visions and pedagogical practices that combine hope, agency, politics, and moral responsibility as part of a broader emancipatory discourse. Academics have a distinct and unique obligation, if not political and ethical responsibility, to make learning relevant to the imperatives of a discipline, scholarly method, or research specialization. But more importantly, academics as engaged scholars can further the activation of knowledge, passion, values, and hope in the service of forms of agency that are crucial to sustaining a democracy in which higher education plays an important civic, critical, and pedagogical role.

C. Wright Mills (2000, p. 181) was right in contending that higher education should be considered a "public intelligence apparatus, concerned with public issues and private troubles and with the structural trends of our time underlying them." He insists that academics in their roles as public intellectuals ought to transform personal troubles and concerns into social issues and problems open to critique, debate, and reason. Matters of translation, connecting private troubles with larger systemic considerations were crucial in helping "the individual become a self-educating [person], who only then would be reasonable and free" (Mills, 2000, p. 186). Yet, Mills also believed, rightly, that that criticism is not the only responsibility of public intellectuals. As Archon Fung (2011) points out, they can "also join with other citizens to address social problems, aid popular movements and organizations in their efforts to advance justice, and sometimes work with governments to construct a world that is more just and democratic."

Academics as public intellectuals can write for multiple audiences, expand those public spheres, especially the many sites opening up online, to address a range of important social issues. A small and inclusive list would include the relationship between the attack on the social state and the defunding of higher education. Clearly, in any democratic society, education should be viewed as a right, not an entitlement, and suggests a reordering of state and federal priorities to make that happen. For instance, the military budget can be cut by two thirds and the remaining funds can be invested in public and higher education. There is nothing utopian about this demand given the excessive nature of military power in the United States. Addressing this task demands a sustained critique of the militarization of American society and a clear analysis of the damage it has caused both at home and abroad. Brown University's Watson Institute for International Studies, along with a number of writers such as Andrew Bacevich, has been doing this for years, offering a treasure trove of information that could be easily accessed and used by public intellectuals in and outside of the academy. Relatedly, as Angela Davis, Michelle Alexander, and others have argued, there is a need for public intellectuals to become part of a broader social movement aimed at dismantling the prison-industrial complex and the punishing state, which drains billions of dollars in funds to put people in jail when such funds could be used to fund public and higher education. The punishing state is a dire threat to both public and higher education and to democracy itself. It is the pillar of the authoritarian state, undermining civil liberties, criminalizing a range of social behaviors related to concrete social problems, and intensifying the legacy of Jim Crow against poor minorities of color. The American public does not need more prisons; it needs more schools.

Second, academics, artists, journalists and other cultural workers need to connect the rise of subaltern, part-time labor in both the university and the larger society with the massive inequality in wealth and income that now corrupts every aspect of American politics and society. Precarity has become a weapon to both exploit adjuncts, part-time workers, and temporary laborers and to suppress dissent by keeping them in a state of fear over losing their jobs. Insecure forms of labor increasingly produce "a feeling of passivity born of despair" (Standing, 2011, p. 20). Multinational corporations have abandoned the social contract and any vestige of supporting the social state. They plunder labor and perpetuate the mechanizations of social death whenever they have the chance to accumulate capital. This issue is not simply about restoring a balance between labor and capital, it is about recognizing a new form of serfdom that kills the spirit as much as it depoliticizes the mind. The new authoritarians do not ride around in tanks, they have their own private jets, they fund right-wing think tanks, they lobby for reactionary policies that privatize everything in sight while filling their bank accounts with massive profits. They are the embodiment of a culture of greed, cruelty, and disposability.

Third, academics need to fight for the rights of students to get a free education, be given a formidable and critical education not dominated by corporate values, and to have a say in the shaping of their education and what it means to expand and deepen the practice of freedom and democracy. Young people have been left out of the discourse of democracy. They are the new disposables who lack jobs, a decent education, hope, and any semblance of a future better than the one their parents inherited. They are a reminder of how finance capital has abandoned any viable vision of the future, including one that would support future generations. This is a mode of politics and capital that eats its own children and throws their fate to the vagaries of the market. If any society is in part judged by how it views and treats its children, American society by all accounts has truly failed in a colossal way and, in doing so, provides a glimpse of the heartlessness at the core of the new authoritarianism.

Finally, there is a need to oppose the ongoing shift in power relations between faculty and the managerial class. Too many faculty are now removed from the governing structure of higher education and as a result have been abandoned to the misery of impoverished wages, excessive classes, no health care, and few, if any, social benefits. This is shameful and is not merely an education issue but a deeply political matter, one that must address how neoliberal ideology and policy has imposed on higher education an anti-democratic governing structure that mimics the broader authoritarian forces now threatening the United States.

Conclusion

In conclusion, I want to return to my early reference to the global struggles being waged by many young people. I believe that while it has become more difficult to imagine a democratic future, we have entered a period in which students and disenfranchised youth all over the world are protesting against neoliberalism and its instrumentalized pedagogy and politics of disposability. Refusing to remain voiceless and powerless in determining their future, these young people are organizing collectively in order to create the conditions for societies that refuse to use politics as an act of war and markets as the measure of democracy. And while such struggles are full of contradictions and setbacks, they have opened up a new conversation about politics, poverty, inequality, class warfare, and ecological devastation. The ongoing protests in the United States, Canada, Greece, and Spain make clear that this is not—indeed, *cannot be*—only a short-term project for reform, but a political movement that needs to intensify, accompanied by the reclaiming of public spaces, the progressive use of digital technologies, the development of public spheres, the production of new modes of education, and the safeguarding of places where democratic expression, new identities, and collective hope can be nurtured and mobilized.

Academics, artists, journalists, and other cultural workers can play a crucial role in putting into place the formative cultures necessary to further such efforts through the production and circulation of the knowledge, values, identities, and social relations crucial for such struggles to succeed. Writing in 1920, H. G. Wells insisted that "history is becoming more and more a race between education and catastrophe" (Braindash). I think Wells got it right, but what needs to be acknowledged is that there is more at stake here than the deep responsibilities of academics to defend academic freedom, the tenure system, and faculty autonomy, however important. The real issues lie elsewhere and speak to preserving the public character of higher education and recognizing that defending it as a public sphere is essential to the very existence of critical thinking, dissent, dialogue, engaged scholarship, and democracy itself. Universities should be subversive in a healthy society, they should push against the grain, and give voice to the voiceless, the unmentionable, and the whispers of truth that haunt the apostles of unchecked power and wealth. These may be dark times, as Hannah Arendt once warned, but they don't have to be, and that raises serious questions about what educators are going to do within the current historical climate to make sure that they do not succumb to the authoritarian forces circling the university, waiting for the resistance to stop and for the lights to go out. Resistance is no longer an option, it is a necessity.

Acknowledgment

This chapter was originally published as Giroux, H. A. (2013, October 29), Public intellectuals against the neoliberal university, in *Truthout*. It is reprinted here with permission.

Notes

1 I have taken this idea of linking Lorde's notion of poetry to education from Smith (2011), "Humanities are a Manifesto," pp. 48–55.

2 For a series of brilliant analyses on public education, inequality, read everything that Michael Yates writes. He is one of our national treasures.

3 See Fraser (2013), "Politics of Debt in America." On the history of debt, see Graeber (2012), *Debt: The First 5,000 Years*.

4 On this issue, see the brilliant essay by Giroux (2012), "On the Civic Function of Intellectuals Today," pp. ix–xvii.

5 I have used this example in other pieces, and I use it again because of its power and insight.

6 This issue is taken up in great detail in Ferguson (2012), *Predator Nation*.

7 See, especially, Newfield (2008), *Unmaking the Public University*.

References

Alvarez, L. (2012). Florida may reduce tuition for select majors. *New York Times*. Retrieved from www.nytimes.com/2012/12/10/education/florida-may-reduce-tuition-for-select-majors.html

Arendt, H. (1977). *Between past and future: Eight exercises in political thought*. New York: Penguin.

Aronowitz, S. (2008). *Against schooling: Education and social class*. Boulder, CO: Paradigm.

Bessie, A. (2013). The answer to the great question of education reform? The number 42. *Truthout*. Retrieved from truth-out.org/opinion/item/19356-the-answer-to-the-great-question-of-education-reform-the-number-42

Borradori, G. (2004). Autoimmunity: Real and symbolic suicides—A dialogue with Jacques Derrida. In G. Borradori (Ed.), *Philosophy in a time of terror: Dialogues with JurgenHabermas and Jacques Derrida* (pp. 121). Chicago: University of Chicago Press.

Braindash. (n.d.). *H. G. Wells*. Retrieved from www.braindash.com/quotes/h_g_wells/human_history_becomes_more_and_more_a_race between_education_and_catastrophe

Brown, W. (2006). *Regulating aversion: Tolerance in the age of identity and empire*. Princeton, NJ: Princeton University Press.

Castoriadis, C. (1997). Democracy as procedure and democracy as regime. *Constellations, 4*(1),10.

Collini, S. (2013, October). Sold Out. *London Review of Books. 35*, 20–24. www.lrb.co.uk/v35/n20/stefan-collini/sold-out

Cunningham-Cook, M. (2013). Re-imagining dissent. *Guernica Magazine*. Retrieved from www.guernicamag.com/interviews/re-imagining-dissent

Ferguson, C. H. (2012). *Predator nation: Corporate criminals, political corruption, and the hijacking of America*. New York: Crown Press.

Foley, S. (2010, March 24). Tony Judt: 'I am not pessimistic in the long run.' *The Independent* (London). Retrieved February 1, 2014, from www.independent.co.uk/arts-entertainment/books/features/tony-judt-i-am-not-pessimistic-in-the-very-long-run-1925966.html

Frank, T. (2012). It's a rich man's world: How billionaire backers pick America's candidates. *Harper's Magazine*. Retrieved from harpers.org/archive/2012/04/0083856

Fraser, S. (2013). The politics of debt in America: From debtor's prison to debtor nation. *TomDispatch.com*. Retrieved from www.tomdispatch.com/dialogs/print/?id=175643

Fung, A. (2011). The constructive responsibility of intellectuals. *Boston Review*. Retrieved from www.bostonreview.net/BR36.5/archon_fung_noam_chomsky_responsibility_of_intellectuals.php

Giroux, S. S. (2012). On the civic function of intellectuals today. In G. Olson & L. Worsham (Eds.), *Education as civic engagement: Toward a more democratic society* (pp. ix–xvii). Boulder, CO: Paradigm.

Graeber, D. (2012). *Debt: The first 5,000 years*. New York: Melville House.

Howe, I. (1990). *This age of conformity. Selected writings 1950–1990*. New York: Harcourt Brace Jovanovich.

Howe, S. (2003). Edward Said: The traveller and the exile. *Open Democracy*. Retrieved from www.opendemocracy.net/articles/ViewPopUpArticle.jsp?id=10&articleId=1561

Jaschik, S. (2010). Making adjuncts temps—Literally. *Inside Higher Ed*. Retrieved from www.insidehighered.com/news/2010/08/09/adjuncts

Kelly, A. R. (2013). David Graeber: 'There has been a war on the human imagination.' *Truthdig*. Retrieved from www.truthdig.com/avbooth/item/david_graeber_there_has_been_a_war_on_the_human_imagination_20130812.

King, Jr., M. L. (1991). The trumpet of conscience. In J. M. Washington (Ed.), *The essential writings and speeches of Martin Luther King, Jr.* (p. 644). New York: Harper Collins.

Lorde, A. (1984). Poetry is not a luxury. In *Sister outsider: Essays and speeches*. Freedom, CA: Crossing Press.

McCarthy, G. (2007). The social edge interview: Zygmunt Bauman. *The Social Edge*. Retrieved January 6, 2013, from webzine.thesocialedge.com/interviews/the-social-edge-interview-sociologist-and-author-zygmunt-bauman

Mills, C. W. (2000). On politics. In *The Sociological Imagination*. New York: Oxford UniversityPress.

Mills, C. W. (2008). *The politics of truth: selected writings of C. Wright Mills*. New York: Oxford University Press.

Morrison, T. (2001). How can values be taught in this university. *Michigan Quarterly Review* (Spring), 276–278.

Newfield, C. (2008). *Unmaking the public university: The forty-year assault on the middle class*. Cambridge, MA: Harvard University Press.

Nussbaum, M. C. (2010). *Not for profit: Why Democracy needs the humanities*. Princeton, NJ: Princeton University Press.

Roy, A. (2001). *Power politics*. Cambridge, MA: South End Press.

Said, E. (2000). *Out of place: A memoir*. New York: Vintage.

Said, E. (2001). On defiance and taking positions. In *Reflections on exile and other essays*. Cambridge, MA: Harvard University Press.

Said, E. (2004). *Humanism and democratic criticism*. New York: Columbia University Press.

Scialabba, G. (2009). *What are intellectuals good for?* Boston: Pressed Wafer.

Scott, D. L. (2012). How the American university was killed, in five easy steps. *The Homeless Adjunct Blog*. Retrieved from junctrebellion.wordpress.com /2012/08/12/how-the-american-university-was-killed-in-five-easy-steps

Smith, M. N. (2011). The humanities are a manifesto for the twenty-first century. *LiberalEducation* (Winter), 48–55.

Spivak, G. C. (2010). Changing reflexes: Interview with Gayatri Chakravorty Spivak. *Works and Days, 55/56* (Vol. 28), 8.

Standing, G. (2011). *The precariat: The new dangerous class*. New York: Bloomsbury.

Wilderson III, F. B. (2012). Introduction: Unspeakable ethics. In *Red, White, & Black*. London: Duke University Press.

Williams, Z. (2012). The saturday interview: Stuart Hall. *The Guardian*. Retrieved from www.guardian.co.uk/theguardian/2012/feb/11/saturday-interview-stuart-hall

Wolin, S. S. (2010). *Democracy, Inc.: Managed democracy and the specter of inverted totalitarianism*. Princeton, NJ: Princeton University Press.

Zernike, K. (2009). Making college 'relevant.' *New York Times*. Retrieved from www.nytimes.com/2010/01/03/education/edlife/03careerism-t.html?pagewanted=all&_r=0

Chapter 2

Audience Matters

Laurel Richardson

Only once before in my life have I had writer's block. That was twenty-five years ago. I was to give the Presidential Address to the North Central Sociological Association. But Postmodernism had frozen my hand. What could I possibly write? How could I speak for anyone, even myself? What's a "self"? Doubt ruled. Theory had tied my tongue, left me speechless.

I did recover.

And I have had a wonderful time at the Postmodern Fairgrounds riding on the Tilt-a-Whirl, Dodgem Cars and roller coasters—the Millennium Force, Mindbender, The Great Global Scream Machine. Many in this room have also been at the Postmodern Fair.

So, here we are. Bruised but unbroken. Welcoming others, and so sad about those who are not with us.

When I was asked to give the Keynote at the 2013 International Congress of Qualitative Inquiry (ICQI), I was excited, honored, and flattered. I have spent much of my career trying to reach diverse audiences. I had walked-the-walk and thought I could probably just talk-the-talk in my sleep.

Qualitative Inquiry Outside the Academy edited by Norman K. Denzin and Michael D. Giardina, 61–70. © 2014 Left Coast Press, Inc. All rights reserved.

The talk's title came easily—Audience Matters. Lots of leeway. But I struggled. So come with me now as I talk about *my* matters regarding audience.

In my undergraduate days at the University of Chicago, I was deeply influenced by my Social Science II professor, David Riesman. His writing and teaching style were unpretentious; his mind omnicurious. When I grew up, I wanted to be one of the people Riesman lauded in his book, *The Lonely Crowd*. Those people had what he called "the nerve of failure," or "the courage to face aloneness and the possibility of defeat in one's personal life or professional work without being morally destroyed" (Riesman, 1954, pp. 33, 55).

My Social Science II class was reading *The Lonely Crowd* in its 1953 paperback edition. I believe it was the first academic research-book published in paperback. At the same time, our Humanities II class had a writing assignment: Argue against the publication of academic treatises in paperback books.

Well, I argued that inexpensive books readily available to the uneducated masses were as potentially dangerous to the academic institution as publication of the Gutenberg Bible had been to the established Church. Paperback books were the first onslaught; they would lead to an unmitigated disaster, the collapse of the institutions of higher education. The masses might learn something on their own. Give birth to their own ideas without the midwifery of the academy. Make professors obsolete. Knowledge is power. Power to the People?!?

I got an "A" on my essay. I was a sixteen-year-old clearly lacking the "nerve of failure."

Fast forward.

At the close of the defense of my dissertation—studies in the sociology of pure mathematics—I was asked what I planned to do with my doctorate.

"OH, share my love for sociology. Write for regular people," I said. Enthusiastically.

The male examiners lounged in their 1960s regulation professorial sage green corduroy suits with skinny, knit ties. Their throats bulged as they took a collective gasp. They shook their graying heads in unison like a choir of lizards.

I was so naïve.

I had given the "wrong" answer. The wrong side of my brain was in gear.

But they didn't flunk me.

What seems especially surprising to me as I look back on this experience is that my graduate seminars taught the ideas of Georg Simmel, Karl Marx, George Herbert Mead, C. Wright Mills, Erving Goffman, William Foote Whyte, Nathan Glazer. These were sociologists whose writing styles and sociological interests were accessible to regular people. But for me to declare that I wanted to follow a *public intellectual* path was judged by the examiners as unworthy of their huge investment in my education. The department's first woman. Bad enough I had gotten married and had a child. Now this. After all their work, my sights were not set on university teaching but on reaching regular people. The third leg of the stool.

My having passed into their exalted realm was overshadowed by the obvious fact that I had disappointed them. *"Just like a woman."*

That dissertation defense experience, I think, shaped the DNA of my career: double strands, running in opposite directions. One strand has science-oriented academics as its audience. I publish work that follows scientific protocols. This work does not disappoint the lounge lizards—nor me. I like the beauty and orderliness; I like feeling smart and powerful when my statistical predictions hold. And, if I had not engaged in this standard work, I would not have gotten a toehold into becoming a full professor at a top-flight department in a major research university.

The other strand, the literary one, has all manner of audiences in mind. With the *New York Times* bestselling "non-fiction" book, *The New Other Woman*, and my subsequent book tour (radio, television, bookstores), I hoped to reach "regular" women. I wrote my gender text, *Dynamics of Sex and Gender*, like a mystery novel, with both students and their mothers in mind. The co-edited interdisciplinary anthology, *Feminist Frontiers* (now in its tenth edition), brought literary-sociological analysis to humanities students. I wrote a mass-market magazine advice column that gave sociological "answers" to people's questions. I publish poetry and creative nonfiction in literary magazines, give workshops for non-academics, and serve on non-standard editorial boards. This year, I wrote a sociologically grounded literary-narrative, *After a fall: A sociomedical sojourn.*

Because, audience always matters to me, writing this keynote address should have been a shoe-in.

But, months passed and I could not get started. I had writer's block. And I had it bad. Postmodern theory could not be blamed, now. It had not left me speechless. It was not *doubt* that I had a corner on the truth; rather, it was doubt that I would have anything *new* to say—anything I hadn't already said in writings now entombed in the eight file drawers that inhabited the north wall of my study—and the six drawerfulls that moldered in the basement.

A poem I wrote long long ago came to mind:

EULOGY

Some think only
Printed Words
     In tomes
In stacks
By spider webs
     Entombed
Have value.
Some of my words are there.
Recall them now?

But I didn't want to recall them. I wanted to say something new.

So, I imagined a speech in which I would talk a little about my undergraduate, graduate, and career-long concern with reaching diverse audiences. Then, I would cheer the new ways audiences are reached through blogs, videos, and YouTube. I'd celebrate new venues like computer screens, movie marquees, dance studios, homeless shelters, hospices, buses, galleries, National Public Radio (NPR). The creativity and chutzpah of qualitative inquiry researchers is mind-bending and world-altering.

Great idea!

But it didn't resolve my writer's block. Everyone at this ICQI conference, I thought, surely knows about these projects! They're the ones who have done them!!

My anxiety about writing the Keynote grew like Google.

Perhaps, I thought, if I go through those 14 file drawers of my writings, I will find something new to say. I hired a non-academic young friend, Tina, to help me create an "archive." Together we went on a three-month search and destroy mission.

Anything to avoid writing.

We came across articles and projects that were not published or funded or finished. Lots of them. My first thought was that they were failures, and I should toss them in the trash. But I wanted to talk about them, and dear Tina was my interested audience.

These old projects became new because I was seeing them through new sets of eyes—Tina's non-academic ones and my older ones. Two new audiences.

The first failed article we came upon in my file drawers dated back to 1963. I had submitted an article to the *American Sociological Review* entitled, "Women in Science: Why So Few?" The editor rejected it with one sentence. "This paper was obviously written by a woman because no one but a woman would be interested." I cried, then I buried that paper. Who was I to challenge the esteemed editor's wisdom? What did I know? I had neither confidence nor chutzpah.

"What's this huge stash?" Tina asked. She had brushed aside a spider web and opened the bottom drawer of a file cabinet in the basement.

I looked over her shoulder onto 20 inches or so of papers. "Oh," I said. "That's the archive from my 15 minutes of fame."

In 1972, my honors methods class researched what I came to call "the changing door ceremony." The students became participant-observers, norm violators, journal keepers, and interviewers. I wanted them to understand how cultural values are inscribed through everyday interactions. Who opens doors for whom? Are there social patterns? Is the Woman's Movement affecting everyday interactions?

"Send me something—anything," an East Coast professor wrote. He had a contract for a qualitative research anthology. I sent him "The Door Ceremony." He rejected it with a handwritten note. "Gender?!? Too trendy. Patriarchy? Too strident."

Hello!

I was untenured. And my department, fearing I would never fully recover from a coma I had following a car accident, had delayed my tenure bid—even though I did have (more than) enough peer-reviewed publications to warrant tenure. But, I submitted the "Door Ceremony" paper to the American Sociological Association's 1973 conference in New York City. At least I would have a department-funded trip to the Big Apple, I thought, before I became applesauce.

But a different fate befell me.

"Hand That Holds Doorknob Rules World," headlined the front page of the *New York Times* Sunday Op-Ed section. The journalist, Israel Shenker, and his paparazzi had come to hear my paper. Shenker's article, written with sensitivity, good-will, and humor, was peppered with pictures of me going in and out of doors. Shenker quoted me as saying, "I know where the power rests in my department."

I also learned about the power of the *New York Times* to create audiences for "news." Shenker's article was cited in every major U.S. and international newspaper. Because of the publicity, my sociology department was bombarded with mail and phone calls. A temp was hired to handle the commotion.

Requests for the article came from professors, priests, psychiatrists, physicists, and prisoners. Two of my "pen-pals" threatened me. The police were called. Two door manufacturing companies wrote. One asked for 200 copies of the article. People wrote seeking advice on other gender issues: *Should older women date younger men? Shouldn't unwed fathers be sent to prison? Is it okay for men to cross-dress?* People wrote seeking help. TOP SECRET. *Help me prove that the Masons murdered Kennedy!* Amy Vanderbilt wrote asking for my help on revising her etiquette book. Journal editors asked to publish the paper. Presses invited me to write a *whole* book. The *Today Show, NBC, CBS, ABC* wanted me ... yesterday, if possible.

One of Ohio State University's trustees just happened to be in Tokyo when the *New York Times* article was published there in Japanese, in which the trustee just happened to be fluent. The trustee called the provost to ask about my status. "Tenure her," the trustee said. The provost called my department. "Tenure her," he said. And so they did.

I have never written about any of this.

As I write about it now, I realize that the "door ceremony" is a politically and personally apt metaphor. Not only was I opening doors for feminist qualitative research, *men* outside my department were opening for me the precious tenure door.

"What do you want to do with all these news clippings and letters?" Tina asked.

"Let's put them in a binder," I said, "and move on!"

Even after my fifteen minutes of fame, not all doors were opened to me. We find three more rejected articles in my files: (1) religiosity and Women's Studies classes; (2) feminism and shopping boycotts; and (3) women survivors of the Holocaust. All three had been submitted to feminist journals. No audiences for them, I was told. In a surly curly blue-pen addendum a woman editor added "Unlike *your Times* apotheosis."

But something much worse than journal rejection happened. I had co-authored these papers with four different untenured colleagues. Two were men. After each of the rejections, not only did our academic collaborations cease, our value in each other's eyes diminished. Our incipient friendships withered. Their tenure bids were turned back. I still feel guilt about giving them false hope based on my ignorance/naivety of the politics of "audience" construction.

"What about a book on women and spirituality?" I asked my editor at *The Free Press*. "None of my Long Island friends would be interested," she said. "Why don't you write a book about unwed mothers?" I accepted a large advance and did perhaps a dozen interviews. What I learned troubled me. I returned the advance.

I moved on, again.

Shopping Malls!! Great idea. What fun it would be to study safe spaces for women where they can bond through "criticizing the clothes," as my granddaughter calls our shared ventures. I raised the topic of "female bonding" to the powerful man in my department who would determine my promotion to full professor. "There's nothing to learn there," he said. I listened, abandoned the project, got promoted to full professor.

Surely, one would think, by the mid-nineties finding academic audiences for my research interests would be a walk in the park. In 1995, I submitted a paper to *Symbolic Interaction* entitled

"Standing in the Gateway: AIDS and Community Impact." My interest was in how AIDS helpers came to devote time, energy, and compassion to People With Aids, and how these helpers managed problems of loss, burn-out, and grief. What community support did they receive? And how did they perceive the potential impact of AIDS on different communities? No one had studied any of these issues.

The editor thought the paper "very nicely written and very interesting ... several passages quite moving" but that its contribution was "practical and motivational." The editor suggested I write a different paper. I didn't. I buried the one I did write. The time was not right for AIDS research on caretakers or for *Symbolic Interaction* to value the "practical and motivational."

I hunkered down.

Graduate students needed financial support and ethnographic experience. I applied for a university grant to study an urban park, The Park of Roses. This park was a safe space—day and night—for everyone: gays, ethnic and racial minorities, pedigreed and mixed-breed dogs on and off leashes, children, families, blue-haired youth, tree-hugging women, inter-racial weddings, Wiccan rituals, Christian memorial services, rock and cello concerts, poetry readings, sonnets, free verse, rap. How was a culture of acceptance and *respect* of difference being passed on? How was this safety accomplished through everyday interactions?

The grant proposal was rejected by my own university when I was a full professor serving on their two most prestigious university committees—the Distinguished Visiting Research Professor Committee and the Athletics Committee—and after I had been the recipient of their first Affirmative Action Award. It was not *me* they were rejecting; *it was socio-politically engaged ethnography.* A dismal 17th century welcome to the 21st century.

When I review these "failed" articles and projects, I see they have three variables in common: (1) They are interesting, valuable, projects; (2) Gatekeepers determined whether there were audiences; and (3) Me.

It was I who did not persist. It is I who had let projects fall. In each case, it was I who lacked the "nerve of failure." I had accepted the judgment of the Gatekeepers.

If it were not for publishers such as Left Coast Press, Sage, Guilford, Routledge, and Sense and editors such as Mitch Allen, Norman Denzin, Yvonna Lincoln, Art Bochner, and Carolyn Ellis, I would not have had any venues for publishing my transgressive work. They were Gatekeepers who opened the gates.

On January 5, 2012, I had major surgery on my left ankle. I feared the surgery because in my childhood, whenever I was weak, ill, or disabled, I was abandoned by those who supposedly loved and cared for me. But my month in rehab undid that lifelong narrative. Rehab was a life-changing experience.

I embraced the Truth that I am only temporarily-abled.

I needed to write about it. I obsessed.

I wrote furiously. Both of my DNA career strands intertwined. Sociological and literary understandings entwined.

It did not take a "nerve of failure" to send the manuscript to Mitch Allen at Left Coast Press because I knew he would give it a respectful critique.

Now, 16 months later, *After a Fall: A Sociomedical Sojourn*— joins Left Coast Press's New Books List. It is one of 15 new qualitative academic books. Here at this conference. Not merely available as a paperback, but available now worldwide as an E-Book! E-power to the people!

Editors, publishers, and conference organizers are the ones who bring together like-minded people. It is they who have built the foundation for our free-standing edifice. It is they who have had the "nerve of failure"—the willingness to risk disapprobation and financial loss so all of us have that extra oomph to be true to our callings, our own unique DNAs.

At the risk of sounding "practical and motivational," I implore you to keep taking risks. Believe in your projects. Become Gatekeepers who open gates for others. Be permission givers. Have the "nerve of failure."

And so, at last I understand why I have had a writing block about this keynote. You are my REAL audience, my people, community, the audience that matters the most to me intellectually and emotionally.

I have been anxious that this speech not disappoint.

References

Riesman, D. (1954). *Individualism reconsidered, and other essays.* Glencoe, IL: Free Press.

Part II
With

Chapter 3

Politics and Public Policy, Social Justice, and Qualitative Research

Maria Mayan and Christine Daum

Politics and Public Policy

"It's political!" "It's politics!" This is often our response when a decision is made that we do not like. We either believe the decision is inappropriate—that a better one could have been made—or we believe that the process by which it was made was unfair. In such circumstances, it is quite correct to blame "politics," as politics are about values and influencing others of the importance of some values over others.

Public policy is derived from values and comprises a series of choices that are intended to change behavior to produce socially desirable outcomes (Nakamura, 1987). Much quoted is the definition: "Public policy is whatever governments choose to do or not to do" (Dye, 1972, p. 3). "Not to do" maintains the status quo. Public policy frames programs and services that government offers (and does not offer), such as subsidized housing, child and elder care, income support, and health services. Consequently, public policies are overt statements on what government values. Politics is the process of how decision-makers influence and are influenced by others to take specific courses of action.

Qualitative Inquiry Outside the Academy edited by Norman K. Denzin and Michael D. Giardina, 73–91. © 2014 Left Coast Press, Inc. All rights reserved.

The policies we argue for, both personally and professionally, reveal what we value and the kind of society in which we want to live.

Social Justice

When we refer to public policy for "socially desirable outcomes," we enter the social justice arena. Social justice has multiple meanings and components (e.g., restorative, procedural, distributive, and economic justice) (Rawls, 1971) that refer to the "morally proper distribution and redistribution of resources in society" (Stadnyk, Townsend, & Wilcock, 2010, p. 331). Social justice examines how the distribution of advantages and disadvantages in society are due to social, political, and economic values and structures (Smith, Jacobson, & Yiu, 2008). Public policies cement these advantages and disadvantages, creating inequity in the distribution of living conditions, assets, opportunities for employment, access to knowledge, access to health services, social security, a safe environment, and opportunities for civic and political participation (United Nations, 2006). These inequities are what we identify as intolerable and take up as social justice issues.

Qualitative Research

Just as politics and policy are about values, so, too, is research. Research is always directed. Simply by the questions we choose to pursue and how we choose to work, we are stating our values, the stories we believe need to be told, and what we consider to be a social injustice.

Qualitative research[1] is well positioned to address social justice issues because it makes the personal public. Qualitative researchers use sensitivity, flexibility, and creativity to try and make sense of life—and inequity—as it unfolds. We take time to explore the many and ever-evolving facets of disadvantage. Connecting with people and taking risks to expose disadvantage—and the politics behind it—can result in motivations and recommendations for the morally proper re-distribution of resources. Indeed, engaging in qualitative research for social justice reasons can be one of the most humanizing activities we do.

Norman Denzin has positioned the pursuit of social justice through qualitative research at the core of every International

Congress of Qualitative Inquiry since its inception in 2005. In 2011 he wrote, "Qualitative researchers are called upon to make their work relevant. They are encouraged to pursue social justice agendas, to be human rights advocates, to do work that honors the core values of human dignity" (ICQI, 2011). Two years later, he challenged qualitative researchers to take action: "We share a commitment to change the world, to engage in ethical work what makes a positive difference" (Denzin, 2013, p. 4). But what have we accomplished since the Congress began?

The theme of this volume is "Qualitative Research Outside the Academy." Yet the phrase *outside the academy* is troublesome for us because of how we position ourselves and our research.

Positioning Ourselves and Our Assertions

We are applied researchers. The ultimate goal of many applied disciplines (e.g., public health, occupational therapy, human ecology, nursing, social work), including our own, is to improve people's quality of life. It involves creating a "good society" in which people's basic (e.g., adequate food, shelter) and higher (e.g., social involvement, leisure) needs are met (Bergland & Narum, 2007). Quality of life and social justice are both about people having equitable access to resources that enable them to participate in society. At their core, our research interests have quality of life and social justice aims. Yet this still does not explain our discomfort with *outside the academy*.

First, to have an *outside*, an *inside* is also needed. We interpret *inside the academy* to mean research that does not engage directly with people or communities. This could include using data that are in the public domain (e.g., media content, government, or historical documents), writing conceptually or with the aim to advance theory, and taking up autoethnographic forms of research.

Conversely, we infer *outside* the academy to be research that involves interacting with people as sources of data. For example, we interview and then write up our "findings." This would encompass most qualitative research done today, yet this still does not capture how we work.

We consider our research to be *along-side* the academy and the community. Affiliated with the academy, we are required to work within demands (e.g., funding constraints, publication expectations). The underlying reasons for our research, however, span beyond publication and contribution to a body of knowledge. Our inspiration, ideas, and methods come from issues encountered in our practice and through dialogue with community members, social service and health care providers, and decision makers. Our research is practical, and social change foregrounds our projects. We see ourselves as facilitators of the research, providing methodological and theoretical expertise as well as contributing our own experience on the topic. We are integrated with our communities and, thus, do not align ourselves *inside* or *outside*, but *along-side* the academy and the community.

We believe that working *along-side* the academy and community is vital to making practical, observable, and timely changes that benefit individuals and communities facing social injustices. We believe that many researchers play it safe. They retreat to the *inside* or go *outside* (using people as data sources alone) and then write up research on social justice issues from within the academy.

Once a community member asked us, in slightly more vivid words, "What have you done for me lately?" This chapter is about answering that question. It is about making our work as qualitative researchers committed to social justice more and directly relevant to those living with inequity through community-based participatory research (CBPR). We outline the nature of CBPR and why we believe it is vital for qualitative research with social justice aims, and then describe what CBPR demands from those who choose this approach. We propose that to "take action," qualitative researchers need to sincerely consider what they are willing to say, do, and risk—working *along-side* the academy and community—in explicit pursuit of social justice.

Community-based Participatory Research

As outlined, one way to address social justice is to do research *on* social justice issues from the safety of the academy. Another is to do research on social justice issues using approaches entrenched in social justice principles. CBPR is such an approach.

CBPR is an umbrella term coined by Israel, Schulz, Parker, and Becker (1998) for diverse approaches (e.g., Action Research, Participatory Action Research, Collaborative Research, Community Based Research) that engage communities in the research process for social justice aims. CBPR stems from traditions that exist on opposite ends of a continuum with respect to the type, extent, and goal of community involvement (Wallerstein & Duran, 2003). Research that has practical, utilization-focused (i.e., problem-solving), and social change purposes sits on one end of the continuum. These "Northern" approaches are less participatory and have roots in Kurt Lewin's (1997) *Action Research*. Research that has emancipatory purposes and seeks social justice is at the other end. These approaches stem from "Southern" traditions, in particular Paolo Freire's (1970) *Pedagogy of the Oppressed*, and are highly participatory.

Regardless of whether CBPR takes a more Northern or Southern tradition, all CBPR centers on a particular community and what it (and not the academic) defines as a priority or issue of importance. The research is driven by the desire to make things better in and with a particular community. This purpose is underscored throughout the research process from its conception to its completion. Because the research is focused on generating knowledge to solve a particular problem, and thereby improving the day-to-day lives of its members, it has the dual purposes of knowledge generation *and* action.

Such research focuses on a "community" as a group of people associated by geography or shared experience (e.g., a First Nations reserve, an inner city, a homeless population, a patient group, a refugee group) and includes not only those living with inequity but their natural supports (e.g., families, friends), social service and health care providers, decision makers, and community leaders (Mayan & Daum, in press). Since not all people in the community are able to or want to participate in the research, those who do come together to form a partnership. The term "partnership," then, is used to represent the working group that is made up of community and academic partners.

Community partners ensure that the CBPR project is community-driven. They are guides to a community's ways of knowing and expression (e.g., diaries, sharing circles, games, and story-telling) and can advise on what questions to ask—and to avoid—that will invite deeply embedded experience to be both told and heard. They suggest how to maneuver hierarchies, navigate gatekeepers, and ally with champions. They make certain that research protocols and materials are tailored to be sensitive to the community context and culture (Macaulay et al., 1999). As such, CBPR can often engage those who live with inequity, are vulnerable, and remain hidden (e.g., teen fathers, homeless individuals). And because CBPR includes those who have a detailed and nuanced understanding of what they consider to be a relevant problem, partners are sincerely invested in working together to find solutions.

Academics dedicated to social justice often choose a CBPR approach because it engages partners in defining and telling their own stories with the explicit and collective aim to participate in altering the policies, programs, and services that organize and structure inequity.

Why CBPR Is Vital for Qualitative Research with Social Justice Aims

CBPR Illuminates the Complexity of an Issue

CBPR can illuminate the complexity of a social justice issue because community partners are diverse and hold multiple perspectives on the issue. Living day-to-day with an issue often provides vital insight into it. Indeed, autoethnography is built on this premise. Hearing and learning about a person's first-hand perspective through autoethnography can be penetrating. The ardor that is present in excellent autoethnographies is multiplied in CBPR because partnerships allow diverse partners with similar and dissimilar lay and professional experiences to "have their say." Partners do not invite one story but multiple stories, which credits multiple realities that we accept ontologically as qualitative researchers. By working in partnership, everyone is obliged to see an issue from many angles. In particular, when lay stories and knowledge are presented that do not match dominant models of understanding, we cannot ignore them. As partners' stories confirm and collide with each other, and against dominant understanding, the complexity of the issue is developed and illuminated.

For example, one of our projects focused on the high rates of tuberculosis (TB) transmission in resource-poor countries, especially among those individuals living with HIV. While TB is almost non-existent in resource-rich countries, some resource-poor countries have over 50% of their populations living with HIV and TB. Recently, the South African government committed to providing

Isoniazid Preventive Therapy (IPT), a proven chemoprophylaxis, to people living with HIV and latent tuberculosis infection (TB bacteria that live in the body) to decrease mortality rates. Those trying to implement IPT recognized that treatment alone was not enough. A CBPR project[2] and corresponding partnership were then established with diverse groups: lay community researchers; nurses and physicians from the local hospital and outlying areas; mini-bus drivers (who hear passengers' chats and concerns); and local community advisory boards comprised of such diverse people as faith healers, politicians, and school representatives. From these perspectives, we learned that monetary support became available upon HIV diagnosis so that many community members chose to become infected with HIV to access these grants. Additionally, because IPT pharmaceuticals have street value, many people infected sell their medication to provide for themselves and their families. Traditional medicines and the role of community healers also spoke to the invisible health and social care system operating at the community level. To decrease the transmission and burden of TB, we need to understand the myriad of issues beyond the biomedical story.

CBPR Draws Attention to Neglected Issues

Qualitative researchers, in general, are really good at addressing the questions people would rather not have answered: those topics that people purposefully want to neglect or are neglected out of ignorance. A CBPR partnership may be initiated to bring forth those issues that are too remote or uncomfortable to manage alone. Or neglected and uncomfortable issues may emerge and be cultivated after people begin to feel comfortable with each other.

For example, people may join a CBPR project because they believe that individuals with intellectual disabilities are unjustifiably limited in their access to opportunities for employment and health services. Through numerous discussions, the issue of supporting individuals with intellectual disabilities to become parents—who may not be fully capable of parenting—moves quietly yet firmly into the conversation. Such an issue has been neglected and, if brought to the fore in the past, muzzled.

This example not only highlights how attention can be brought to neglected issues but also reinforces how social justice issues, and the policies created (or not) to address them, are undeniably about values. Moreover, influencing policy on highly value-laden issues is tricky. Having a CBPR partnership from varying organizations, including government, "at the table" means that the issue may be gently yet confidently moved through political channels.

CBPR Invites Debate

Many qualitative researchers are guided by critical theory and frame their research to examine and explain social inequity. That same critical lens is brought to bear in CBPR in a practical way when partners consider what was, what is, and what should be and draw on historical, local, and even global examples and experiences. These conversations invite vigorous debate as partners consider the following questions: What does this mean to me? How does this fit with my community? How is my understanding incomplete? Arguments and counter arguments among community and academic partners are exchanged to question assumptions and scrutinize otherwise hidden or misunderstood practices. In this way, we mirror Brinkmann's (2007) "epistemic interview" to take "advantage of the knowledge-producing potentials inherent in our conversations" (p. 1117). Drawing on Ellis's *Emotional and Ethical Quagmires in Returning to the Field* (1995), researchers using CBPR practice what she wrote:

> I would consider people in my research settings an audience. … I would talk more with community members about what I was doing. … I would, when appropriate, ask them to read what I had written and challenge my interpretations and consider negotiating with them the ultimate decision about whether to include sensitive information. (p. 88)

Debate does not serve to have one perspective "win," to come up with one meaning. Debate ensures all possible meanings are recognized. CBPR thus enables an epistemology whereby knowledge claims are justified to be "true" according to those living with an inequity and other supporters (i.e., natural supports, social service and health care providers, decision makers, community leaders). And because the research is about people's lives in practice, not in theory, community partners not only want to be heard, but want to ensure action toward ameliorating the problem is sound. There is a lot at stake. Of course, there is never "the solution," but partners propose the best solution, for now, given time, place, strengths, and limitations, knowing that life keeps moving.

In a CBPR project that involved 16 partners, including local government, the partnership was in the process of identifying "next steps" in the context of ethics. We made a suggestion. A local government partner turned to us and asked, "Do you think you are smarter than us?" Our suggestion was interpreted as dismissive of the partners' experience and as if we, as academics, could be the only authority in acting ethically. While this was unnerving and upsetting at the time, it demonstrated that the partnership environment invited honesty and debate, opening up the conversation to what would be ethically appropriate.

CBPR Decenters Academic Authority

With postmodernism, qualitative researchers became attentive to the authority of the researcher in all aspects of the research process. We were challenged to consider who we were representing in and who benefitted from our research. Were we telling the story of the researcher or the researched (Pillow, 2003)? We began to write layered texts to enable readers to fill the spaces with their own interpretations. We were convinced that, indeed, "writing is not an innocent practice" (Denzin, 1999, p. 568). We also started painting and drawing, illustrating comic books, creating poetry, stories, and performing plays. We were intent on allowing others to interrupt the researcher's account.

Interestingly, CBPR was introduced to community health in 1998. The same postmodern undertones that challenged us to do qualitative research differently also challenged a different approach to health research. Evident of these undertones, some of original principles upon which CBPR was built explicitly decenter academics' and other traditional power holders' authority. For example, early CBPR texts stated that not all partners have equal power (e.g., members living with the inequity vs. academics vs. government officials) and insisted that the partnership determine how it was going to manage and correct these power differentials at the inception of and throughout the project (Wallerstein & Duran, 2003). As a government partner once said, what she enjoyed about our group was that everyone "leaves their ego at the door." Early texts also outlined that different kinds of knowledge exist (e.g., academic, practical, cultural, professional) and that the assumption of working in partnership is that all knowledge is needed for addressing the problem (Israel et al., 1998). Thus, the academic is just one member in the partnership. As another community partner once said, "We rise and fall together."

And there is nothing better than having partners challenge interpretations, sculpt the findings, and determine how they are represented. They can determine how to layer their texts or communicate their stories to reveal their complexities and hidden contributors to inequities. CBPR lends itself beautifully to plays, sculpture, film, collage, and text, and oftentimes with partners as the actors, artists, and writers. In this way, partners make sense of their stories and do not attempt to edit or censor their own or others' experiences.

Decentering of the academic is best exemplified when engaging in CBPR with First Nations peoples. The Kahnawake Schools Diabetes Prevention Project, a partnership between the Mohawk community of Kahnawake and academics, was established to prevent Type 2 diabetes (Macaulay et al., 1999). The community and academics created a community advisory board (CAB) comprised of over 40 representatives from organizations, services, and the community at large. In addition to defining the project's vision and initiatives, the CAB developed a Research Code of Ethics based on the community's values. The Code established authorship guidelines for publications and presentations and outlined how disagreements regarding data interpretation would be managed. Because it was decided that data belonged to the community, rather than to the academics, it was returned to the community at the end of the project, halting future analysis unless approved by the CAB.

CBPR Dissuades the "Us and Them" Dichotomy

Qualitative researchers despise dichotomies. Yet when qualitative researchers refer to *outside* the academy, we create an *inside* the academy and, by extension, a *them* and an *us*. We divide ourselves into non-academics and academics, people who do not do research and those who do. But are the people that live with injustice incapable of critical thought and critique, unable to understand and articulate their own issues?

In CBPR, an assumption is that every member in the partnership, regardless of title, position, or past experience, brings strengths and knowledge needed to address the injustice. Thus, CBPR assists in eliminating this divide by acknowledging community partners as being theorists, philosophers, well-read, well-spoken, and having skills, connections, and the capacity to do something about the inequity they live with. Thinking otherwise is patronizing and paternalistic. Have we, as qualitative researchers, not learned from Spivak's (1988) work on the subaltern and the notion that the more powerful make decisions about others, dismissing those living with an issue by saying, "We know best"?

CBPR acknowledges that academics are also citizens and community members who can bring their own experience of the issue to the table. We occupy worlds and roles where we are partners, parents, friends, neighbors, caregivers, concerned community members, and so on. CBPR allows us as academics to use our research skills but also to participate as people who may have experience with the inequity. CBPR actually accepts that many times we do indeed focus our research on those things that we have experienced personally and, therefore, do not even begin to claim "objectivity."

Instead of being unsure of whom our work is reaching and for what purpose, qualitative researchers concerned with social justice should work *with* the people who we say our research aims to help. Let us treat our research participants the same way we would treat people in our personal lives. Ellis (1995) reminds us, "Make decisions the same way you make them in your everyday lives" (p. 89). In doing so, we rid ourselves of the notions of *inside* and *outside* and *us* and *them* and come back to our notion of *along-side* the academy and the community. We should think about research for social justice aims as a collective of people working on a problem together and desiring the same end—an injustice ratified.

CBPR Is Change Oriented

Social justice involves making society a better place to live. This requires an improvement in current conditions. CBPR is inherently change-oriented. It closes the gap between research and action, resulting in changes and benefits to communities, academics, and institutions.

Community benefits from involvement in CBPR projects are multiple and well-documented (e.g., Cashman et al., 2008; Israel et al., 1998). Community partners "find" each other, generate momentum, and mobilize their resources. Often, relationships developed through the CBPR project remain after it formally ends. This is critical as the complexity of social justice issues require continued commitment and multiple strategies to make change.

Academics, too, benefit from CBPR. We benefit from working with community partners, but less discussed is how working with service providers and policy makers results in a better understanding of the systems in which policy makers operate. Academics gain a more sophisticated understanding of overt and covert agendas, how decisions are made, who the key players are, and how to position a message. We learn alongside policy makers to know what is amenable to change now and in the near and distant future, what will garner "quick wins," and where more incremental change is needed.

Yet even less attention has been given to the role of CBPR in institutional change. If qualitative researchers are serious about social justice, then ultimately those who live marginalized lives must become leaders—government officials, industry leaders, and academics—to create knowledge for the advancement of their own communities. CBPR can play a pivotal role in this enterprise. By working with both marginalized communities and the systems that support them, other ways of knowing become real and legitimized. These other ways of knowing challenge existing structures, including the meritocracy model[3] on which our institutions are based. CBPR partners challenge the notion of "merit" itself and the structuring and hiring of people into decision-making positions based on merit, as measured by education, standardized tests, and credentials. Of course there is hard work put into achievements, but those who are rewarded within this meritocracy model fail to acknowledge that we hold these positions because of the structures we put in place. Few First Nations people are in positions of power and have places in the academy. Their knowledge and credentials do not fit the normative. And we spend time trying—indeed with very good intentions—to get those who are marginalized to fit into our dominant and established structures. But then we perpetuate the meritocracy logic.

In its place, we need to create structures that fit other ways of knowing. Instead of squeezing people into our structures, how can our structures change to accommodate other knowledge and experience? What and who has to change? This extends not only to government but to our research institutions and methodology. We typically create opportunities for "empowerment" and stop. People still have to empower themselves within the given and smothering structure and are often blocked.

CBPR is well positioned for change at the institutional level, as it is openly political and aims for policy change, even if it is those policies that protect and legitimize our society's institutional structures in which we are rewarded.

Summary

CBPR obliges that qualitative researchers respect the multiple perspectives on an issue, revealing its complexity and creating space where neglected issues can be brought forward. It creates an environment where partners can debate, not to win but to have their own assumptions challenged. CBPR explicitly decenters the authority of the academic and, in doing so, dissuades the use of "us and them." And above all, CBPR is change oriented. CBPR ties us to these spaces, not as academics or community members, but as partners, not allowing us to simplify that which is complex.

What CBPR Demands

While our aim is to argue for the worth of CBPR for projects with social justice aims, we do not purport that CBPR is the panacea of research. We do not ask all qualitative researchers to abandon their current research practices in favor of CBPR. Indeed, we acknowledge that CBPR can be difficult and in some circumstances highly problematic. Much has been written on strategies for successful CBPR projects (e.g., Flicker, Savan, McGrath, Kolenda, & Mildenberger, 2008; Israel et al., 1998; Seifer, 2006). To conclude this chapter, we go beyond this literature to highlight what we believe CBPR demands of academics in addition to skills such as conflict resolution and facilitation. We uncover the underbelly[4] of doing this kind of work.

Willingness to Expose Our Values and Politics and Act Upon Them

As qualitative researchers, we are told that to do good qualitative research we need to expose our theoretical allegiances and our assumptions and beliefs about how the world works, the nature of reality, and how to get at reality. We do this, for example, by positioning ourselves, including ourselves in our writing, and practicing reflexivity, as best we can.

In addition, when we choose to use CBPR, we expose even more about ourselves. CBPR forces us to develop and act upon our values in the context of political agendas. By using CBPR, not only is the research political, but the academic is drawn into politics. It is risky. We must be willing to expose personal values, overtly align ourselves with a community, and act politically. We put ourselves into a difficult position. We must write for publication to keep our positions in the academy but also must act politically to bring about the change we agreed upon as a partnership. Our deans and our community partners hold us accountable.

Work with Those in Power

Academics using CBPR are often drawn to Pierre Bourdieu's work. As a public intellectual, he argued to "respect the complexity of problems" (cited in Garrett, 2007, p. 232) and was considered an activist, a "foe of neo-liberalism and defender of embattled public services" (p. 225). Yet, Bourdieu (2001) contended that public intellectuals need to be independent of those in power, reasoning that "there is no genuine democracy without genuine opposing critical powers" (cited in Garrett, 2007, p. 232). We agree and see the role of an academic to be independent of those in power so as to interrogate established conventions and truths.

In the case of CBPR, we see working with those in power essential. We need to engage directly and meaningfully with those in power in order to respect "the complexity of problems." The change-orientation of our work demands that the partnership include partners who know the public policy system, have credibility within it, and can navigate through it. The principle that all partners can bring their personal experiences with the issue to the table also invites work with power holders. Does it mean that individuals who hold power cannot appreciate the history behind an issue and articulate what it means to live a better life? Do those in power not have children with mental health issues, parents who live in elder care, brothers and sisters who fight addictions, neighbors or friends who are immigrants or refugees that face barriers due to language, education, or socioeconomic status? Indeed, some of the policymakers we have worked with can tell us about the devastating effects of their policies. If we do not allow people in power to participate, are we not complicit in essentializing?

Critique, Not Criticize

Which qualitative researcher did not change fundamentally after being exposed to the work of Edward Said? In the list of his many contributions, he ensured that we would always think, at least twice, each time we wrote something about someone. And like Bourdieu, he wrote about the role of the public intellectual as independent of those in power and more directly of "the scoffer whose place it is publicly to raise embarrassing questions—to be someone who cannot easily be co-opted by governments or corporations" (cited in Posner, 2003, p. 30).

To that we say, in a less sophisticated manner than Said, that you catch more flies with honey than vinegar. We argue from a CBPR perspective that if you are fair, genuine, and seek good, you have a better chance at working well with people to achieve a common end. Simply put, people will not change when you embarrass or humiliate them, or tell them what to do; they shut down. We know that relationships are the key to any good work, and that there is tremendous satisfaction when partners say, "We did it together." Thus, to achieve social change, we must sit and participate with others to solve a problem, pushing when we can, pulling back when we need to, knowing the leverage points, and knowing what is static. And on the matter of being "co-opted" by working with government: working together does not mean we have been co-opted. If we think this way, it dismisses our integrity, our training, and our stead.

Critiquing Our Own System

Perhaps our greatest learning from being involved in CBPR is for partners (including us as academics) to openly critique their own systems. How can we do this when our natural inclination is to protect ourselves, our practice, and our systems? How was the policy-maker introduced earlier able to articulate that her ministry's policies were disadvantaging women and keeping them, in this case, in poor housing conditions? We do not want to critique what we value—to bite the hand that feeds us.

When we, as academics using CBPR, engage partners, participate *with* them, and include their perspectives to develop the complexity of the problem and ameliorate injustice, we are better able to ask: What are we protecting in our systems and why? Why do we feel threatened? When partners are able to sit down in an exchange and critique their own systems, the real political work that is needed for social change can happen. Fingers are not pointed; we have a shared problem, albeit a complex one, and we work within our own spheres of influence—no matter how small—to change.

We are responsible for what we replicate. If we do not critique our own systems, we may create and recreate structures that perpetuate injustice.

Summary

What does CBPR demand of academics? It demands a willingness to have an open mind and to work not only with those living with the inequities but also with those in the systems that on a day-to-day basis do what they can, when they can, to assist in making peoples' lives better. If we participate directly with those in power, we can better see the complexity of issues and advocate for change from this informed position. And if we can critique our own systems first, we are better partners for each other and can identify how our systems are complicit in the inequities our society creates.

Inside, Outside, and Along-side

For the purposes of social justice, should qualitative inquiry be *outside*, *inside*, or *along-side* the academy? Some days, it may feel like *up-side down* inquiry. If qualitative researchers seriously consider what Norman Denzin has been encouraging us to do for years, pursue social justice through qualitative research, we need to sincerely ask ourselves, "What are we trying to accomplish with our work?" If "taking action" is our answer, then we propose that "a desk is a dangerous place from which to view the world" (le Carre, as cited in BrainyQuotes, n.d.). Qualitative researchers need to work *along-side* the academy and the community in an equitable partnership to become political in the explicit pursuit of social justice.

Notes

1 While we prefer the word "inquiry" over "research," this chapter presents community-based participatory *research*, not inquiry. Consequently, we use the term "research" throughout.

2 Thank you to Jody Boffa, PhD candidate, Department of Community Health Sciences, Faculty of Medicine, University of Calgary, for her lead on this study.

3 We thank Daily Laing, MA, research assistant, for her thoughts on this section.

4 Thank you to Maxi Miciak, PhD candidate, Department of Rehabilitation Science, University of Alberta, for coining this term.

References

Bergland, A., & Narum, I. (2007). Quality of life: Diversity in content and meaning. *Critical Reviews in Physical & Rehabilitation Medicine, 19*, 115–139.

Bourdieu, P. (2001). *Acts of resistance: Against the new myths of our time.* New York: Polity.

BrainyQuotes. (n.d.). John le Carre quotes. Retrieved December 11, 2013, from www.brainyquote.com/quotes/authors/j/john_le_carre.html#FhY0q7kl Gk3mwkfy.99

Brinkmann, S. (2007). Could interviews be epistemic? An alternative to qualitative opinion polling. *Qualitative Inquiry, 13*, 1116–1138.

Cashman, S. B., et al. (2008). The power and the promise: Working with communities to analyze data, interpret findings, and get to outcomes. *American Journal of Public Health, 98*, 1407–1417.

Denzin, N. K. (1999). Two-stepping in the '90s. *Qualitative Inquiry, 5*, 568–572.

Denzin, N. (2013). *Welcome from the director, ninth international congress of qualitative inquiry.* Retrieved from www.icqi.org/wp-content/uploads/2013/04/QI2013-Final-Program-042413.pdf

Dye, T. R. (1972). *Understanding public policy.* Englewood Cliffs, NJ: Prentice Hall.

Ellis, C. (1995). Emotional and ethical quagmires in returning to the field. *Journal of Contemporary Ethnography, 24,* 68–98.

Flicker, S., Savan, B., McGrath, M., Kolenda, B., & Mildenberger, M. (2008). 'If you could change one thing...' What community-based researchers wish they could have done differently? *Community Development Journal, 43*(2), 239–253.

Freire, P. (1970). *Pedagogy of the oppressed.* New York: Seabury Press.

Garrett, P.M. (2007). Making social work more Bourdieusian: Why the social professions should critically engage with the work of Pierre Bourdieu. *European Journal of Social Work, 10,* 225–243.

International Congress of Qualitative Inquiry. (2011). *Seventh international congress of qualitative inquiry.* Retrieved December 12, 2013 from www.icqi.org/qi2011/index.html

Israel, B. A., Schulz, A. J., Parker, E. A., & Becker, A. B. (1998). Review of community-based research: Assessing partnership approaches to improve public health. *Annual Review of Public Health, 19,* 173–202. Retrieved from http://www.annualreviews.org/journal/publhealth

Lewin, K. (1997). *Resolving social conflicts and field theory in social science.* Washington, DC: American Psychological Association. (Original work published in 1948.)

Macaulay, A. C., Commanda, L. E., Freeman, W. L., Gibson, N., McCabe, M. L., Robbins, C. M., & Twohig, P. L. (1999). Participatory research maximises community and lay involvement. *British Medical Journal, 319,* 774–778.

Mayan, M., & Daum, C. (in press). Generating and applying qualitative evidence: The potential of community-based participatory research. In K. Olson, R. Young, & I. Schultz (Eds.), *Handbook of qualitative research for evidence-based practice.* New York: Springer.

Nakamura, R.T. (1987). The textbook policy process and implementation research. *Review of Policy Research, 7,* 142–154.

Pillow, W. (2003). Confession, catharsis, or cure? Rethinking the uses of reflexivity as methodological power in qualitative research. *International Journal of Qualitative Studies in Education, 16,* 175–196.

Posner, R. A. (2003). *The public intellectuals: A study of decline.* Cambridge, MA: Harvard University Press

Rawls, J. (1971). *A theory of justice.* Cambridge, MA: Belknap Press of Harvard University Press.

Seifer, S. (2006). Building and sustaining community-institutional partnerships for prevention research: Findings from a national collaborative. *Journal of Urban Health-Bulletin of the New York Academy of Medicine, 83,* 989–1003.

Smith, D., Jacobson, L., & Yiu, L. (2008). Primary health care. In L. Stamler & L. Yiu (Eds.), *Community health nursing: A Canadian perspective* (2nd ed., pp. 111–124). Toronto: Pearson Prentice Hall.

Spivak, G. (1988). Can the subaltern speak? In C. Nelson & L. Grossberg, *Marxism and interpretation of culture* (pp. 271–313). Chicago: University of Illinois Press.

Stadnyk, R. L., Townsend, E. A., & Wilcock, A. A. (2010). Occupational justice. In C. H. Christiansen & E. A. Townsend (Eds.), *Introduction to occupation: The art and science of living* (2nd ed., pp. 329–358). Upper Saddle River, NJ: Pearson.

United Nations. (2006). *Social justice in an open world: The role of the United Nations*. New York: United Nations.

Wallerstein, W., & Duran, B. (2003). The conceptual, historical, and practice roots of community based participatory research and related traditions. In M. Minkler & N. Wallerstein (Eds.), *Community-based participatory research for health* (pp. 27–52). San Francisco: Jossey-Bass.

Chapter 4

Thinking *Through* Theory

Contemplating Indigenous Situated Research and Policy

Margaret Kovach

Cree scholar Neal McLeod introduces *wîsahkêcâhk* in his 2007 book *Cree Narrative Memory*. *wîsahkêcâhk* is known in Plains Cree culture as the transformer. *wîsahkêcâhk* stories tell of the transformer deftly moving through the terrain of Cree narrative expressing itself, then re-imagining itself, in the consciousness of the Cree as the culture re-affirms itself generation upon generation. *wîsahkêcâhk* invites the imaginings of those who participate in Cree society and the understandings that the transformer inspires. "With regard to *wîsahkêcâhk*, there are many voices and many perspectives" (McLeod, 2007, p. 99). In these stories, as McLeod states, the nature of the transformer is only limited by the imagination of those who sit spellbound in the midst of its mystery. The transformer stirs us to think, and then think again. In the immediacy of a routinely fashioned life *wîsahkêcâhk* waits to visit, arriving with the intentionality of the paradoxically aloof provocateur and, in doing so, stops us short. Whether prompting a jarring halt in daily 'business as usual' or a less startling lull, when the transformer visits we notice. *wîsahkêcâhk* medicine does not so much direct as offer pause to listen to what we know, consider what we do not know, and think about what it is, exactly, that we are doing. If I were a Cree storyteller, and if this were a research story told by a fire, it would be in broaching theory talk that I would halt the flow of words, sit silent for a moment, knowing that at any moment *wîsahkêcâhk* will be entering the circle.

Absorbed in completing this writing task, I am not paying attention to my immediate situatedness, which is a desk cluttered with journal articles, books, orange Post-it notes, yellow highlighter pens, and an assortment of coffee cups from this most recent writing venture. Moving my mouse, I nudge Neil McLeod's *Cree Narrative Memory* against Kerry E. Howell's *The Philosophy of Methodology* perilously positioned amid the muddle on my desk. The nudge causes a chain reaction, the books slide, my coffee mug topples, and hot java smudges a red-inked underlined note on my essay outline—"theory moves through research."

Theory in qualitative research is a certainty, but like the intangible *wîsahkêcâhk* that moves with a maverick's covertness, theory in research can perplex. This is unfortunate, as the nature of theory implies suppositions that when left unquestioned flourish—particularly when the consenting majority favors a normative theory. Stringer (2014) states that theory is not necessarily right or wrong, "but that it focuses on particular aspects of the situation and interests them in particular ways" (p. 38). Whether theory impels a felt experience of liberation or oppression, whether it is contested or accepted, theory as both form and substance subsists through research that informs policy.

Indigenous peoples endure so-called 'capacity building' policy that is largely born of outsider imaginings built upon specious theoretical suppositions of what is and isn't good for Indigenous people. If the Indigenous voice is not being heard in the research theory that shapes Indigenous policy development, whose voice, then, is being relied upon? How trustworthy is this voice in offering an accounting of Indigenous people's lives? To omit the Indigenous voice in the theory-research-policy relationship is to be complicit in reproduction of dubious policy development. Theory unexamined, valorized through research and manifested in policy, poses, indeed has posed, great risk for Indigenous people. However, such a conjecture assumes that research, as a theory-laden exercise, does impact policy.

Klemperer, Theisens, and Kaiser (2001) offer this perspective on the linkage between research and policy:

> In our experience, the relationship between policy making and policy research resembles "dancing in the dark", where the dancers do not completely see each other, the movements are complex, and the environment influences the flow of the dance. (p. 197)

Klemperer et al. (2001) go on to illustrate specific ways in which research factors into the policy process. Citing Carol H. Weiss's work, the authors articulate different ways that research influences policy development. This typology includes: a) "Problem-solving research"; b) "Political uses of research"; and c) "Research used for enlightening purposes" (p. 200). Problem-solving research is specific research focused on a particular issue as a means to help develop and clarify policy on that issue. Political use of research involves the use of research to support political opinions already established. Finally, research for enlightening purposes helps give greater insight to a policy concern and "may help in the process of shaping ideas or conceptualizations of the problem" (p. 200).

Policy within Indigenous education (primary, secondary, and tertiary) is a good example of the theory, research, and policy dynamic in action. Policy discourse in Indigenous education in Canada is more often than not geared toward closing the Aboriginal "achievement gap." Certainly, this has merit given that a report on *Bridging the Aboriginal Education Gap in Saskatchewan* by economist Eric Howe "shows that a North American Indian male who drops out of school has lifetime earnings of only $362,023. If he just completes high school his earnings more than double" (Howe, 2011, p. 8). For a non-Aboriginal male in Saskatchewan who drops out of high school his lifetime earnings are $693,273 (Howe, 2011). The *Campaign 2000 "2011 Report Card on Child and Family Poverty in Canada"* (Family Service Toronto, 2011) reports that the child poverty rate for 1996–2006 for children under 18 living in low income two-parent families was 52% for Aboriginal families, while for all children it was 18%. Education is, as Blair Stonechild puts forth in his appropriately titled book, *The New Buffalo: The Struggle for Aboriginal Post-secondary Education in Canada*, critical to addressing such inequities. The difficulty is that the Indigenous student achievement gap discourse tends to be motivated by an economic imperative loaded with deficit theorizing.

An aware Canadian only has to consider the recent Conservative federal government's proposed bill on First Nations education, *Working Together for First Nations Students*. The research found in the policy guide for this initiative, *Developing a First Nations Education Action: Discussion Guide* (Aboriginal Affairs and Northern Development Canada, 2012), cites achievement gap research using "lag behind" (p. 1) language to describe First Nations student abilities. The proposed response is that tighter funding, limited jurisdiction, and increased controls by the federal government are what is going to make the difference in graduation rates of First Nations students. Assembly of First Nations Chief Shawn Atleo stated in a recent interview that the new bill "is on the verge of potentially imposing an 'assimilationist' educational system on aboriginal children that repeats the mistakes of residential school" (Kennedy, 2013, para. 1). Aboriginal columnist Doug Cuthand from the *Saskatoon Star Phoenix* made this comment: "It's an old fashioned, top-down colonial approach that was supposed to have been put to bed 40 years ago with the adoption of the First Nations policy of Indian control of Indian Education" (Cuthand, 2013, A1). Strength-based theorizing that considers the possibility of anti-racist, culturally responsive schooling, based upon the strength of Indigenous cultural values, as a way to encourage student engagement is not what is being privileged in this approach. The power of culture, as articulated by the kokums and mosoms, is not being heard.

Within an Indigenous context, policy, and the research that informs policy, has often been from the outside looking in. In focusing on research, much has been extractive and has worked to mummify Indigenous culture. This has left a lingering distaste of research by Indigenous peoples (Tuhiwai Smith, 2013; Denzin & Lincoln, 2005). The production and reproduction of research laden with assumptions about Indigenous people has arisen from non-Indigenous situated, one-eyed seeing theorizing. Such theorizing has been the bane of the Indigenous community. Given the impact of theory manifested in research and policy, it is imperative, right at the start, that researchers are clear on what assumptions are being put out there in the form of theory. Unpacking how theory functions in research is useful in showcasing its pervasiveness.

Unpacking Theory

Traveling into the abstract language of research theory, I am reminded of a document I came across a number of years ago when I was an undergraduate post-secondary student. The report, entitled *What Was Said? The Taking Control Project*, was an inquiry into post-secondary education. In the 1986 report Cree educator Sid Fiddler posed a question pertinent then and relevant now to my research instructor self. I now appreciate this as a *wîsahkêcâhk* question. He asked: "How can you relate what is being taught to what the hell is happening on the reserve?" (cited in Stalwick, 1986, p. 7). He prefaced this question by pointing out that the abstract nature of education can hinder the inclusion of community knowledge. Knowing the risks, it remains necessary to venture into the fray of 'the abstract' so as to examine how theory is implicated in research.

I would like to differentiate between what is understood as a conceptual framework or paradigm in qualitative research and methodology. A framework or paradigm for qualitative inquiry can be described as an "an interrelated set of assumptions, concepts, values, and practices that comprise a way of viewing reality" (Schwandt, 2007, p. 122). A framework, or paradigm, includes broad, abstract assumptions and actions related to research. Examples of qualitative frameworks include positivism, transformative, constructivism, and, increasingly, the recognition of an Indigenous/Indigenist paradigm. Methodology can be described as relating to a specific research project and is the process by which a researcher goes about responding to the research question (Howard, 2013; Stringer, 2014). Examples of methodology include participatory action, feminism, grounded theory, and Indigenous methodology. The qualitative framework or paradigm and methodology are connected, but for the purposes of this discussion, theory will be situated within a discourse on methodology. This makes explicit an additional assumption of this commentary—methodology involves both theory and methods.

In this section, three definitional terms will be relied upon to describe and differentiate research theory. The use of definitional terms within the production and reproduction of theory can arguably work to oversimplify intrinsic complexities that surround the articulation of theory in research. However, I am including definitional terms in this chapter because I find them useful in unpacking what is meant by theory in research methodology and how theory is located within methodology, including the design, methods, and analysis in research. Finally, I find these definitions useful in making visible how research is permeated with theory and how, when unleashed from the 'laboratory,' this research influences the policy and practice that flow from it.

The following definitions are presented in a linear fashion, but the appearance of theory in research is not a linear process. While admitting to the possibility of oversimplifying the complexity of theory, I do fully respect that research theory travels through *wîsahkêcâhk* territory, where switchbacks, detours, and any number of alternative routes may be part of the terrain. In fact, I find the language of flux and movement associated with an Indigenous paradigm to be a more precise descriptor of the nature of theory in research.

The definitional terms used to describe ways that theory makes appearance in most qualitative methodologies include: a) *personal theory* (situatedness); b) *framework theory*; and c) *substantive (or substantiated) theory*. The terminology used in this section is borrowed from qualitative research (Howell, 2013; Schwandt, 2007). It is noted that there is a range of methodologies within qualitative inquiry and that these definitional terms can be found among approaches of an interpretive tradition. *Substantive theory*, in particular, is a term found in grounded theory (Charmaz, 2006). It ought to be noted that perspectives on the role of theory and subjectivities in qualitative methodology can differ. In referencing the work of Anfara and Mertz (2006), Mansor Abu Talib (2010) puts forward that researchers approach theory in qualitative research in various ways. This ranges from those who acknowledge the role of theory (Guba & Lincoln, 1994) to those who argue that theory "does not typically have a solid relationship with qualitative research (Merriam, 1997; Schwandt, 2007)" (Tavallaei & Abu Talib, 2010, p. 571).

Personal theory is the pre-existing beliefs and assumptions that a researcher brings to a research project. Howell (2013), who utilizes the term "personal theorizing" (p. 27), describes this as understandings that an individual holds arising from his or her individual experience. I am beginning with personal theory because it is most closely associated with one's own embodied, situated knowledges that exist before and beyond any particular research project. In qualitative research the subjectivity of personal situatedness is recognized as valid knowledge (Finlay, 2002; Richardson & St. Pierre, 2005). The process of participant reflection and centrality of life narrative in research appears in one of the earliest qualitative research projects, a study of the Polish peasant in Europe and America (1918–1920), by sociologists Thomas and Znaniecki. This study had its origins at the Chicago school of sociology in the early 1900s (Abbott & Egloff, 2008) and is cited as one of the first qualitative studies insisting upon the inclusion of subjectivity in a socially situated life. "The idea of 'the self' in *The Polish Peasant* is relational, situational and sequential, with writing a life, seriality and temporality seen as essential for gauging the processes of social becoming" (Stanley, 2010, p. 147).

As qualitative methodologies have progressed from their early ethnographic roots (early 1900s) to more positivist leanings (1960s) to more critically transformative strategies found in current approaches, there has been an invitation to reveal the situatedness and positionality of both participant and researcher in research (Denzin & Lincoln, 2005). As Richardson and St. Pierre (2005) suggest, critical self-reflection "evokes new questions about the self and subject; remind[s] us that our work is grounded, contextual, and rhizomatic; and demystif[ies] the research/writing process" (p. 965). They say that honoring one's own situatedness through self-situating "can evoke deeper parts of the self, heal wounds, enhance the sense of self—or even alter one's sense of identity" (p. 965). Finlay (2002) suggests that critical reflexivity is inseparable from contemporary qualitative inquiry and "is now the defining feature of qualitative research (Banister et al., 1994)" (p. 211). Personal theory is the life knowledge (including beliefs) that we bring to the research.

A *framework theory* is a focus on, and alignment with, a set of beliefs and assumptions associated with qualitative research methodologies. It is closely associated with what Guba and Lincoln (1994) reference as a paradigm or set of "basic beliefs" (p. 107). In his book, *Action Research*, Ernest T. Stringer uses the term "theory of the *method*" (2014, p. 39). The consideration of a framework theory generally occurs at the front-end of a specific research project and is, commonly, a theoretical orientation formalized in existing literature. The term *formal theory* in this context is synonymous with established theory found in research discourse. Examples include feminist, post-modernist, relativist, critical theory. The framework theory in this context is that which has often been defined in previous theoretical, customarily academic, writings. Those in the academy who have had the privilege to represent themselves have historically defined and established such theories. A framework theory emerges from a particular cultural context and from a particular voice.

Critical theory is an example of a framework theory. It is a particular theoretical perspective that assists in focusing research in a particular way. Bohman (2013) offers this perspective on critical theory, "A critical theory provides the descriptive and normative bases for social inquiry aimed at decreasing domination and increasing freedom in all their forms" (para. 1). Thus, research that integrates a critical theory perspective will have as a focus power and privilege. Often critical theory is associated with decolonizing research.

The choice of framework theory is quite significant because it is foundational in guiding research method choice and analysis. The framework theory is more often than not linked with personal theory in qualitative methodologies because researchers, being human, tend to gravitate toward theoretical framing that is congruent with (i.e., not repellent to) their own personal belief system. While the use of established theories in qualitative methodologies is the norm, there exists space for the establishment of emergent framework theories, of which Indigenous theory is an example.

Substantive theory has arisen from the methodological enterprise and language of grounded theory methodology. Substantive theory differentiates from personal theory and framework theory in that substantive theory emerges from the data of a specific research project. In articulating what is meant by substantive theory, grounded theorist Kathy Charmez (2006) offers this description:

Most grounded theories are substantive theories because they address delimited problems in specific substantive areas such as a study of how newly disabled young people reconstruct their identities. (p. 8)

Howell (2013) defines substantive theory as "derived from data analysis" and includes "rich conceptualizations of specific situations" (p. 27). Substantive theory, then, is closely associated with data and occurs in the research phase when one is working with the data to make meaning. One's own personal theory and subjectivities are implicated in the building of substantive theory within a singular research project. This is based upon the argument that research subjectivities can never be divorced from one's research choices and interpretations. Furthermore, the framework theory that is applied within a research design will impact the substantive theory arising from the data.

Theoretical choices in research shape-shift and evolve according to experience and knowledge (Howell, 2013). As Charmaz's (2010) states: "The theory [grounded or substantive] *depends* on the researcher's view: it does not and cannot stand outside of it" (p. 130). In a well-considered research design, there is evidence of a relationship between personal theory, framework theory, and situated theory.

Revealing how an aspect of a phenomenon functions in relationship to the larger phenomenon is instrumental in discerning its significance. Knowing the function of firewood in building a fire helps clarify its import, and so tending to the firewood is rudimentary. In much the same way, knowing the different forms that theory takes in research is basic to appreciating its role. Theory as form then becomes less of an enigma and a more transparent process. In considering personal theory, framework theory, and substantive theory as form (or a 'place-saver') the task then is to consider the 'type' or substance of theory being proposed. The next section references Indigenous theory to more specifically consider theory as that which focuses on a situation in a specific way Stringer (2014) and that which understands a situation from a particular perspective. Indigenous theory is a particular theoretical orientation with specific attributes and characteristics. A main argument throughout has been the importance of

Indigenous situated voice in the theory-research-policy dynamic. Indigenous theory has much to offer here.

Indigenous Theory

Within Indigenous methodologies, an Indigenous theory can be useful in demystifying and concretely grounding methodology in Indigenous situated knowledge. The rationale for briefly addressing Indigenous theory is to illustrate that: a) an Indigenous theoretical perspective in research is possible and b) Indigenous theory is a viable theoretical approach well positioned to situate Indigenous experience. Personal theory (or situatedness) is valued within Indigenous philosophy and, thus, Indigenous theory. Consequently, the assumptions arising from this theoretical perspective (Indigenous theory) are grounded within Indigeneity itself, thereby offering an Indigenous insider-out approach to research.

The term *Indigenous paradigm* is common to Indigenous research and is used to articulate an Indigenous belief system. As with other qualitative paradigms (e.g., transformative, constructivist) an Indigenous research paradigm can be described as a set of assumptions, values, and practices that comprise an approach or perspective. Indigenist or Indigenous methodologies are founded upon this paradigm (Kovach, 2010; Wilson, 2008). Because of their paradigmatic orientation, Indigenous methodologies are well positioned to integrate theory steeped in Indigenous philosophy.

Indigenous philosophy and, subsequently, Indigenous theory are of an ancient, but ever evolving, set of beliefs and practices arising from tribal cultures. Writings on the nature and characteristics of Indigenous philosophy have seen growth within academic publication, including writing by such authors as Vine Deloria, Jr., Willie Ermine, Leroy Little Bear, and Marie Battiste. Much of this writing, documenting Indigenous community-based knowledges, shows a shared set of beliefs among Indigenous peoples globally. Such beliefs include the acknowledgment of process, wholeness, and the collective. In his article, *Jagged Worldviews Colliding*, Blackfoot scholar Leroy Little Bear (2000) writes:

Arising out of the Aboriginal philosophy of constant motion or flux is the value of wholeness or totality. The value of wholeness speaks to the totality of creation, the group as opposed to the individual, the forest opposed to the individual trees. It focuses on the totality of the constant flux rather than the individual trees. (p. 79)

Of the totality, flux, and collectivity, Mohawk scholar Brant Castellano (2000) delineates the esteem assigned to spiritual, experiential, and holistic knowledges and the significance of oral transmission within Indigenous beliefs and practices. Within the metaphysics of Indigeneity, the symbiosis of individual and collective endure.

Perkins (2007) identifies several components of Indigenous theory while reminding that definitional categories and components are themselves antagonist toward the holistic nature of Indigenous theory. These components include: the "concept of harmony or balance"; "importance of place and history"; "experience, practice, and process"; the holistic and collective nature of Indigeneity; and "the cyclical and genealogical nature of time" (p. 64). Maori scholar Graham Hingangaroa Smith further conveys specific characteristics of Indigenous theory. According to Smith (cited in Kovach, 2010) Indigenous theory is culturally contextualized, born of community, articulated by a theorist knowledgeable of Indigenous worldview; change orientated; transferable, but not universal; flexible; theoretically engaged, not isolationist; critical; and accessible.

Threaded throughout an Indigenous theoretical perspective is the value of personal knowledge and the practice of communicating what has been learned. Vine Deloria, Jr. (as cited in Deloria, Jr., & Wildcat, 2001) had this to say about why Indigenous people relate personal experience: "We share our failure and successes so that we know who we are and so that we have confidence when we do things" (p. 46). Through this connection there is empathy and support, along with concrete practical guidance. Knowledge is personally situated but collectively sourced. Deloria, Jr., went on to say that tribal knowledges help us "to see our place and our responsibility within the movement of history as it is experienced by community" (p. 46). Collective notions of place, responsibility, and history anchor personal understandings and actions.

Personal situatedness allows for acknowledgement of kinship and community in personal realizations. The practice and protocol of self-situating with the purpose of acknowledging those who have held us up is increasingly found within research and scholarship by Indigenous authors (Cardinal, 2001; Coram, 2011; Debassige, 2010; Iwama, 2009). Within community, the protocol of introduction is a sign of respect and functions as a way for others to situate who we are within kinship and community systems.

The value of personal theory or situatedness within Indigenous theory asks, or rather requires, that Indigenous experience be included. In and of itself, this is a remedial, restitutional, and radical proposition. In Indigenous theory the totality of theory, in all its forms, is valued. Indeed a criterion of an Indigenous framework theory is to place oneself within one's own life and social context. Further, it is the articulation of personal theory and framework theory steeped in Indigeneity that ultimately leads to situated theory with an Indigenous sensibility.

The *wîsahkêcâhk* Hypothesis

In connecting back to policy, the absence of Indigenous situated theorizing has led to a ground swell of both research and policy promoting a deficit theorizing approach to Indigenous people. Such research and policy initiatives have pierced the Indigenous community with a 'gap' focused, victim-blaming sting. In the third edition of *The SAGE Dictionary of Qualitative Inquiry*, Schwandt (2007) speaks to the uses of theory. Here he quotes R. Alford's arguments that research responds to both theoretical and empirical questions. The theoretical questions posed include "Why did something happen? What explains this? Why did these events occur? What do they mean?" (p. 293). If we were to consider, for example, the experience of Indigenous student engagement in Canadian educational institutions, how would an Indigenous theory respond to these theoretical questions: How may this be different from the existing normative perspective? Would this shift thinking? In shifting thinking, would actions change? Would knowing the myriad ways that theory functions in research help to demystify how deficit theorizing of Indigenous peoples perseveres?

Research and policy impacting Indigenous communities have never been apolitical, nor have they been atheoretical. Whether visible or not, both are inevitably imbued with suppositions and conjectures. This essay offers some big picture connections. It begins with the premise that there is a connection between theory, research, and policy. In reflecting upon unexamined theory in an Indigenous context, we see that more often than not outsider theorizing in research and policy has diminished rather than upheld Indigenous peoples. Unpacking the different forms that theory takes in research—as in personal, framework, and substantive theory—offers insight into its persuasiveness. Moving toward an Indigenous theory, as a particular approach, provides a way forward toward a more fully Indigenous situated theorizing.

Within Indigenous country, for too long theorizing of Indigenous people, culture, and experience has occurred from an outsider situated vantage point. As research involving Indigenous peoples continues to be highly fundable, the production line, drive-through approach often trumps a more meditative one. All too frequently, it seems as if it is the same old song until there is a shift in energy—a book topples, coffee spills. Alertness expands and responsive intensifies. *wîsahkêcâhk*—the transformer—has entered the room. *wîsahkêcâhk* has the potential to trouble even the most theoretically complacent researcher, and in doing so, changes things. The shrewd transformer interrupts the habitual and makes space for us to pause, reflect, think, and think again. And in the often stagnant, deficit theorizing of Indigenous peoples in research and policy discourse, both thinking again and changing things couldn't hurt.

References

Aboriginal Affairs and Northern Development Canada. (2012). *Developing a First Nation Education Act: Discussion Guide*. Ottawa: Canada.

Abott, A & Egloff, R. (2008). The polish peasant in Oberlin and Chicago: The intellectual trajectory of W. I. Thomas. *American Sociologist 39* (4), 217–258.

Abu Talib, M. (2010). A general perspective on role of theory in qualitative research. *The Journal of International Social Research, 3*(11), 570–577.

Anfara, V., & Mertz, N. T. (2006). *Theoretical frameworks in qualitative research.* Thousand Oaks, CA: Sage.

Bannister, P. Burman, E., Parker, I., & Tindall, C. (1994). *Qualitative methods in psychology: A research guide.* Buckingham, UK: Open University Press.

Bohman, J., (2013). Critical theory. In E. N. Zalta (Ed.), *The Stanford encyclopedia of philosophy* (Spring 2013 ed.). Retrieved from plato.stanford.edu/archives/spr2013/entries/critical-theory

Brant Castellano, M. (2000). Updating Aboriginal traditions of knowledge. In G. J. Sefa Dei, B. L. Hall, & D. G. Rosenberg (Eds.), *Indigenous knowledges in global contexts: multiple readings of our world* (pp. 21–36). Toronto: University of Toronto Press.

Cardinal, L. (2001). What is an Indigenous perspective? *Canadian Journal of Native Education, 25*(2), 180–182.

Charmaz, K. (2006). *Constructing grounded theory: A practical guide through qualitative analysis.* Thousand Oaks, CA: Sage.

Coram, S. (2011). Rethinking Indigenous research approval. *Qualitative Research Journal, 11* (2), pp. 38–47.

Cuthand, D. (2013, October 25). Aboriginal Education Act a regression to 1950s. *The Saskatoon Star Pheonix*, A13.

Debassige, B. (2010). Re-conceptualizing Anshinaabe mino-bimaadiziwin (the good life) as research methodology: A spirit centred way in Anishinaabe research. *Canadian Journal of Native Education, 33*(1), 11–28.

Deloria, Jr., V., & Wildcat, D. R. (2001). *Power and place: Indian education in America.* Golden, CO: American Indian Graduate Centre and Fulcrum Resources.

Denzin, N., & Lincoln, Y. (2005). Introduction: The discipline and practice of qualitative research. In N. Denzin & Y. Lincoln (Eds.), *The SAGE handbook of qualitative research* (3rd ed., pp. 1–32). Thousand Oaks, CA: Sage.

Family Service Toronto (2012). *2011 report card on child and family poverty in Canada: Revisiting family security in insecure times.* www.campaign2000.ca/reportCards/national/2011EnglishRreportCard.pdf (accessed February 4, 2014).

Finlay, L. (2002). Negotiating the swamp: The opportunity and challenge of reflexivity in research practice. *Qualitative Research, 2*(2), 209–230.

Guba, E. G., & Lincoln, Y. S. (1994). Competing paradigms in qualitative research. In N. Denzin & Y. Lincoln (Eds.), *Handbook of qualitative research* (pp. 105–117). Thousand Oaks, CA: Sage.

Howe, E. (2011). *Bridging the Aboriginal education gap in Saskatchewan.* Retrieved from www.gdins.org/node/230

Howell, K. E. (2013). *An introduction to the philosophy of methodology.* London: Sage.

Iwama, M., Marshall, M., Marshall, A., & Bartlett, C. (2009). Two-eyed seeing and the language of healing in community based research. *Canadian Journal of Native Education, 32*(2), 3–23.

Kennedy, M. (2013, October 10). Stephen Harper's First Nation Education Act might continue assimilation, Shawn Atleo says [Postmedia News]. Retrieved from www.canada.com/life/Stephen+Harper+First+Nation+Education+might+continue+assimilation+Shawn+Atleo+says/9007822/story.html

Klemperer, A., Theisens, H., & Kaiser, F. (2001). Dancing in the dark: The relationship between policy research and policy making in Dutch higher education. *Comparative Education Review—Special Issue on the Relationship Between Theorists/Researchers and Policy Makers/Practioners, 45*(2), 197–219.

Kovach, M. (2010). *Indigenous methodologies: Characteristics, conversations, and contexts.* Toronto: University of Toronto Press.

Little Bear, L. (2000). Jagged worldviews colliding. In M. Battiste (Ed.), *Reclaiming Indigenous voices and vision* (pp. 77–85). Vancouver: UBC Press.

McLeod, N. (2007). *Cree narrative memory—From treaties to contemporary times.* Saskatoon, Canada: Purich.

Merriam, S. B. (1997). *Qualitative research and case study in education.* San Francisco: Jossey-Bass.

Perkins, U. (2007). Pono and the *Koru*: Toward Indigenous theory in Pacific island literature. *Hulili: Multidisciplinary Research on Hawaiian Well-being, 4*(1), 59–65.

Richardson, L., & St. Pierre, E. (2005). Writing: A method of inquiry. In N. Denzin & Y. S. Lincoln (Eds), *The SAGE handbook of qualitative research* (3rd ed., pp. 959–978). Thousand Oaks, CA: Sage.

Schwandt, T. A. (2007). *The Sage dictionary of qualitative inquiry.* (3rd ed.) Thousand Oaks, CA: Sage.

Stalwick, H. (1986). *Study guide no. 1—What was said. Taking Control Project.* Regina, Canada: University of Regina.

Stanley, L. (2010). To the letter: Thomas and Znaniecki's *The Polish Peasant* and writing a life, sociologically. *Life Writing, 7*(3), 149–151.

Stonechild, B. (2006). *The new buffalo: The struggle for Aboriginal post-secondary education in Canada.* Winnipeg, Canada: University of Manitoba Press.

Stringer, E. T. (2014). *Action research.* (4th ed.). Thousand Oaks, CA: Sage.

Tavallaei, M., & Abu Talib, M. (2010). A general perspective on role of theory in qualitative research. *The Journal of International Social Research, 3*(11), 570–577.

Tuhiwai Smith, L. (2013). *Decolonizing methodologies: Research and Indigenous Peoples* (2nd ed.). London: Zed Books.

Wilson, S. (2008). *Research is ceremony: Indigenous research methods.* Winnipeg, Canada: Fernwood.

Chapter 5

Confronting Old Habits Overseas

An Analysis of Reciprocity between Malawian Stakeholders and a Canadian University

C. Darius Stonebanks

Are they useful to us? Can they fix our generator? Can they actually do anything?
—Smith (1999, p. 10)

Perhaps fewer words in an academic text had a greater impact on those of us carrying out research outside of the campus and "in the field" than Linda Tuhiwai Smith's questioning of the simple worth of a researcher. Akin to an old joke often repeated in the Northern communities of Canada, that a traditional Inuit family consists of mother, father, two children, and an anthropologist, Smith's opening wit in *Decolonizing Methodologies* quickly resulted with many having deep reservations over what research *actually* meant. Critical questions posed, such as "Whose research is it? Whose interest does it serve? Who will benefit from it?" (Smith, 1999, p. 10), left me, personally, both encouraged that someone in academia was finally asking fundamental questions and simultaneously petrified that my own answers would fall short. Inexorably, academics engaged in any kind of research with human participants will increasingly find themselves tangled within the dilemma of risk versus benefits and who ultimately profits. Research within Indigenous communities

Qualitative Inquiry Outside the Academy edited by Norman K. Denzin and Michael D. Giardina, 107–127. © 2014 Left Coast Press, Inc. All rights reserved.

takes on an extra dimension of concern, given a history of government or academic based studies "on" communities that were far too often horrific (Hodge, 2012). Canada's *Tri-Council Policy Statement: Ethical Conduct for Research Involving Humans* (TCPS2, 2010) makes note that in the case of Indigenous communities "justice may be compromised when a serious imbalance of power prevails between the researcher and participants" (p. 109), which does signal an encouraging awareness of past and ongoing inequity while fostering future conditions of justness. After many years of working with pre-service teachers in Cree communities (Stonebanks, 2007), when I read Smith's book in 2000 and those simple words essentially stating, "What have you actually done?" it was humbling to recognize that good intentions are clearly not enough, and hiding behind words like "social justice" and "transformative" means nothing if community has limited participation and cannot corroborate positive change. Moving towards equitable research in communities that self-identify as having great need, a fundamental commitment to equity must be *lived*, all the while recognizing that all parties should be made aware that qualitative research is often complex, messy, and cannot make promises of pain-free or especially life altering outcomes (Watts, 2008). This effort of clarity is even more important when working with the most vulnerable of participants, especially in the context when "development" is often seen as an understandable means of survival, with any discussion of "ends" being relegated to memories of broken promises. This chapter chronicles the initial development process of working collaboratively with community members in the growth of a university Experiential Learning Project (ELP) (see, e.g., Boud, Keogh, & Walker, 1985; Cantor, 1997; Damron & Otis, 2005; Lempert & De Souza, 1995; Long et al., 2010; O'Connor, 2009) called Praxis Malawi, while trying to shake off old habits (by all parties) associated with research outside of the academy.

In 2009, a group of Bishop's University professors began an interdisciplinary "overseas" project situated in the rural region of Kasungu, Malawi, that would primarily encourage undergraduate and graduate students to develop creative and concrete applications for the theoretical learning they acquired in their area of studies that related to the core principle of alleviating human suffering. "Praxis" was an essential guiding concept in our project,

with the understanding that it can be one of the most empowering and intimidating words uttered in academia. On the one hand
it allows students to dream of possibilities that could be; on the
other hand it can immobilize even the most experienced professor when he or she considers application of theories in "the real
world," especially when related to beliefs of social justice. Given
this reality, one of our main educational goals was to facilitate a
new generation of university students and partnership communities to demystify theory through application, while at the same
time embracing humility in our endeavors and the complexity of
the pursuit towards a common good. Praxis Malawi embraces this
challenge and encourages all members to work in collaboration to
consider and act upon ethical possibilities for change. Our choice
of Malawi, known as "the warm heart of Africa," as a location for
collaborative research was based on a simple reality: Malawi is one
of the poorest countries in the world (The World Bank). Per capita
government expenditures, citizen income, and access to education are woefully low in a country that prides itself on being and
self identifies as a culture of caring and hospitality. Recognizing
that there is great need all over the world, our focus on Malawi is
grounded on the establishment of a positive and equitable human
relationship with our community stakeholders, with partnership
being a key component. While living in a rural village (situated
in the Chilanga region of Kasungu, Malawi), students from multidisciplinary backgrounds engage in creating and exploring their
own research interests in conjunction with professors, peers, and
members of the Makupo community. The result of a five to seven
week fieldwork experience is meant to encourage students to creatively expand their own borders of learning through a spirit of
reciprocal participation and active dialogue.

An ongoing concern in such an endeavor is that, although
students from developed nations typically report fulfillment from
ELP activities either closely or loosely associated with higher
learning institutions, to what extent these efforts benefit the communities is, at the very best, not clear. Prominent scholars, such
as Smith (1999), argue that such relationships do much for the
university and little for the communities they frequent and ultimately abandon. This is certainly a position we have witnessed in
Malawi, with many community members expressing deep concern

that, like many other foreign groups, our time with them would be temporary, that we would engage in piecemeal work and, ultimately, would never return. Shared by community members is the overwhelming experience that, at the end of the research process, Indigenous knowledge (Abdullah & Stringer, 1999; Kincheloe & Semali, 1999; Maurial, 1999; Simpson, 2004) is removed from the local site and employed for purposes that have little to do with improving Indigenous communities and social institutions (G. Smith, 2000; Mutua & Swadener, 2004). Relationships between many organizations are typically described as being one-sided, with local Indigenous persons having little to do with the formulation of projects. The hopes expressed are that, at the very least, short-term monetary compensation and possible exposure to their living conditions can be derived from association. For many, "development" as enacted by foreigners is seen as an industry unto itself, with little vision to long-term humane commitments.

Recognizing the subjectivity that is interwoven in qualitative methods (Denzin & Lincoln, 2000), it should be noted that between my own Iranian heritage and my academic and in-the-field colleague Arshad Taseen's Indian heritage, we have our own memories of this unequal and clouded relationship after witnessing foreign military and Peace Corp volunteers in India and Iran. Although foreign military objectives in one's home country rarely meet anything but tragic ends, the case of the volunteer is often more ambiguous, but nonetheless still a relationship of one-sidedness, despite what is often the best of intentions (Viorst, 1986). Understanding that the rapport between "volunteer" and community is steeped in a history of power imbalances, our own moral guide as university co-investigators was to carry out collaborative research where such experiences would not be forgotten or repeated, we therefore utilized a Participant Action Research (PAR) (Carr & Kemmis, 1986; Jordan, 2003; McNiff, 1993; Stringer, 2007; Zuber-Skerritt, 1996) approach to facilitate desired expectations.

Through PAR, we documented and analyzed collaboratively efforts with community members, with the focus of this chapter on the perceptions of building towards reciprocity with a Canadian university. Our primary intent continues to be in working with community members in the region of Kasungu, Malawi, to develop a transfer of a knowledge-based educational project that is both sustainable and reciprocal. To what end this knowledge transfer manifests was, in great part, a responsibility taken on by community to define, while we all worked towards establishing a model in which reciprocal learning and knowledge transfer would eventually be deemed, by all parties, to be equitable. In a short time, we realized that the roots of the relationship between one of the economically poorest countries in the world and one of the richest would reveal old habits of consciously and unconsciously romanticizing expectations built on long standing histories. Many of these habits were not necessarily valued or believed by anyone; rather, they manifested as any other practices do—we are simply accustomed to them. Japhet Chiwanda,[1] known as Chief Makupo in his official capacity, did a great deal to elucidate personal experience while encouraging understanding of public perceptions. Chief Makupo has been a part of our project building from the outset, and has stood as a stalwart activist for his community, both locally and at large. Elected through a matrilineal system of what is termed as "traditional authority," Chief Makupo epitomized our in-field collaboration. Not solely in regard to organizational authority and responsibility, but in regard to making clear the research baggage of what has been.

We are in deep problems. And you have come to help alleviate those problems. [Chief Makupo, 2011]

As is evidenced by Chief Makupo, his initial response to what reason Canadian university students and professors would come to a rural village in Malawi indicates a relationship where one is in a position of power to give, and the other is simply passive to receive. Even at the date in which Chief Makupo made the statement, the University side of the research team had spent enough time living in the impoverished areas of Malawi to acknowledge the reality of Chief Makupo's words. We recognized the urgency of the statement; however, we were troubled by what they would lead to in regard to expectations. On the surface, when Chief Makupo made the statement of "problems" in a meeting of elders, stakeholders, and Bishop's University professors, it resonated with the community, but troubled us as professors and students that we were, despite our best intentions, reproducing old models of "development" as charity that had only marginally improved the lives of the most vulnerable. A post-secondary graduate himself, who, like many other Malawians, found himself living in humble rural villages when professional employment ended, Chief Makupo understood the subject of Malawi's "problems" in great depth. It is with the respect of his knowledge in daily lived experiences, and the knowledge of others, while valuing our own, that we obliged ourselves as a group to better understand the meaning of what a relationship with a Canadian University, via an ELP, could accomplish.

Central to our research objective has been the production of a transformative set of knowledges and education that could sincerely be called useful by community members. Working toward this goal, we engaged in a critical form of PAR (Kemmis & McTaggart, 1987; Wadsworth, 1998), all the while aware that the vast majority of academic based work "on" local people began and concluded with the community having little or nothing to do with the research process (Goldie, 1995). As many have already stated (Deloria, 1969; Howard, 1995; Maurial, 1999), the hierarchy that exists in such relationships usually results in submissiveness in the researched and ultimate control by the researcher, and it must be acknowledged that even in situations where such observations are made, the same relationships exist only with the façade of equity language masking old habits. Ultimately, the end result of knowledge being removed from the Indigenous community and employed for purposes that have little to do with improving Indigenous life (G. Smith, 2000; Mutua & Swadener, 2004; Stonebanks, 2007) continues to be the norm, despite calls for change. Moreover, another tragic observation is that many academics that make calls for sweeping modifications in research methods are far too often those who do not enact or live change where needs are so great. Often, the answer to the "research conundrum" has been to simply do nothing (Stonebanks, 2008), with a new model of criticality moving from critical thinking/inquiry to simply being disparaging of those who attempt to animate emancipatory goals. The version of PAR, to which we have committed ourselves, makes great effort to unravel old assumptions, understand their roots, and move forward into new spaces equipped with openness to experiences that will shape social inquiry and transformation. In this model, reflections on the past, present, and expected outcomes were encouraged by all participants, while the categories of participation, action, and research were blurred (Baum, MacDougall, & Smith, 2006). Such a methodology directly relates to the overall goal of helping promote reciprocity in developing Praxis Malawi as a project that attempts to break the traditional restrictions that are often unconsciously steeped in academic research. The concerted effort is to use a variety of qualitative tools to gain as much information as possible from all participants and to move away from the traditional model and relationship of the researcher and researched (Stonebanks, 2008). In such a collaborative mode of knowledge production, the interaction between a myriad of inquirers and participants becomes especially important and celebrated. In deciding how to produce community-based, new knowledge for this research, we utilized the "Generative Curriculum Model" (Ball, 2004), which lends itself perfectly for a community-based education partnership between the community of Malawi and a university-based group, all moving towards a common research goal. As Ball notes, "A generative approach focuses on uncovering new, community-relevant knowledge sources, considering knowledge that resides in communities, and creating fresh understandings from reflection and dialogue" (p. 460). This holistic exemplar gains further support as it is grounded in emancipatory ideology (Freire, 2005), which respects and facilitates local voices, so that the development of the Malawi Project is truly reciprocal.

During the dry season in Malawi (late spring/early summer for Canada) 2011, we began actively initiating dialogue with the Chilanga community, with our host village, Makupo, acting as a central meeting spot, to better understand possibilities for our combined time and efforts together. The village of Makupo, located in the Chilanga, Kasungu, region, accommodates our university group of approximately 15 Canadian students and professors, for what has been an annual learning event since 2009.

Audio and videotaped conversations were carried out in group and private formats, and we publically noted that, as is often the case with ethnographic methods, rich conversations occurred when recording devices were not present. Three large community meetings, held during the dry season, included community members from the villages in the Chilanga area, consisting of village elders, leaders, and professional representatives (clergy, education, etc.). A series of questions were posed at the meetings for group consideration, with opportunity for reflection spanning no less than a week between gatherings. Although English is formally the language of education and commerce in Malawi, Francis Jumbe and Undeni Mtekateka, our on-site coordinators, acted as translators for those community members who felt more at ease expressing opinions in the local language of Chewa. Translations of English were given when community members were unsure of their comprehension as well. Our objective was not to extensively quote individual community members for future publications, rather, in keeping with local tradition, to develop consensus to guide research projects. After introductions and ceremony, we began the meeting by giving our group a common direction and working targets to achieve.

> The only way that this relationship between Bishop's University and the Kasungu region will be sustainable is if we all agree that we're having a mutual, beneficial relationship and if we all believe it's equitable. So by having these meetings and then having interviews and conversations with you individually, we are trying to build our project into something that is sustainable. So, we have all of our fine administrators and teachers and chiefs in the area at this meeting. And we want to know what you think you can get out of this relationship, where you will benefit as much as we think our students benefit. But we can't build it properly, equitably if we don't have your input. [Stonebanks, 2011]

We clarified with the community that our primary goal was to create emancipatory conditions in Malawi and committed that the all-consuming obsession in academia to publish papers or present at conferences must be a distant second. All participants were encouraged to dialogue between meetings, meet with each other, or with us as a group or individually, and report back their conclusions and considerations to the public forum. If we did not record the conversations through electronic means, and it was made clear that this was completely acceptable, we simply engaged in informal conversations. If we participated in informal dialogue that created profound shifts in forward movement, we asked permission to chronicle the conversation via journaling for the sake of collective comprehension. One of the first points of discussion was to understand the community's perception on *why* university students would come to Malawi and what the community thought everyone was gaining out of this relationship. Throughout our time in Malawi, we have always attempted (in our minds in any case) great clarity in explaining a university perspective for our presence in Malawi, including what we believe may be the limitations inherent to ELPs. Field, experiential, place based or situated learning in developing nations amongst students of higher education in developed countries has grown in popularity for the past fifty years. However, the benefits to either the students or the Indigenous peoples have often been questioned amongst academics, particularly those coming from a critical, Indigenous, post-colonial or decolonizing theoretical framework. Once more, such narratives relating to our own native countries reveal similar conclusions as we all too often read criticisms, in this example by Peace Corps volunteers, of cultural norms and perceptions in India and Iran not meeting Western standards (Viorst, 1986). With the majority of such projects taking on an "exposure tourism," almost voyeuristic characteristic that has usually developed through a "top-down" design, the benefits to the communities in which the students reside can often result in a moment of profound personal growth in the student, but can often leave only superficial or temporary positive impact for the Indigenous population. Despite our attempts to give clarity to the project, it quickly became evident that community members were unclear on what we actually did compared to other organizations and agencies. One village elder thanked us for boreholes that we did not contribute to, and another for solar lights that we did not install. A teacher from a local school commenced giving public thanks to us for a variety of accomplishments for which we clearly could not take credit.

I think Bishop's University is an advantage to us. There are many advantages. For example, I will speak on behalf of my school. There are computers there. We didn't have any computer. And no student knew how to use computers. But after that donation, by now at least three quarters of the students know how to use computers and that is a very big advancement to the school. We can also talk of donation of fees to orphaned students; students who otherwise could not have learned. They had no hope of education. Because of you, Bishop's University, you have donated fees to those students and by now they are learning. Without Bishop's University, that would not have happened. Another point is you'd come and teach our students some areas which we did not cover. You come and cover those subjects and students as well as teachers benefit from Bishop's University because you come and relieve them, you come and relieve us in the teaching of some subjects. Even reading, which we can only do through a donation of books. We have some books from Bishop's University in the library which students are reading by now. That is a very big advantage to this school. And you sometimes help us with teaching and learning aids. That is a very big advantage. And as of now there are some officers from Bishop's University who are coming to the school to introduce reading clubs, art clubs, which is a very big advantage. Our students did not know much reading. They didn't know how good it is to be reading. But because of Bishop's University, some students now know how good it is to read, because reading is the gateway to success. [Mr. Isaiah, 2011]

With further conversations with Mr. Isaiah, we came to understand his reasonable perspective of development, because it had been a passive experience. With very few development advocates taking the time to explain who they were or even what they were doing in our community, why would any of us think differently? Dialogue with women of the village of Makupo echoed Mr. Isaiah's understandable assessment of what we actually contributed to the community. Their perspectives were compounded by the reality that the majority of work they had carried out to date with our group focused on the service aspect of our stay in Malawi; signifying the long standing problem of women being relegated to the peripheral edges of development projects. When asked what students were learning in the community, Lisha, a resident of Makupo, responded that they learn about "food, culture and language." When another resident responded about benefits in return, she indicated material gain.

When the students come here, they always bring with them some items which they donate to the schools which helps (pause) which helps not only our children but also other children from the surrounding area. [Chinue, 2011]

With responses exemplifying that either our own attempts to clarify have met with little success or that fundamental and immediate economic needs outweigh anything as lofty and super-fluous as "reciprocal knowledge transfer," who exactly benefits from such relationships has always been a point of concern. With poverty being our own pressing motivator for instigating research work in Malawi, it only seems reasonable that economics be a concern for residents as well. However, whatever funding we put into the local community through fair compensation for work being carried out to support the project came at a consequence to fostering a sense of community beyond village borders. With multiple stays in the village of Makupo, it became evident that the influx of money and, consequently, influence was not seen as equitable to other villages. As is understandable in a moribund economy, wealth distribution became a point of concern. It was Chief Makupo who noted that other elders from far away villages commented to him that they saw the glow of solar powered LED lights emanating from his village. The clear question was whether or not old ways of tightly possessing foreign organizations for strictly local gain were being repeated, or if the village itself was going to spearhead something entirely different and more equi-table. Our conversations within the group meetings allowed us to discuss implementing projects in a new model, which prompted others from outside the village to express hopes for change. Mr. Joah (a teacher), sympathetic to the misunderstanding of his col-league, Mr. Isaiah, as to what foreign agency did what and for whom in his community, expressed a possible reason:

> People may be confused because they thought this group and this project was only particularly for the Makupo residents. But now my understanding is that it is not. For this knowledge project, it involves Kasungu as a district. So that is a differ-ence. So people may have been confused. This project is not particularly for Makupo residents. People were confusing that. [Mr. Joah, 2011]

Worries about "ownership" of such relationships are unfor-tunately part and parcel of the kinds of projects that community members are used to experiencing. As is typical of such over-seas experiential learning programs, we live in a village with no electricity or running water for up to six or seven weeks. For the mainstream Canadian undergraduate student who is attracted to an overseas ELP, his or her motivation to participate in such an experience has overwhelmingly been based on humanitarian reasons (Stonebanks, 2013). Comparatively and understandably, the primary motivations for the community members to work with foreigners are due to severe economic and health needs. By observing the monetary gain of our university association with Malawi, in no way do we mean to call into question the legitimacy of the culture of hospitality and welcome that is entrenched in the Malawian culture, yet it is a part of the relationship that requires acknowledgment and assessment. When asked about the great laughter that was heard from the women preparing dinner for the students, through translation, Chinue smiled and discussed how the presence of university students would bring much needed economic relief for the mothers of the village:

> She said the laughter you heard yesterday, was because they were discussing your visit, and that you shouldn't stop coming here because that's part of helping the mothers. Because they need help. So they were happy. And they're hoping that you can continue to come so that they can get help. When they're working they get money to help their families. And that happiness and love; it's all about [filling] the needs. [Chinue via Undeni, 2013]

A group of university students living in a fairly typical rural sub-Saharan village represents a sum of money that would otherwise not be available. This is, once again, not to suggest in any way that economic gain was the sole motivator for villagers to accept us into their community, nor that university students are not expecting participation in activities to bolster their future earning power. During one of our many public conversations with elders, the idea was forwarded that perhaps the community would be better served by Canadian universities simply raising money and sending it without student presence. After careful consideration, many elders returned with the answer that such efforts had been tried in the past with little result of change to community. Moreover, students who participated in similar dialogue acknowledged that experiential learning in Malawi had the potential for meaningful change to personal worldviews and ongoing global responsibility, which would not be attained through the simple act of monetary charity from a distance.

The subject of simply turning the university model of partnership with Chilanga away from a research orientation and towards a more exposure tourism model was brought up to the community. We even went so far as making the bold prediction to community members that Canadian undergraduate students would perhaps even be more attracted to a form of exposure tourism that would relieve them of the stressors of coursework related to ELPs. Upon hearing the word "tourism," Chief Makupo responded emphatically:

> You are not tourists! You are not tourists. A tourist is someone who comes and sees the guesthouse. "Oh yes, see Kasungu mountain? *Yes.* To the national park? *Yes.*" And he goes! But you are asking questions which will benefit us in the future. So you're not a tourist. You're educating us. [Chief Makupo, 2013]

Products of our own dialogical philosophical background, the question was asked in return, "Well then, how are you educating us?" The Chief's answer was swift and clear:

> Ah! Well, this environment to you is pretty new. We educate you by giving you whatever you are looking for from us. Yes. You ask us questions, we answer you, and we educate *you*. You ask questions, you answer, *you educate*. [Chief Makupo, 2013]

Certainly, echoing Chief Makupo's sentiments on the tourist compared to the committed partner, our intent was to move away from the "feel good" educational sightseer model to a transfer of knowledge based project where both parties acknowledge equity and sustainability. But clearly, we discovered that this is not an easily achievable act. So often, far too often, words like "sustainability," "transformative," "collaboration," and "equity" are just that in academia, *words*. Words to be debated, but not lived. As with praxis, writing them on paper and presenting critiques at academic conferences is one thing, but living them is an entirely different matter. This is a challenge that is equally difficult for our community partners, given the long standing relationships that are clearly built on a top-down model, regardless of how such inequities are repackaged. In the 21st century, the term "Third World country" has largely given way to the popular designate and repackaged "developing nation."

Whereas "Third World" suggests rankings that have been evaluated, handed out, and registered, "developing nation" denotes care, possibility, and the promise, if not the appearance, of upward mobility. The terms may have changed, but both still share their own subtext of hierarchy. First, Second, and Third World definitions indicate a race in which some countries win, some do not get it, and some are just losers. Although ideological differences exist between First and Second, separating each other until Second admits fault, Third World countries still have potential to be winners, to "get it," if they just had a little help. And many people from First World countries in the West did just that; they travelled abroad to help. Del Mar (2011) notes, "Most went to Africa in the 1960s to share the American way of life" (p. 349), and certainly these volunteers did so with the best of intentions, even if the experience was permeated with an impression of the older sibling teaching something to his or her younger brother or sister. In an attempt to move away from this relationship, the power to set direction to our work was forwarded to community members at a group meeting.

> What we would like to do is take those needs you indicate, and make a list of those needs and take it to the university. Now, if you are here, in the field, you are able to read the people in the Kasungu area far better than what we can. And maybe if you help us develop and identify these needs, it would be really appreciated. I've gone to Kasungu city, I've tried to see many things, and the simple needs of the people here are not being met. It is being met from *outside*. If you buy cooking oil for instance, it comes from outside of Malawi. I mean, it can be made here in the village. There is so much growth of peanuts, but nobody makes oil with it, and it's simple to do it. But it comes pre-packaged to Lilongwe, and they fill up bottles in the city and then they sell it to you. Lumber, it all comes from the north. You just said agriculture, everything, it comes from outside. Or if it is here, it's just a small amount of people who are doing it, but they're not doing it together. [Taseen, 2011]

Our attempts were to clarify that expertise had to be mutually identified, understood, and respected. The culture of pacifity, reinforced by years of colonialism, needed to be identified. In regard to these pecking orders imbedded between outside organizations and local community, the relationship between developed and developing nations had to be discussed aloud, with admission that we have not really veered that significantly from preceding processes of thought or implementation. In the past, the relationship between these older and younger sibling nations may have been more top-down, more stern tough love, whereas the current association is one in which knowledge is transferred via nurturing and scaffolding. Even with the growth of maternalism (Christensen & Hewitt-Taylor, 2006; Fischer, 2006), neither escapes the attitude of superiority associated with paternalism (Shiffrin, 2000), and an overall sense of idealization of "doing good" permeates both. For those of First World, developed or privileged nations who work in or with Third World, developing or underprivileged countries, the volunteer is at the forefront. And with the volunteer, romanticism is never far behind. That romanticism, which has long been a part of volunteerism and work overseas, needs to be a subject addressed by all parties. With the observation that the "growing trend of the 'globalisation of poverty,' which has its roots in the polarization of incomes both within nations and between them; the rich are getting richer and the poor poorer" (Dine, 2001, p. 81) requires immediate concern. A serious consideration is the need to examine the continued matter realistically and honestly, in which notions of working *with* communities abroad must be stripped of the failings of romanticism, paternalism, and even maternalism when it comes in the form of condescension (Waaldijk, 2012). In the not so distant past, organizations in the 1960s like Canadian University Service Overseas (CUSO) and the American Peace Corps were steeped in the noble and naïve convictions that sending the relatively privileged abroad to volunteer in the most economically moribund economies would eventually benefit them from prolonged contact. Over time, modified romanticism shifted from the belief that the individual could do something for the village to the village being able to do something for the individual (del Mar, 2011). Mirrored in Hollywood blockbusters, from *Lawrence of Arabia* (1962), to *Dances with Wolves* (1990), and then *Avatar* (2009), we see a popular trend in which whereas at one time the individual in the village aspired to the idea of helping the natives, now the dream is that the village will help the individual. The romantic idea of the individual travelling abroad to spread his or her knowledge to the less fortunate has now become fused with a sense that a spiritual void can be filled by returning to a "simpler," almost anti-modern life. Whatever idea of commitment between university agencies and community that may carry objectives like "transformation," the one who is transform-ing is not entirely clear. Clarity in regard to dedication towards mutually agreed upon goals has now become an openly discussed notion amongst all participants. As Mr. Joah noted:

> There should be dedication. And, there should be trust. Because when you're doing things with two parties (pause) sometimes some people can ... *cheat*. Trust, dedication and we should also (long pause) it should be *open* to *everybody*. So that everybody should see what is happening. We had discussed this as well last meeting. I think it's different from what you are talking about. Now I think there's going to be more openness. [Mr. Joah, 2011]

Essentially, our ongoing research documents and analyzes a practical research based road map of the development (which began in the Spring of 2011) and ongoing implementation of a reciprocal ELP based education model in a developing country. The transparencies that Mr. Joah spoke to stand at the forefront of moving towards change, and that openness has certainly not been a part of past relationships. It is messy and time consuming, and most of our universities do not have the patience or commit-ment in such endeavors where the results usually valued at the institutional level have nothing to do with long-term and tangible emancipatory goals.

Despite the fact that over a million students, in the United States alone, are engaged in some form of "studying abroad" (Zhou et al., 2008), we are still left with the fact that very little literature exists on the development process of university based experiential learning programs/projects, field place learning, and internship programs (ELPs). Even less literature exists in which the local Indigenous community has an equal voice in the creation of the educational program. This reciprocal and respectful nego-tiation process found within the PAR methodology is central to our ongoing research goals. As researchers engaged in this type of inquiry, we want to be continuously aware of what Warrior (2001c, p. 123) calls the "death dance of dependence." Far too often, this is a dance that has manifested into a dichotomy of all or nothing when it comes to knowledges and research, and coun-ters the principles of dialogue and respect. The dedication of our research model is that we seek to not only continue to uncover the yet to be explored systemic failures of ELPs through community stakeholders' perspectives, but also examine the community's vision of what these programs should be accomplishing and how to attain such goals. In carrying out this research we strongly believe that it should potentially and profoundly reshape schooling views on ELP programs connected with development. In this sense, we are looking to perpetual work with the community to lay the academic and practical groundwork towards the autonomy and accountability that such programs must attain. For let us not forget, "Even a number of quality scientists will tell you that statistics are, in some ways, the icing on the cake when you do your science" (Duffield, *The End of the Line*, 2009).

As we build and amass our data, it is hard to shake the feeling that we are going over audio and video recordings and typing transcriptions for the sake of validity towards conferences and publications. A completely self-serving process that may, only *may*, have only the slightest bit of interest to some of the members of our community participants. It is hard to escape the feeling that much of what we are uncovering is already intimately known by community members, and yet at the same time in the direction of project as a means to make profound change, we are truly in our infancy. Even five years into the project, we realize that breaking old modes of working with local communities is a difficult and time-consuming effort. In 2012 and as Chief Makupo played an increasingly prominent role as the leader responsible for facilitation between university and community, he pulled one of us aside and said, "We have been playing games with you up until now." Short-term gain was a necessity to assure in the face of overwhelming histories of romanticized encounters with both parties silently knowing commitment is absent. "Up until now, we *have been playing games*," he emphasized and repeated. His admission was astonishingly honest and clear. This version of "the dance of dependence" was one built on the strong evidence that we would not be a long term commitment in their daily lives, but the chief was ready to risk much and abandon that paradigm in place of optimism.

Late into our first public meeting, Doug Miller—an educator whose commitment to Malawi began with CUSO in the 1960s, was then bound by family through marriage to a local teacher, and now continues on as an activist for the Kasungu region—reflected on the challenges and possibilities of dialogue and action that would be fundamentally different than what community members experienced in the past:

> It's not enough that Canadians come and absorb from you. They have to give something back. It has to be sharing. It has to be equal. It has to be respectful. So that's why I am hoping the project from Bishop's University is going to help us learn how to do this so that the sharing is equal. And that's why we are working together so closely on this. But it's not a mathematical formula. It cannot be A plus B, equals C. It's learning from our side and your side, so that everybody benefits. So sometimes we will make mistakes. Sometimes it will not always be successful. But that's what respect is about. That's what being equal is about. To be able to talk to each other and say we must change it, we must do it this way, we must try something else. And so the future will bring what the future brings and we look forward to (pause) *collaboration*. [Miller, 2011]

It seemed apt to conclude our gathering at this point, with his words encapsulating the ideals of which we needed to be continuously aware and, ultimately, towards where we hoped to be heading.

Acknowledgments

With thanks to Arshad Taseen, Barbara Hunting, Melanie Bennett-Stonebanks, Japhet Chiwanda, and the Bishop's University Senate Research Committee.

Notes

1 Mr. Chiwanda is the only participant whose name has been used with permission; all other names are pseudonyms.

References

Abdullah, I., & Stringer, E. (1999). Indigenous knowledge, Indigenous learning, Indigenous research. In L. Semali and J. L. Kincheloe (Eds.), *What is Indigenous knowledge? Voices from the academy* (pp. 143–155). Bristol, PA: Falmer.

Ball, J. (2004, January 1). As if Indigenous knowledge and communities mattered: Transformative education in First Nations communities in Canada. *American Indian Quarterly, 28*, 454–479.

Baum, F., MacDougall, C., & Smith, D. (2006). Participatory action research. *Journal of Epidemiology & Community Health, 13*(10): 854–857.

Boud, D., Keogh, R., & Walker, D. (Eds.) (1985) *Reflection: Turning experience into learning*. London: Kogan.

Cantor, J. A. (1997). *Experiential learning in higher education: Linking classroom and community*. Washington, D.C.: George Washington University.

Carr, W., & Kemmis, S. (1986). *Becoming critical: Education, knowledge and action research*. London: Falmer.

Christensen, M., & Hewitt-Taylor, J. (2006). Empowerment in nursing: Paternalism or maternalism? *British Journal of Nursing, 15*(13), 695–699.

Damron, D., & Otis, C. (2005, February 20). Mentoring from across the pond: Reflections on promoting (experiential) learning in international internships. Paper presented at the annual meeting of the American Political Science Association Teaching and Learning Conference. Washington, D.C.

del Mar, D. (2011). At the heart of things: Peace Corps volunteers in Sub-Saharan Africa. *African Identities, 9*(4), 349–361.

Deloria, V. (1969). *Custer died for your sins*. New York: Macmillan.

Denzin, N. K., & Lincoln, Y. S. (Eds) (2000). *Handbook of qualitative research* (2nd ed.). Thousand Oaks, CA: Sage.

Dine, J. J. (2001). Multinational enterprises: international codes and the challenge of 'sustainable development.' *Non-State Actors & International Law, 1*(2), 81–106.

Fischer, M. (2006). Addams's internationalist pacifism and the rhetoric of maternalism. *NWSA Journal, 18*(3), 1–19.

Freire, P. (2005). *Pedagogy of the oppressed*. New York: Continuum.

Goetz, J., & LeCompte, M. D. (1993c). *Ethnography and qualitative design in educational research*. San Diego, CA: Academic Press.

Goldie, T. (1995). The representation of the Indigene. In B. Ashcroft, G. Griffiths, & H. Tiffin (Eds.), *The post-colonial studies reader* (pp. 172–175). New York: Routledge.

Harding, S. (1998). *Is science multicultural? Postcolonialisms, feminisms, and epistemologies*. Bloomington: Indiana University Press.

Hodge, F. (2012). No meaningful apology for American Indian unethical research abuses. *Ethics & Behavior, 22*(6), 431–444.

Howard, G. (1995). Unraveling racism: Reflections on the role of nonIndigenous people supporting Indigenous education. *Australian Journal of Adult and Community Education, 35*(3), 229–237.

Jordan, S. (2003). Who stole my methodology: Co-opting PAR. *Globalisation, Societies and Education, 1*, 185–200.

Kemmis, S., & McTaggart, R. (1987). *The action research planner*. Geelong, Australia: Deakin University Press.

Kincheloe, J. L., & Semali, L. M. (Eds.) (1999). *What is Indigenous knowledge? Voices from the academy*. New York: Falmer.

Lempert, D. H., & De Souza Briggs, X. N. (1995). *Escape from the ivory tower: Student adventures in democratic experiential education*. New York: Jossey-Bass.

Long, S., Akande, Y., Purdy, R., & Nakano, K. (2010). Deepening learning and inspiring rigor: Bridging academic and experiential learning using a host country approach to a study tour. *Journal of Studies in International Education, 14*(1), 89–111.

Maurial, M. (1999). Indigenous knowledge and schooling: A continuum between conflict and dialogue. In L. Semali & J. Kincheloe (Eds.), *What is Indigenous knowledge? Voices from the academy* (pp. 59–77). New York: Falmer.

McNiff, J. (1993). *Teaching as learning: An action research approach*. London: Routledge

Mutua, K., & Swadener, B. B. (Eds.) (2004). *Decolonizing research in cross-cultural contexts: Critical personal narratives*. Albany: State University of New York Press.

O'Connor, K. (2009). Northern exposures: Models of experiential learning in Indigenous education. *Journal of Experiential Education, 31*(3), 415–419.

Panel on Research Ethics, Government of Canada (2010). Tri-council policy statement: Ethical conduct for research involving humans. Retrieved February 4, 2014, from www.pre.ethics.gc.ca/eng/policy-politique/initiatives/tcps2-eptc2/Default/

Shiffrin, S. (2000). Paternalism, unconscionability doctrine, and accommodation. *Philosophy & Public Affairs, 29*(3), 205.

Simpson, L. (2004). Anticolonial strategies for the recovery and maintenance of Indigenous knowledge. *American Indian Quarterly, 28*, 373–384.

Smith, G. (2000). Protecting and respecting Indigenous knowledge. In M. Battiste (Ed.), *Reclaiming Indigenous voice and vision* (pp. 209–224). Vancouver: University of British Columbia Press.

Smith, L. T. (1999). *Decolonizing methodologies*. New York: Zed Books.

Stonebanks, C. D. (2007). *James Bay Cree and higher education: Issues of identity and culture shock*. Netherlands: Sense.

Stonebanks, C. D. (2008). An Islamic perspective on knowledge, knowing and methodology. In N. K. Denzin, Y. S. Lincoln, & L. T. Smith (Eds.), *Handbook of critical and Indigenous methodologies*. Thousand Oaks, CA: Sage.

Stonebanks, C. D. (2013). Cultural competencies, culture shock and the praxis of experiential learning. In E. Lyle (Ed.), *Bridging theory & practice: Pedagogical enactment for socially just education* (pp. 249–277). Nova Scotia: Backalong Books.

Stringer, E. T. (2007) *Action research: A handbook for practitioners.* Thousand Oaks, CA: Sage.

Viorst, M. (1986). *Making a difference: The Peace Corps at twenty-five.* New York: Weidensfeld & Nicolson.

Waaldijk, B.. (2012). Speaking on behalf of others: Dutch social workers and the problem of maternalist condescension. In M. van der Klein, R. Plant, N. Sanders, & L. Weintrob (Eds.), *Maternalism reconsidered: Motherhood, welfare and social policy in the twentieth century.* New York: Berghahn.

Wadsworth, Y. (1998). What is participatory action research? *Action Research International, Paper 2.* Retrieved December 2, 2013, from www.scu.edu. au/schools/gcm/ar/ari/p-ywadsworth98.html

Warrior, R. A. (2001). *Tribal secrets: Recovering American Indian intellectual traditions.* Minneapolis: University of Minnesota Press.

Watts, J. H. (2008). Integrity in qualitative research. In L. Given (Ed.), *The SAGE encyclopedia of qualitative research methods* (Vol. 1, pp. 440–441). Thousand Oaks, CA: Sage.

Zhou, Y., Jindal-Snape, D., Topping, K., & Todman, J. (2008). Theoretical models of culture shock and adaptation in international students in higher education. *Studies In Higher Education, 33*(1), 63–75.

Zuber-Skerritt, O. (1996) *New directions in action research.* London: Falmer.

Media References

Cameron, J., & Landau, J. (Producer), & Cameron, J. (Director). (2009). *Avatar* [Motion picture]. USA: Lightstorm Entertainment.

Costner, K., & Blake, M. (Producer), & Costner, K. (1990). *Dances with Wolves* [Motion picture]. USA: Tig Productions.

Duffield, G. (Producer), & Murray, R. (Director). (2009). *The End of the Line.* [Documentary]. UK: Arcane Pictures.

Spiegel, S. (Producer), & Lean, D. (Director). (1962). *Lawrence of Arabia* [Motion picture]. UK: Horizon Pictures.

Chapter 6

Global Reform Policies Meet Local Communities

A Critical Inquiry on the Children's Act in South Africa

Beth Blue Swadener and Bekisizwe S. Ndimande

There can be no keener revelation of a society's soul than the way in which it treats its children.

—Nelson Mandela (quoted in Bakan, 2011)

At the time of this writing (December 2013), the world was mourning the death of former President Rolihlala Nelson Mandela of South Africa. There are many reasons for doing so, especially as we remember his commitment to human rights issues in South Africa and around the world. Under apartheid, South Africa did not honor international human rights declarations because of its institutionalized policy of racism and discrimination, which grossly violated human rights. Apartheid was, in fact, instituted the same year (1948) that the framework for human rights was declared. Therefore, over the four decades of apartheid, the rights of Indigenous peoples in South Africa were not recognized, including the rights of their children, who had no official protections. Their schools were segregated and underfunded (Ndimande, 2006; Nkomo, 1990), and were not protected against such things as hunger, abuse, child labor, and abusive and oppressive laws.

Qualitative Inquiry Outside the Academy edited by Norman K. Denzin and Michael D. Giardina, 128–145. © 2014 Left Coast Press, Inc. All rights reserved.

This chapter focuses on human rights policies, practices, and attitudes in South Africa, and especially on the Children's Act of 2007, which covers a range of children's rights issues, including protection, provision, and participation. We draw from interviews with parents and professionals regarding the implementation of the Children's Act in South Africa. First, we discuss the human rights evolution from apartheid to post-apartheid as a context to this discussion. Second, we connect the broader discussion of children's rights, particularly as they are formulated in the UN Convention on the Rights of the Child (UNCRC, 1989) and the African Charter on the Rights and Welfare of the Child (1990) to the perspectives of Black parents and professionals whom we interviewed in South Africa. Third, we draw from the interviews to analyze ways in which children's rights and the Children's Act are understood and interpreted within communities, particularly within Indigenous communities.

Lastly, we discuss themes that emerged from this study, foregrounding perspectives of the participants, as well as drawing some initial conclusions about these themes based on theories that analyze social contradictions and inequalities that persist in post-colonial Africa. We frame our analysis within anti-colonial theories (Biko, 2002; Cary, 2004; Dei, 2011; Fanon, 1963; McLeod, 2000; Myers, 2001; Ngugi, 1993; Skutnabb-Kangas & Dunbar, 2010). Further, we engage a critique of neoliberal policies in sub-Saharan Africa (Bond, 2005; Brock-Utne, 2000; Desai, 2002; Pillay, 2002; Swadener, Wachira, Kabiru, & Njenga, 2007) to show the limitations of policies constructed within Western perspectives and implemented in an African country with little attention to the local cultural values as they relate to children.

Universal Children's Rights and the Case of Post-Apartheid South Africa

It was not until the release of Rolihlala Nelson Mandela from prison in 1990 and the ultimate demise of apartheid in 1994 that South Africa began to legally institute human rights issues for all, including the rights of the child. The democratic Constitution (1996) played a major role in the recognition of human rights. It provides for rights necessary for the child to develop in a socially conducive environment and be supported in meeting social and physical needs. Specifically, Section 28 (a1) of the Bill of Rights states that every child has the right to basic nutrition, shelter, health care, and social services; it further stipulates in Section 29(1) that everyone has a right to a basic education.

The key statement of human rights in relation to children is the United Nations Convention on the Rights of the Child. The CRC, through its 54 articles and comments, frames children's rights in three broad categories: protection, provision, and participation. Several articles relate to the protection rights of children. These include Article 19, which protects children from violence, abuse, and neglect. Provision rights refer to children's rights to food, clothing, shelter, (free) primary education, and health care. Participation rights refer to children's rights to get and share information (Article 13), so long as it is not damaging to themselves or others, and the right to express their views and to have those views given due weight in all matters affecting them. It is also important to note that protection, provision, and participation rights are not mutually exclusive. These distinctions in broad categories and more subtle aspects of children's rights served as analytic frames in this study.

While there has been legislation focused on children since the 1920s, the Children's Act (2005, amended in 2007) was the first act in South Africa, other than the South African Schools Act (SASA, 1996), that spoke directly to the rights of *all* children. Some of the broad areas it covers include the care and protection of children, early childhood development prevention and early intervention, the provision of child and youth care centers, child welfare services, early childhood development programs, the protection of children from abusive treatment, the provision of health care to children, caring for children with disabilities, advocating for parental responsibilities and rights, children's rights to education, as well as all other important social aspects necessary for raising children in a democratic environment. As evident in its preamble, this act bears strong democratic principles of raising and protecting children.

The Children's Act becoming law was an important milestone in the nation, but it also started a national debate, as reflected in the national media (e.g., *Citizen*, 2007; *Mail & Guardian*, 2007; *Sowetan*, 2007; the *Herald*, 2005; *Witness*, 2007). Those in favor of the Act observed that it addresses decades of child neglect and abuse, and regulates parents' and other adults' control over children. Those who opposed it warned that this act may lead the nation to unforeseen erosion of children's normal behavior (*Mail & Guardian*, 2007). These reactions and interpretation of the Act are complicated. They are influenced by conflicting constructions of childhood and socio-cultural experiences and values. Our exploratory study sought to better understand and contextualize reactions to and interpretations of the Children's Act and children's rights more generally. We further sought to understand the perspectives of those shaping policy and practice related to children's rights. This study examined the views of communities, particularly Black communities, and professionals who work with children. We focused on how these individuals viewed the Children's Act in the contexts of protection, provision, and participation rights (Ndimande & Swadener, 2013).

Methodology

This collaborative study utilized qualitative methods, primarily conversational interviews and document analysis. The first author is a European-American researcher and the second is an Indigenous South African researcher. Both researchers have previously worked with South African Black communities on various educational projects. The first author has also done work in sub-Saharan Africa, particularly Kenya, since the mid-1980s. We built on a decolonizing methodologies framework (Denzin, Lincoln, & Smith, 2008; McCarty, 2009; Mutua & Swadener, 2004; Ndimande, 2012; Skutnabb-Kangas & Dunbar, 2010; Smith, 1999; Swadener & Mutua, 2008) and utilized a critical analysis of discourse and constructs employed on behalf of children and their rights and voices, particularly those in Indigenous communities. According to Smith (1999), decolonizing research challenges underlying colonizing practices in research, which involve "discovery," exploration, and appropriation in research.

We conducted semi-structured conversational interviews with parents and professionals. Interviews with parents were conducted in participants' homes in two different Black townships in Gauteng province. This was a focus group interview with five parents. Interviews with professionals were typically conducted in their place of work. We conducted individual interviews with a social worker and a school administrator. In both focus group and individual interviews, the interview questions were open-ended, asking about a range of issues, including three broad topics: (1) definitions of a child, (2) what participants knew and thought about children's rights, and (3) how they viewed the Children's Act of 2007 and its implications.

Initially, we recruited three parents for the focus group interview and five professionals, who were also parents, for individual interviews. Seven of the participants were Indigenous and had grown up under apartheid, and one participant was a non-Indigenous South African. We considered the Indigenous participants to represent some of the many Indigenous cultural values in South Africa, although we did not assume they were spokespersons for their ethnic group. We recruited professionals based on their roles working in agencies serving children and families. The interview sessions lasted for one to two hours each, and it took a month to complete the interviews with all the participants. In addition to the interviews, we analyzed the Children's Act as well as related policy documents.

We translated some of the interviews into English, when Indigenous languages were used. The use of these languages was important for several reasons. Parents were able to respond in *IsiZulu* and *SeSotho*, the most frequently spoken Indigenous languages in Gauteng province. This allowed for expression of their thoughts without the barriers of using a second language. We do not suggest, however, that Black parents are unable to speak or communicate in English. These parents grew up in a state, including its schools, which forced them to learn and speak colonial languages. Part of this approach is meant to affirm a decolonizing framework in research, positioning marginalized people in the center of research. All interviews were transcribed and data were analyzed using qualitative narrative analysis. This included the use of open coding, based on the research questions, and noting particular phrases, discourse patterns, issues raised, and identities of our participants.

Themes and Issues

This section provides a summary of the themes and issues raised by participants. We present findings related broadly to participants' views on children's rights in policy and practice. We also wish to explain that our participants described a child in unique ways. Most of the participants viewed a child as one who is still dependent upon parents and adults, and whose growing independence is governed by cultural values and practices. For them, a child is not determined by a fixed age, but she or he remains a child forever in the parent's or other elder's eye. We believe this definition is important in that it is closely linked to the cultural constructions of childhood and the roles of children in their communities.

Views of Children's Rights in Policy and Practice

Children's rights, as stipulated in the Convention on the Rights of the Child and the African Charter on the Rights of the Child, are often grouped into three broad categories—protection, provision, and participation. This section discusses positive, negative, and contradictory views of children's rights in each of these broad categories. Contrasts between specific stakeholder groups (e.g., parents and professionals, particularly social workers) are discussed.

Protection

Protection rights refer to prevention of abuse, violence, and other violations of children's rights to safety and well-being. All participants spoke to the broad need for children to be protected from a range of potential risks, including child abuse, exploitation, trafficking, and HIV/AIDS. This was particularly the case for professionals, including Emma,[1] a social worker. She told us that there are many vulnerable children in Black townships in Gauteng, including those who head households because they have no parents or guardians taking care of them. Emma said she had found 329 children from such households with no support, completely on their own in the year of our interview.

Emma further told us that the Act is good because it creates a national register for children, stating:

> It creates a national register; section A will create a register of children's names [those who have been abused], hopefully with

good provisions for confidentiality, and Section B will create a register of perpetrators, and not just those convicted but those from children's court and labor hearings, etc.

According to Emma, it had been very difficult previously to convict people who abuse children, but now with the Act introducing a register, it is possible. Emma said that the Act requires that anyone working with children must disclose current and past child abuse findings against them, and a check of registry will be done. In addition, the Children's Act was heralded for leading the fight against child trafficking. It makes provisions for possible ways to be able to prosecute those who are involved in child trafficking and to go forcefully after the child trafficking syndicate.

When parents discussed protection rights, it was often in reference to changing views and laws related to physical child discipline. While most felt that it was a good trend to find alternatives to corporal punishment, this topic raised contradictory reactions from many, who saw the role of traditional discipline as maintaining cultural values such as respect for elders, including parents and teachers, become less important. When referring to her own childhood, Semakaleng stated:

> My father was *so* strict— and would threaten to beat us. One day I had to sing a song that goes like this, "*Bontate babangwe balapisa, babogale, batau,*" [some fathers are as strict and as harsh as lions]. It calmed him down. ... Given this background, I understand why there is more talk of children's rights but I am not happy with the interruption of ... traditional practices.

One implication raised by both parents and teachers was that, with children's rights being introduced and increasingly emphasized in schools, children seem to think that anything they want to do is within their rights, including those practices which are not culturally accepted.

Provision

This second broad category of rights most often came up in talking about issues of poverty, social inequities, and health-related concerns—particularly issues associated with the high incidence of HIV/AIDS and the resulting phenomenon of child-headed households.

Emma mentioned the great efforts to provide for children who head households, i.e., those who are vulnerable and live on their own:

> We brought in community women to act as caregivers and trained them [the children]. This empowered local mothers to link with NGOs and be there for children. We also provided school supplies, files for documents such as parents' death certificates … [provided] grants to access paperwork written so that children could track needed documents.

Provision rights also included access to education and health care, especially for children with disabilities. Seipati, parent and education administrator, stated that there were "huge gaps for children with disabilities—from resources for physical needs to preventing and dealing with abuse, especially in hostels." Other issues included lack of provision for basic care and nutrition.

Parents did not question their role in providing for children's needs and considered this an important children's right. Parents also stated that they were happy that public schools are now in a position to provide a safer space for their children. According to Semakaleng, children's rights were also connected to the education of poor children. For instance, she told us that children who are on welfare grants are provided with tuition waivers at school and are put on lunch programs. Children of low income can now receive free school uniforms and books through to grade 12.

Some parents said that schools were best situated to provide for and exemplify children's rights because most parents in the township were not familiar with the concept of rights as promulgated by the Children's Act. They viewed schools as conduits to provide these rights to children. As Ntombi stated, "Parents look to teachers to raise their children. … Some parents did not finish school themselves or never received proper education, such as the 15-year-old mothers in the townships—parental responsibility is also important for children's rights." One of the important provisions where schools were involved focused on the rights of girls. Seipati observed that teen pregnancy is unavoidable. In the past, schools would not allow teenagers to attend school if pregnant. However, the Children's Act reversed this practice. Pregnant teenagers can now attend school, i.e., be treated the same as teenage fathers.

Participation

Participation rights are often the least understood and most controversial category of child rights (Una, 2010). As previously discussed, these include a range of ways that children can access and share information, be consulted about issues affecting them, and express their citizenship rights. Professionals in this study appeared to appreciate the role of children's more active engagement, voice, and participation rights. Some of the parents, however, felt that children were becoming overly "empowered" in ways that showed disrespect for elders and cultural traditions.

One of the positive views on child participation rights came from Seipati, who spoke to the importance of children finding a voice, engaging with democratic decision-making, and having greater participation in their school community. She stated:

> We now have RCLs (Representation Councils of Learners), whose focus is to build leaders. ... [These] are part of school governance; two student members sit on the governing body of the school. [In] case of expulsions, this body can "hear" these cases and represent the students involved.

While parents and teachers both commented on the importance of children knowing their rights and participating more fully as young members of a democratic society, they tended to be critical and cautious of some of the unintended consequences of greater child voice. As one of the parents who is also a teacher, Nunu, put it, "In schools, according to new laws, discipline guidelines, etc., you cannot reprimand; you can, up to a point, but children know their rights and will say, 'Don't shout at me,' and then the teacher may need to write a letter to parents or explain their actions." This view was echoed by others who felt that there might even be an unintended hierarchy of rights, with children increasingly at the top.

Tensions and Contradictions

Our findings pointed to the complexities and contradictions in the ways in which children's rights and the Children's Act were understood or "read" by participants. None of the participants opposed the introduction and strengthening of children's rights. In the media coverage analyzed, the concept of children's rights was welcomed, embraced, and discussed as something that was necessary for the children of the new South Africa. However, some parents were concerned about the ways in which some rights were defined and/or implemented, many of which involved cultural tensions and ways in which children's rights discourse was shaping family and community patterns of interaction. Because of these concerns, we argue that the Children's Act was a desirable endeavor, but that it came with contradictions and complexities in terms of understanding children's rights within the cultural context of local communities (Ndimande & Swadener, 2013).

Our data revealed that parents and community leaders were concerned about issues related to cultural and religious values. For instance, one of the major concerns for parents regarding a provision of the Children's Act was that they did not agree that teenage girls should have a right to abortion without parental knowledge and consent. They were also concerned about the Act's provision of contraception to children age 12 and above without the consent of parents. For them, such laws threaten to erode Indigenous cultural values dictating that children cannot engage in birth control or abortion without the knowledge of their parents. Many parents and community leaders perceived such rights as antithetical to their cultural values and practices, which emphasize the need for children to be guided by the parent, rather than children making decisions, particularly decisions of that magnitude, without their parents' or guardians' knowledge.

Even those who supported the Act were still conflicted on certain of its sections. For instance, some parents expressed views that the Children's Act gives more power to children and that this has caused many children to disrespect adults, something that is not acceptable in several local communities, including but not limited to Indigenous ones. The notions of rights at school and the need for respect of elders, etc., at home created tensions. NomaSonto, one of the parents who is also a teacher, articulated what she called the "disconnect of rights," as modeled through the school, and those which should be linked to cultural practice:

> There has been a strong reaction to the Children's Act—many have freaked out regarding introducing children to contraception and abortion issue! There are cultural arguments against it—parents and teachers will say, "This is not in our culture."

Some other comments embodied an implicit critique of child rights documents and policies as reflecting Western values that were often misunderstood by children and even their teachers. As a mother and a teacher, Ntombi puts it, "I had a chance to teach Life Orientation. ... [I]t is difficult to teach this—the language of these concepts is English and these are very difficult for children to understand and many misunderstand!" Her interpretation of rights discourse as "English"—read Western and dominant—raises issues of how or to what extent child rights concepts are interpreted in Indigenous languages, knowledges, and practices.

Discussion

Our findings reflect the complexities and challenges of enacting policies that reflect universal assumptions about children and their place in society—particularly in the already complicated set of relations found in a postcolonial, post-apartheid setting such as South Africa. The "global politics of educational borrowing and lending" (Steiner-Khamsi, 2004) and the circulation of neoliberal Western policies through international agreements and funding-related requirements are part of the landscape in which child rights legislation is adopted in the Global South. While we do not argue against the Children's Act and the CRC, data from this study underscore the importance of taking a culturally nuanced view of ways in which the CRC and national legislation such as the South African Children's Act are understood, enacted, critiqued, resisted, and adapted.

We have grouped the discussion into three broad categories: (1) the policy-practice gap, (2) persistent neocolonial tendencies, and 3) lack of mechanisms to support the Children's Act. Two set of theories informed our analysis and are reflected in the discussion and conclusions. First, we engage theories that critique the influence of neoliberalism in post-apartheid South Africa. Second, we engage anti-colonial literature that is critical of policies and social reforms guided by colonial ideologies.

Policy-practice Gap

In the participants' discourse, as well as in national media accounts, our data provided evidence of gaps between policy on paper and policy in practice, as related to children's rights and the

Children's Act. This policy-practice gap reflected gaps between formal/legal structures and more informal/traditional values and practices. Parents tended to convey the sense that policies they were aware of in the Children's Act often did not reflect their cultural values or childrearing views. Some expressed the concern that parents and communities were not sufficiently consulted in establishing child rights policies and that some of the ideas represented more Western views and were inconsistent with respect for elders and the local community structures.

In making sense of participants' views of the children's rights and the Children's Act as they relate to the policy-practice gap, it is important to situate the findings in the post-apartheid context of South Africa. Post-apartheid policy changes cannot be understood outside the broader policy framework and the influence of Western institutions such as the World Bank and the International Monetary Fund (IMF) in sub-Saharan Africa (Brock-Utne, 2000; Swadener, Wachira, Kabiru, & Njenga, 2007). Put simply, social policies in the post-apartheid government are associated with and influenced by the Western discourse of economy, race, culture, gender, class, and politics. This policy-practice gap is exemplified by South Africa's adoption of neoliberal policies, which devalue a bottom-up approach in planning and implementing policies, in this case the Children's Act. Bond (2005), Desai (2002), Pillay (2002), and others argue that post-apartheid social policy is influenced by neoliberal politics. Neoliberalism, it could be argued, is concerned about the individual; it does not consider collective participation or communal values in which the individual lives. This is a challenge in a nation like South Africa which has a long tradition of local community participation and practices local values.

This, together with the increasing role of Western consultants in national policy formulation, has come to reveal how international "specialists" come to inform local policies. Such policies do not necessarily reflect the views and aspirations of poor and marginalized peoples, but only those who are privileged and more inclined to Western values than African. The issue of cultural difference and racial privilege becomes critical in creating the *disconnect* between those who propose these policies and the majority of the people who are culturally different and in a less privileged socio-economic status, thus less likely to be asked to participate in the formulation of these proposals.

We argue that the policy-practice gap that has led to the lack of consultation among diverse South African communities can turn an otherwise strong document with good intentions into a more controversial one. In the next section, we further analyze the Children's Act within the discourse of anticolonial theories. We use this literature to draw implications for the post-apartheid South African context and children's rights.

Persistent Neocolonial Tendencies

Issues of children's rights in post-apartheid South Africa cannot be discussed outside the historical context of colonialism, apartheid, and decades of marginalization of the subaltern groups in this nation. Colonialism and apartheid were not simply about economic dominance and segregation of communities by race, but mainly about the denial of human rights of the oppressed. While the post-apartheid democratic Constitution advocated for human rights, this discourse happens within the neocolonial field of power, i.e., the laws and the definition of rights as constructed within the Western discourse.

Anti-colonial literature is part of the decolonizing agenda that forces both the colonized and the colonizers to break away from the colonial frames of reference with a renewed subjectivity (Dei, 2011). Anti-colonial scholars (Biko, 2002; Cary, 2004; Dei, 2011; Fanon, 1963; McLeod, 2000; Myers, 2001; Ngugi, 1993) remind us that more authentic decolonization of African countries involves actively challenging colonial ways of knowing and interpretation of the social policies in post-colonial nations. Unless colonial discourse is challenged, postcolonial states will continue to be undermined and excluded in terms of cultural, socio-economic, and political decision-making. Cary (2004), for instance, argues that the former colonized are embedded in a messy terrain left behind by their colonizers manifested institutionally, culturally, socially, and spiritually. This literature explicitly argues that ideas of social reform, no matter how progressive they may appear, are typically formulated and informed by the unequal ideological relations of power between the former colonies and colonizers, with the ideas of the latter becoming the yard stick to judge between good and bad values and social norms.

Lack of Mechanisms to Support the Children Act

We were struck by the interviews that spoke to a pervasive lack of structures to help poor and marginalized children to benefit from the new law. For instance, the professional we interviewed was concerned that social workers were stretched very thin in terms of their duties to support the act. Although the Department of Social Development passed a budget to help with the implementation of the act, funding remains a major challenge. As Emma stated, "Social workers are now mandatory reporters and no longer are police the only mandatory reporters, which is problematic. [Social workers] ... are already stretched thin and no funding for hiring more, [nor] training for these issues."

In the interview Emma was concerned that there were insufficient trained officials from the Labor Department in school districts. This created a concern about whether the Act would be successfully implemented. As Emma pointed out, once there were no trained Labor Department officials, then the Act might not be fully enforced. She pointed out that without trained officials, including teacher union leaders, human resources officials can simply turn away and avoid dealing with abused children because they lack knowledge of or deny the extent of abuse issues in children. This is indeed a serious concern and calls for proper mechanisms to support this important act so that children can live a safe and respected environment. South Africa is moving in the right direction, but needs to pay attention to the concerns revealed in our analysis.

Conclusion

Our findings show that the Children's Act of 2007 embodies good intentions with important and necessary policies intended to protect and empower the children of South Africa. Yet, there are also tensions, contradictions, and unintended consequences that reveal the complexities and challenges of enacting laws and policies that reflect universal assumptions about children without a careful consideration of the contexts in which they operate. While post-apartheid South Africa is part of the global society, it has a unique and complicated history of colonialism and apartheid, which has not yet been expunged. This is also exacerbated by the neoliberal influence on policies, which denies a bottom up participation from communities. This policy-practice gap becomes crucial in the relationship between the people who have been included or excluded in formulation and implementation of this act.

Since this act does little to explicitly recognize African childrearing perspectives and beliefs of what constitutes childhood, it can be viewed as embodying implicit Western cultural values as universal. We argue that this can be viewed as an embodiment of persistent colonial assumptions that often do not take into account the complexities of local cultures. As a recommendation, we believe that, in this nation with a 79% Indigenous population, such policies should be revised and be framed with more effort to include the input and recommendations of Indigenous communities, as well as the ideas of other communities whose cultural backgrounds are not Western—for example, the Indian communities in South Africa. This allows for broad based participation on important decisions about children, cultures, and rights. The dissemination of information is important, and information should be available in all languages, not just in English. Through forums and debates, these policies can be discussed and modified to fit the context and goals defined by the communities. In addition, there have to be efficient mechanisms to support this act.

As we conclude this chapter, thousands of people, including hundreds of world leaders, are gathered in Johannesburg to attend the memorial service of the first democratically elected president of South Africa, Rolihlala Nelson Mandela. President Mandela led the fight to restore human dignity and the rights of the oppressed people in South Africa. He led the fight for the rights of children. Indeed, the first democratic Constitution in South Africa provided a foundation for the Children's Act of 2007, whose tension and contradictions need urgent attention for the children to be protected, given the opportunity to thrive, and to be given a voice through this Act.

Acknowledgments

This is a revised version of Ndimande B. S., & Swadener B. B. (2012). Children's rights and cultural tension in South Africa, *International Journal of Equity and Innovation in Early Childhood. 10*(1), 79–92.

We would like to acknowledge Claudio Chris Gutierrez, for the careful read of the data to an extent that this point was underscored in the Lack of Mechanisms to Support the Children Act discussion above.

Note

1 All names used in this research are pseudonyms.

References

African Charter on the Rights and Welfare of the Child, adopted by the Twenty-sixth Ordinary Session of the Assembly of Heads of States and Government of the OAU, Addis Ababa, Ethiopia, July 1990. OAU Doc. CAB/LEG/24.9/49 (1990), *entered into force* Nov. 29, 1999.

Bakan, J. (2011). *Childhood under siege: How big business targets children.* New York: Free Press.

Biko, S. (2002). *I write what I like: Selected writings.* Chicago: The University of Chicago Press.

Bond, P. (2005). *Elite transition: From apartheid to neoliberalism in South Africa.* Pietermaritzburg, South Africa: University of KwaZulu Natal Press.

Brock-Utne, B. (2000). *Whose education for all?: The recolonization of the African mind.* New York: Falmer Press.

Capazorio, B. (2005, December 19). Children's Act welcomed, but still contentious. The *Herald*, 4.

Cary, L. J. (2004). Always already colonizer/colonized: White Australian wanderings. In K. Mutua & B. B. Swadener (Eds.), *Decolonizing research in cross-cultural contexts: Critical personal narratives* (pp. 69–83). New York: State University of New York Press.

Children's Act, Act No. 38 of 2005; amended by Children's Amendment Act, Act No. 41 of 2007; Gazzette no. 33076, Notice no. 261, 01 April 2010.

Constitution of the Republic of South Africa, 1996. (As adopted on May 8th 1996 and amended on October 11, 1996).

Dei, G. J. S. (2011). Introduction. In G. J. S. Dei (Ed.), *Indigenous philosophies and critical education: A reader* (pp. 1–13). New York: Peter Lang.

Denzin, N. K., Lincoln, Y. S., & Smith, L. T., (Eds.). (2008). *Handbook of critical and Indigenous methodologies.* Thousand Oaks, CA: Sage.

Desai, A. (2002). *We are the poor: Community struggles in post-apartheid South Africa.* New York: Monthly Review Press.

Du Toit, C. (2007, October, 24). Children have rights too. *Mail & Guardian Online.* Retrieved from mg.co.za/article/2007-10-24-children-have-rights-too

Fanon, F. (1963). *The wretched of the earth.* New York: Grove Press.

McCarty, T. L. (2009). Empowering Indigenous languages—What can be learned from Native American experiences? In T. Skutnabb-Kangas, R. Phillipson, A. K. Mohanty, & M. Panda (Eds.), *Social justice through multilingual education* (pp.125–139). Buffalo, NY: Multilingual Matters.

McLeod, J. (2000). *Beginning post-colonialism*. New York: St. Martin.

Mudzuli, K. (2007, July 5). Clerics urge changes to Child Act. *Citizen*, 3.

Mutua, K., & Swadener, B. B. (Eds.). (2004). *Decolonizing research in cross-cultural contexts: Critical personal narratives*. Albany, NY: SUNY Press.

Myers, W. E. (2001). The rights rights? Child labor in a globalizing world. In W. H. Alan, A. W. Neil, & L. F. Jude (Eds.), *The analysis of the American Academy of Political and Social Science. Children Rights* (pp. 36–55). London: Sage.

Ndimande, B. S. (2006). Parental "choice": The liberty principle in education finance. *Perspectives in Education. 24*(2), 143–156.

Ndimande, B. S. (2012). Decolonizing research in post-apartheid South Africa: The politics of methodology. *Qualitative Inquiry, 18*(3), 215–226.

Ndimande, B. S., & Swadener, B. B. (2012). Children's rights and cultural tension in South Africa, *International Journal of Equity and Innovation in Early Childhood. 10*(1), 79–92.

Ndimande, B. S., & Swadener, B. B. (2013). Pursuing democracy through education rights: Perspectives from South Africa. In B. B. Swadener, L. Lundy, J. Habashi, & N. Blanchet-Cohen (Eds.), *Children's lives and education in cross-national contexts: What difference could rights make?* (pp.169–187). New York: Peter Lang.

Ngobese, N. (August 30, 2007). Parents speak on the Child Act. *Witness*, 11.

Ngugi wa Thiong'o. (1993). *Moving the center: The struggle for cultural freedoms.* Portsmouth, NH: Heinemann.

Nkomo, M. (1990). Introduction. In M. Nkomo (Ed.), *Pedagogy of domination: Toward a democratic education in South Africa* (pp. 1–15). Trenton, NJ: Africa World Press.

Office of the United Nations High Commissioner for Human Rights. (1989). The Convention on the Rights of the Child. Geneva, Switzerland.

Pillay, D. (2002, October 6). Between the market and a hard place. *Sunday Times*, 24.

Skutnabb-Kangas, T., & Dunbar, R. (2010). *Indigenous children's education as linguistic genocide and a crime against humanity? A global view. GálduČála. Journal of Indigenous Peoples' Rights, 1.* Guovdageaidnu/Kautokeino: Galdu, Resource Centre for the Rights of Indigenous Peoples.

Smith, L. T. (1999). *Decolonizing methodologies: Research and Indigenous peoples.* Dunedin, New Zealand: University of Otago Press.

South African Schools Act, (1996). *Government Gazette of the Republic of South Africa*, NO. 84 of 1996, vol 377, November 15, 1996.

Sowetan Editor. (2007, July 5) Sowetan says act fast-tracks kids to adulthood. *Sowetan*, 18.

Steiner-Khamsi, G. (2004). *The global politics of educational borrowing and lending*. New York: Teacher College Press.

Swadener, B. B., & Mutua, K. (2008). Decolonizing performances: Deconstructing the global postcolonial. In N. K. Denzin, Y. S. Lincoln, L. T. Smith (Eds.), *Handbook of critical and Indigenous methodologies* (pp. 31–43). Thousand Oaks, CA: Sage.

Swadener, B. B., Wachira, P., Kabiru, M., & Njenga, A. (2007). Linking policy discourse to everyday life in Kenya: Impacts of neoliberal policies on early education and childrearing. In A. Pence (Ed.), *Africa's future/ Africa's challenge: Early childhood care and development in sub-Saharan Africa* (pp.407–426). New York: The World Bank.

Swadener, B.B., with Kabiru, M., & Njenga, A. (2000). *Does the village still raise the child? A collaborative study of changing child-rearing and early education in Kenya.* Albany: State University of New York Press.

The Universal Declaration of Human Rights. (1948). Retrieved August 20, 2009, from www.un.org/Overview/rights.html

Una Children's Rights Learning Group. (2010). *Children's Rights in Una and Beyond: Transnational Perspectives.* Una Working Paper 7, Belfast: Una

Chapter 7

Freeing Ourselves

An Indigenous Response to Neo-Colonial Dominance in Research, Classrooms, Schools, and Education Systems

Russell Bishop

This then is the great humanistic and historical task of the oppressed: to liberate themselves and their oppressors as well. The oppressors, who oppress, exploit and rape by virtue of their power, cannot find in this power the strength to liberate either the oppressed or themselves. Only power that springs from the weakness of the oppressed will be sufficiently strong to free both.

—Freire (1972, p. 21)

Introduction

This chapter draws from the work that I have been doing over the past 25 years in the field of Māori and Indigenous education within the frame of kaupapa Māori theory. This journey over time has led me from researching the impact of colonization on my mother's Māori family to an appreciation of just what researching in Māori contexts involves. What I learned from that analysis was then extrapolated to re-theorize the marginalization of Māori students in mainstream secondary school classrooms. From this understanding, a means of supporting teachers and leaders to reposition themselves

Qualitative Inquiry Outside the Academy edited by Norman K. Denzin and Michael D. Giardina, 146–163. © 2014 Left Coast Press, Inc. All rights reserved.

discursively and create caring and learning relationships within mainstream classrooms was developed. From these theoretical beginnings a large-scale classroom-based, school-reform project grew and eventually developed into a comprehensive approach towards theory- or principle-based education reform that is being implemented in 49 of the 320 secondary schools in New Zealand.

Fundamental to this theorizing and practice were the understandings promoted by Paulo Freire over 40 years ago, that the answers to the conditions that oppressed peoples found themselves in was not to be found in the language or epistemologies of the oppressors, but rather in that of the oppressed. This realization was confirmed when I understood that researching in Māori contexts needed to be conducted dialogically within the world view and understandings of the people with whom I was working. This realization also led me to understand how dialogue in its widest sense is crucial for developing a means whereby Māori students would be able to participate successfully in education.

Kaupapa Māori Responses

The major challenges facing education in New Zealand today are the ongoing and increasing social, economic, and political disparities within our nation, primarily between the descendants of the European colonizers (Pakeha) and the Indigenous Māori people. Māori have higher levels of unemployment (especially among youth), are more likely to be employed in low paying employment, have much higher levels of incarceration, mental and physical illness, and poverty than do the rest of the population, and are generally under-represented in the positive social and economic indicators of the society. These disparities are also reflected at all levels of the education system.[1]

Along with those of other indigenous peoples in the world who have suffered the impact of colonialism, these disparities reflect major and ongoing power imbalances that, along with socio-economic and political marginalization, have seen major culture and language loss among Māori people, particularly over the past century. This marginalization, culture and language loss, and the ethnic revitalization that has developed from within Māori culture itself in response is the major focus of this chapter. This chapter will demonstrate how theorizing and practice that have grown from within Māori epistemologies have been applied in a number of settings as counter-narratives to the dominant discourses in New Zealand.

Māori People Address the Problem of Educational Disparities

Frustrated with the lack of an effective system response to the problem of educational disparities and language and culture loss, in a Freirean sense, Māori people have undertaken their own response which grew out of the wider ethnic revitalization movement that developed among Māori people in New Zealand during their massive post World War II urbanization. This response initially saw the growth of a discourse of proactive theory and practice, broadly termed *kaupapa* (agenda, philosophy) Māori. Kaupapa Māori seeks to operationalize Māori people's aspirations to restructure power relationships at all levels in society to the point where partners can be autonomous and interact from this position rather than from one of subordination or dominance as has been the situation since the time of the signing of the Treaty of Waitangi in 1840 when the new nation of New Zealand was established. This theorizing drew together an emerging political consciousness among Māori people that promoted the revitalization of Māori cultural epistemologies as a philosophical and productive counter-narrative to the hegemony of neo-colonial discourses. In reference to kaupapa Māori in education, G. Smith (1997) explained this as occurring when "Māori communities armed with the new critical understandings of the shortcomings of the state and structural analyses began to assert transformative actions to deal with the twin crises of language demise and educational underachievement for themselves" (p. 171).

Elaborating on this point in 2003, Smith (2003) identified that the aim was to move from reactive grievance to proactive politics, from negative to positive motivations, from 'decolonization,' which locates the colonizer at the center of the debate, to 'consciousness raising' "which puts Māori at the centre" (p. 2). In short, to promote self-determination (*tino rangatiratanga*) by and for Māori people (Bishop, 1996; Durie, 1995, 1998; G. Smith, 1997; L Smith, 1999), which in Durie's (1995) terms "captures a sense of Māori ownership and active control over the future" (p. 16). However, this call for self-determination is clearly understood by Māori people as being relative, not absolute; that is, it is self-determination in *relation to others*. In Young's (2004) terms, such an approach identifies "a quest for an institutional context of non-domination" (p. 187). To ensure non-domination, "relations must be regulated both by institutions in which they all participate and by ongoing negotiations among them" (Young, 2004, p. 177). Therefore, educational institutional leaders and practitioners should structure and conduct their practices in such a way as to seek to mediate potential tensions by actively minimizing domination, co-ordinating actions, resolving conflicts, and negotiating relationships. In Young's terms, this is an education where power is shared between self-determining individuals within non-dominating relations of interdependence.

Early examples of kaupapa Māori theorizing in practice included the growth of Māori medium education institutions such as Te Kohanga Reo (Māori medium elementary schools), Kura Kaupapa Māori (Māori medium primary schools), Wharekura (Māori medium secondary schools), and Waananga Māori (Māori tertiary institutions). As G. Smith (2003) explains, Māori communities "were so concerned with the loss of Māori language, knowledge and culture that they took matters into their own hands and set up their own learning institutions at pre-school, elementary school, secondary school and tertiary levels" (pp. 6–7). Despite facing many problems, these new institutions continue to make inroads into the general culture of New Zealand to the extent that they are now immutable elements of the wider society.

Simultaneously, a number of other initiatives grew within the philosophical frame of kaupapa Māori. This chapter looks at three examples of how this author was involved in an indigenous people's initiative to *free ourselves* from neo-colonial oppression by creating counter-narratives to the dominant discourses around research, classroom practices, and school and system organization. The chapter also highlights how such an approach has redirected the actions of members of the 'oppressor' groups to discursively reposition themselves through an ongoing process of conscientization in relation to the representations of Māori as a minoritized group.

Kaupapa Māori Research Approaches

An early example of a Kaupapa Māori project was an investigation of what constituted effective approaches to researching in Māori settings undertaken by the author (Bishop, 1996, 2005). In this project, the centrality of the process of establishing extended family-like relationships, understood in Māori as *whanaungatanga*, were used metaphorically as a research strategy to ensure that issues of initiation, benefits, representation, legitimation, and accountability were not being dominated by the researcher's agenda, concerns, and interests within the research process.

In this sense, *whanaungatanga* means that groups (be they of research or classroom participants) are constituted as if they were a *whanau*, or extended family. Metge (1990) explains that to use the term *whanau*, whether literally or metaphorically, is to identify a series of rights and responsibilities, commitments and obligations, and supports that are fundamental to the collectivity. These are the *tikanga* (customs) of the *whanau*; warm interpersonal interactions, group solidarity, shared responsibility for one another, cheerful cooperation for group ends, corporate responsibility for group property, material or non-material (e.g., knowledge) items and issues. These attributes can be summed up in the words *aroha* (love in the broadest sense, including mutuality), *awhi* (helpfulness), *manaaki* (hospitality), and *tiaki* (guidance).

What is central to developing research (and classroom) relationships in this manner is that the *whanau* is a location for communication, for sharing outcomes, and for constructing shared common understandings and meanings. In other words, it is the context within which research (or classroom) activities can take place effectively. In such contexts, individuals have responsibilities to care for and to nurture other members of the group, while still adhering to the *kaupapa* (agenda, purpose) of the group. The group will operate to avoid singling out particular individuals for comment and attention and to avoid embarrassing individuals who are not yet succeeding within the group, and group products and achievement frequently take the form of group rather than individual performance.

This approach gave voice to a culturally positioned means of developing interviewing so as to collaboratively construct research stories (Collaborative Storying; see Connelly and Clandinin, 1990) in a culturally conscious and connected manner by focusing on the researcher's connectedness, engagement, and involvement with others in order to promote self-determination, agency, and the voice of those involved in the interaction (Bishop & Glynn, 1999; Bishop, 2005). Indeed, establishing and maintaining extended family (*whanau*) type relationships is a fundamental, often extensive and ongoing part of the research process that precedes and contextualizes all other activities. This re-ordering of what constitutes the research relationship is undertaken not on terms of or within understandings constructed by the researcher; instead *whanaungatanga* (establishing relationships within Māori discursive practices) uses Māori cultural practices and means of sense-making, such as *hui* (Māori formal meetings), found in Māori decision-making processes in Māori formal meetings on *marae* (Māori formal meeting settings), other extended family settings, and informal day-to-day practices (Bishop, 2005: Salmond, 1975), to set the pattern for research relationships.

Kaupapa Māori in Mainstream/Public School Classrooms

The above-described understanding was then extrapolated to classroom settings (Bishop & Glynn, 1999). This extrapolation suggested that a pedagogy that would be effective for Māori students in mainstream schools would be one that was understandable in Māori epistemological terms, would address the on-going power imbalances and racism that exist in neo-colonial New Zealand, and would create a context that would re-order the relationships between teachers and students in classrooms and mainstream/public schools. In other words, just as *whanau* relationships, *whanaungatanga* re-orders what constitutes the research relationship in classrooms; relationships could also be re-ordered using this organizing metaphor. Similarly, this re-ordering of the pedagogic relationship need not be within the cultural understandings or constructions of the teacher, but instead, processes of *whanaungatanga* that use Māori language, cultural understandings, decision-making processes, means of sense-making, and students' prior knowledge and language would create a pedagogic approach that would more effectively support Māori students' engagement and learning. Such a pedagogy would develop caring and learning relationships that would be culturally responsive

(Gay, 2010) and culturally sustaining (Paris, 2012). In this pedagogic approach, power would be shared between self-determining individuals within non-dominating relations of interdependence (Young, 2004); the maintenance and promotion of Māori culture and language would be central; learning would be interactive, dialogic, and spiralling; and participants would be connected and committed to one another through the process of co-constructing shared common understandings and meanings. Drawing on Gay (2010), Villegas and Lucas (2002)—who identify the importance of a culturally responsive pedagogy—and Sidorkin (2002) and Cummins (1996)—who propose that relations ontologically precede all other concerns in education—I have termed such a pattern Culturally Responsive Pedagogy of Relations (see Bishop, 2008).

How such a pedagogy could be operationalized was then investigated by interviewing Māori students, their families, principals, and teachers in 2001 (Bishop & Berryman, 2006), in 2004–2005, and again in 2007 (Bishop et al., 2007). The interviews were undertaken within the Collaborative Storying approach described above that sought to address the self determination of Māori secondary school students by talking with them and other participants in their education about their understandings of what is involved in limiting and/or improving their educational achievement. These narratives of experience became the foundation of a research and development project called *Te Kotahitanga: Improving the Educational Achievement of Māori students in Mainstream Schools* (Bishop et al., 2003, 2007, 2011), which has been implemented in 49 secondary schools with some 32,000 students, 14,000 of whom were Māori, and 2,000 teachers.

The process of Collaborative Storying from a range of engaged and non-engaged Māori students (as defined by their schools) in five non-structurally modified mainstream secondary schools was very similar to *testimonio* in that it is the intention of the direct narrator (research participant) to use an interlocutor (the researcher) to bring his, her, or their situation to the attention of an audience "to which he or she would normally not have access because of their very condition of subalternity to which the *testimonio* bears witness" (Beverly, 2000, p. 556). In this research, the students were able to have their narratives about their experiences of schooling shared with teachers who otherwise might not have access to them. These vicarious experiences proved to be a very powerful means of facilitating teachers' critical reflections on the part they themselves might be playing in the low attendance, retention, and achievement of Māori students in their classrooms.

Such an approach is consistent with Ryan (1999), who suggests that a solution to the one-sidedness of representations that are promoted by the dominance of the powerful—in this case, pathologizing discourses—is to portray events as were done in the collaborative stories of the Māori students, in terms of "competing discourses rather than as simply the projection of inappropriate images" (p. 187). He suggests that this approach, rather than seeking the truth, or "real pictures," allows for previously marginalized discourses "to emerge and compete on equal terms with previously dominant discourses" (p. 187).

In these recounts of experience, in contrast to the majority of their teachers who tended to dwell upon the problems of what they saw as the children's deficiencies, Māori students clearly identified that the main influence on their educational achievement was the quality of the in-class relationships and interactions they had with their teachers. Most of their teachers were reproducing society-wide power imbalances by explaining Māori students' learning difficulties in deficit terms, the results being the perpetuation of their use of pathologizing practices, which in turn perpetuated the persistent pattern of educational disparities. Such discursive positioning created contexts for learning that Māori students described as being negative and harmful to their developing positive identities for themselves. In addition, relationships between Māori students and their teachers were characterized by teachers having low expectations of Māori students' ability to learn. As a result, Māori students behaved inappropriately and absented themselves from classroom interactions they found to be unacceptable, resulting in a general breakdown in the classroom being a place of concentrated learning for all. This breakdown in relationships creates a downward spiral of lowering teacher expectations, as seen in low levels of the cognitive challenge in lessons, a concentration on the use of traditional transmission pedagogies, less use of effective discursive interactions in classrooms by the teachers, and a consequent lack of engagement and attendance by Māori students in the lessons and learning.

In contrast, the Māori student interviewees explained how teachers could create an alternative context for learning in which Māori students' educational achievement could improve by teachers changing the ways they related to and interacted with Māori students in their classrooms. It was suggested that if teachers were supported to understand the impact of negative, deficit theorizing and subsequent practice on their relationships with students in their classrooms and learn to (re)theorize their actions in ways that were culturally responsive to their students, they would understand how they could be agentic, which in turn would refocus their attentions on the teaching-learning relationship. As a result, teachers would have higher expectations of their students, which would lead to greater engagement by students with learning. In effect, the context that Māori students saw as being supportive of their learning was one where teachers establish caring and learning classroom relationships that they described in terms of whanau-like relationships, *whanaungatanga*.[2]

Based on these observations, Bishop et al. (2003) developed an Effective Teaching Profile (ETP). Fundamental to the ETP is teachers' understanding of the need to reject deficit theorizing as a means of explaining Māori students' low educational achievement levels, and taking an agentic position in their theorizing about their practice. In order to help teachers change their practice the professional development program was developed. It provides teachers with professional learning opportunities where they can critically evaluate where they discursively position themselves when constructing their own images, principles, and practices in relation to Māori and other minoritized students in their classrooms. Teachers are provided with ongoing opportunities to consider the implications of their discursive positioning on their own agency and for Māori students' learning. Teachers are then able to express their professional commitment and responsibility for bringing about change in Indigenous and other minoritized students' educational achievement by accepting professional responsibility for the learning of all of their students, not just those whom they can relate to readily.

As Mazarno, Waters, and McNulty (2005) identified, most educational innovations do not address the "existing framework of perceptions and beliefs, or paradigm, as part of the change process—an ontological approach" (p. 162), but rather assume "that innovation is assimilated into existing beliefs and perceptions" (p. 162). They go on to suggest that reforms that are more likely to succeed are those that are fundamentally ontological in nature, providing participants with an "experience of their paradigms as constructed realities, and an experience of consciousness other than the 'I' embedded in their paradigms" (p. 162). In other words, reforms need to provide teachers with experiences of how discourses can determine their subsequent relationships and interactions. This insight is something pointed out by several theories from a range of perspectives as widely divergent as Bruner (1996) and Foucault (1972). Hence the focus in Te Kotahitanga on rejecting deficit theorizing, for as Sleeter (2005) suggests with reference to American schooling:

> It is true that low expectations for students of color and students from poverty communities, buttressed by taken-for-granted acceptance of the deficit ideology, has been a rampant and persistent problem for a long time … therefore, empowering teachers without addressing the deficit ideology may well aggravate the problem. (p. 2)

In effect, if we think that other people have deficiencies, then our actions will tend to follow our thinking and the relationships we develop, and the interactions we have with these people will tend to be negative and unproductive (Valencia, 1997). That is, despite teachers being well-meaning and with the best intentions in the world, if teachers are led to believe that students with whom they are interacting are deficient, they will respond to them negatively. We were told time and again by interview participants in 2001 (Bishop & Berryman, 2006) and again in 2007 (Bishop et al., 2007) that negative, deficit thinking on the part of teachers was fundamental to the development of negative relations and interactions between the students and their teachers, resulting in frustration and anger for all concerned.

Therefore, far from positioning teachers as having deficiencies, or creating a false dichotomy between teachers being agents and teachers working with a model that 'regulates' them, the learning opportunities offered to teachers in the professional development program provides them with ongoing opportunities to undertake what Davies and Harre (1990) called *discursive repositioning*. This means that they are offered opportunities to draw explanations and subsequent practices from alternative discourses that offer them solutions instead of those that reinforce problems and barriers. Evidence of the effectiveness of this approach is to be found in surveys and interviews conducted with teachers in the project (Bishop et al., 2007, 2011; Meyer et al., 2010; Sleeter, 2011) that demonstrate teachers' appreciation of an approach that offers activities that enable them to experience cognitive dissonance of the sort described by Timperley, Wilson, Barrar, and Fung (2007) in that it is undertaken in a respectful manner that supports teachers as learners. In this way, the program draws from Māori epistemologies by using the metaphor of a 'koha' to explain the process of discursive (re)positioning within the project. A koha is literally a gift that is placed on a *marae* (cultural meeting place) by the visitors (in this case the external professional developers) for the hosts (the teachers) to respond as they see fit. It is up to the hosts to determine themselves if they will accept the gift or not. The visitors cannot impose the gift upon the hosts. However, once the gift has been picked up there is an expectation from the visitors that it will be looked after with respect and cared for in a manner that demonstrates reciprocal responsibility, thus emphasizing the connectedness between host and visitors once the ritualized process of gift giving and receiving has been undertaken.

These central understandings are then manifested in these teachers' classrooms when effective teachers demonstrate on a daily basis that: they care for the students as culturally located individuals; they have high expectations for students' learning; they are able to manage their classrooms and curriculum so as to promote learning; they are able to engage in a range of discursive learning interactions with students or facilitate students to engage with others in these ways; they know a range of strategies that can facilitate learning interactions; they collaboratively promote, monitor, and reflect upon students' learning outcomes so as to modify their instructional practices in ways that will lead to improvements in Māori student achievement; and they share this knowledge with the students (Bishop & Berryman, 2006).

The most recent analyses of the effect of the implementation of the ETP through the professional development program show that the schools who are the most effective implementers of the ETP see Māori student schooling experiences improve dramatically. In addition, participation, engagement, retention, and achievement all show positive gains compared to a comparison group of schools (Bishop et al., 2011; Meyer et al., 2010).

Example 3: Freeing Public Schools and the Education System

The third example is about developing a model for freeing public schools and the education system that supports them from neo-colonial dominance by scaling up; that is, by extending and sustaining effective, Indigenous-based education reform as opposed to education reform that is based on dominant group understandings. Scaling up such education reform has the potential to have a major impact on the disparities that exist in society, because deepening and expanding the benefits of effective education reform programs will change the status quo of historical, ongoing, and seemingly immutable disparities. Nevertheless, claiming that educational reform on its own can cure historical disparities is not the purpose of this chapter; rather, it is clear that educational reform can play a major part in a comprehensive approach to addressing social, economic, and political disparities.

Current approaches to scaling up educational reform have not worked for Indigenous and minoritized students. Most attempts are short term, poorly funded at the outset, and often abandoned before any real changes can be seen, soon to be replaced by some "bold new initiative." In contrast, the model identified in this chapter suggests that educational reforms need to have built into them, from the very outset, those dimensions that will see them sustained in the original sites and spread to others. These elements will allow educational reforms to be scaled up with the confidence that the reform will not only be able to be sustained in existing and new sites, but that, above all, will work to reduce disparities and realize the potential of those students currently not well served by education. Put simply, educational reforms that can be sustained and extended can have an impact on educational and social disparities through increasing the educational opportunities for students previously denied these options, on a scale currently not available in most Western countries.

GPILSEO: A Model for Cultural and Structural Reform

The GPILSEO reform model is based on Coburn's (2003) analysis of conditions necessary for taking a project to scale. This analysis was used by Bishop and O'Sullivan (2005) and Bishop, O'Sullivan, and Berryman (2010) as a useful starting heuristic for considering how to successfully implement and take an educational reform project to scale in a large number of classrooms and schools, and to sustain the achievement gains made in these classrooms and schools. The central understanding of this model is that a reform initiative must have a series of dimensions present from the very outset, at a variety of levels—classrooms, schools, and within the wider system—in order that educational reform can be successful.

In order to ensure achievement gains are made by target students and that these gains are sustainable, the following elements should be present in the reform initiative *from the very outset*. These elements need to include: a means of establishing a school-wide GOAL and vision for improving the targeted students' educational achievement; a means of developing a new PEDAGOGY to depth so that it becomes habitual; a means of developing new INSTITUTIONS and structures to support the in-class initiatives; a means of developing LEADERSHIP that is responsive, transformative, pro-active, and distributed; a means of SPREADING the reform to include all teachers, parents, community members, and external agencies; a means of EVALUATING the progress of the reform in the school by developing appropriate tools and measures of progress; and a means of creating opportunities for the school to take OWNERSHIP of the reform in such a way that the original objectives of the reform are protected and sustained.

For example, in classrooms for a reform initiative to bring about sustainable change, there must be, from the very outset: a *goal* on improving targeted students' (in this case, Māori) participation, engagement, and achievement in the classroom; a means of implementing a *relational pedagogy* to depth so that new ways of relating and interacting are organized and instituted; a means of developing new institutions, such as structured collaborative decision making sessions, so that new ways of relating and interacting are organized and instituted; a means of developing distributed leadership within the classroom where students can participate in the co-construction of curriculum content and learning processes; a means whereby the new classroom relationships and interactions are spread in order to include all students; a means of monitoring and evaluating the progress of all students so as to inform practice; and above all, a means whereby the teachers and their students know about and take ownership of the reform, its aims, objectives, and outcomes.

At a school level there needs to be: a focus on improving all targeted students' achievement across the school; a culturally responsive pedagogy of relations developed across all classrooms that informs relations and interactions at all levels in school and community; time and space created for the development of new institutions within the school, such as induction hui, observations and feedback sessions, structured collaborative decision-making meetings about future pedagogic interactions based on evidence of student progress, and shadow-coaching of specific goals in the classroom—and structures such as timetables and personnel organization need to support this reform; leadership that is responsive to the needs of the reform, pro-active in setting targets and goals, and distributed to allow power sharing; a means whereby all staff can join the reform and for parents and community to be included into the reform; a means whereby in-school facilitators, researchers, and teachers are able to use appropriate instruments to gather evidence/data to monitor the implementation of the reform so as to provide data for formative and summative purposes; and a means whereby the whole school, including the board of trustees, can take ownership of the reform. Ownership is seen when there has been a culture shift so that teacher learning is central to the school and systems, and structures and institutions are developed to support teacher learning—in this way, addressing both culturalist and structuralist concerns at the school level.

The need for system-wide reform: a national policy focus and resource allocation sufficient to raise the achievement of the target students and reduce disparities; a means whereby pre-service teacher education is aligned with in-service professional development so that each supports the other in implementing new relational pedagogies; a review of funding so that salaries for in-school professional developers can be built into schools' staffing allocations and schooling organizations to provide ongoing, interactive, and embedded reform; national level support and professional development for leaders to promote distributed leadership models; collaboration between policy funders, researchers, and practitioners; national level support for evaluation and monitoring that is ongoing and interactive, and that informs policy; national level support for integrated research and professional development that provide data for formative and summative purposes; national ownership of the problem; and the provision of sufficient funding and resources to see solutions in a defined period of time and in an ongoing, embedded manner.

This model therefore encompasses the need to address both culturalist and structuralist positions at the three levels of classroom, school, and system by creating a means of changing the classroom, the culture of the school, and the education system. Cultural change concerns are addressed through goal setting, the development of appropriate pedagogies to depth and the support this requires, and the taking of ownership of the whole reform at each level. Structural concerns are addressed by the development of new institutions; responsive and distributed leadership; the spread of the reform to include all involved; the development of data-management systems within the school to support the reform; and the taking of ownership by the teachers, school, and policy makers of both the cultural and structural changes necessary to reform education to address educational disparities. In this way education can play its part in removing the key contributing factors to poverty among Māori and other minoritized peoples in Aotearoa/New Zealand. Structural concerns are also addressed at a system-wide level when schools are supported at a national level to implement these structural changes.

So overall, this chapter records the development of a means where, just as Paolo Freire predicted it should, educational reform has grown out of the power of the oppressed. It commenced by our initially wresting control over what constitutes research into Māori peoples' lives from the dominant groups. It then meant that we could use this control to establish professional development for teachers that makes sense to Māori students and not just to the teachers (although that happens as well) and then design a model to expand this process to a large number of sites in New Zealand.

Notes

1 In comparison to majority culture students (in New Zealand these students are primarily of European descent): the overall academic achievement levels of Māori students is low; their rate of suspension from school is three times higher; they are over-represented in special education programs for behavioral issues; enrollment in pre-school programs is in lower proportions than other groups; they tend to be over-represented in low stream education classes; they are more likely than other students to be found in vocational curriculum streams; they leave school earlier with less formal qualifications and enroll in tertiary education in lower proportions. For example: 23% of Māori boys and 35% of Māori girls achieved university entrance, compared to 47% and 60% for their non-Māori counterparts in 2009; in 2010, Māori students were twice as likely to leave school at the age of 15 than Pakeha students; only 28% of Māori boys and 41% of Māori girls left school in 2009 with a level 3 qualification or above, compared to 49% and 65% of their non-Māori counterparts (Ministry of Education, 2010a); in 2009, the retention rate to age 17 was 45.8% for Māori , compared to 72.2% of non-Māori; Māori suspension rate is 3.6 times higher than that of Pakeha (Ministry of Education, 2009); and while 89.4% of Māori new entrants had attended pre-school programs in 2010, 98.1% of Pakeha/European new entrants had done so (Ministry of Education, 2010b).

2 See Bishop & Berryman (2006) for details of these analyses by Maori students.

References

Beverley, J. (2000). Testimonio, subalternity, and narrative authority. In N. K. Denzin & Y. S. Lincoln (Eds.), *Handbook of qualitative research* (2nd ed., pp. 555–565). Thousand Oaks, CA: Sage.

Bishop, R. (1996). *Collaborative research stories: Whakawhanaungatanga*. Palmerston North, New Zealand: Dunmore Press.

Bishop, R. (2005). Freeing ourselves from neo-colonial domination in research: A kaupapa Māori approach to creating knowledge. In N. K. Denzin & Y. S. Lincoln (Eds.), *The Sage handbook of qualitative research* (3rd ed., pp. 109–138). Thousand Oaks, CA: Sage.

Bishop R. (2008). Te Kotahitanga: Kaupapa Māori in mainstream classrooms. In N. K. Denzin, Y. S. Lincoln, & L. T. Smith (Eds.), *Handbook of critical and Indigenous methodologies* (pp. 439–458). Thousand Oaks, CA: Sage.

Bishop, R., & Glynn, T. (1999). *Culture counts: Changing power relations in education*. Palmerston North, New Zealand: Dunmore Press.

Bishop, R., & O'Sullivan, D. (2005). *Taking a reform project to scale: Considering the conditions that promote sustainability and spread of reform*. A monograph prepared with the support of Nga Pae o te Maramatanga, The National Institute for Research Excellence in Māori Development and Advancement. Unpublished manuscript.

Bishop, R., & Berryman, M. (2006). *Culture speaks: Cultural relationships and classroom learning.* Wellington, New Zealand: Huia.

Bishop, R., O'Sullivan, D., & Berryman, M. (2010). *Scaling up education reform: Addressing the politics of disparity.* Wellington, New Zealand: NZCER Press.

Bishop, R., Berryman, M., Tiakiwai, S., & Richardson, C. (2003). *Te Kotahitanga: The experiences of year 9 and 10 Māori students in mainstream classrooms.* Wellington, New Zealand: Ministry of Education.

Bishop, R., Berryman, M., Cavanagh, T., & Teddy, L. (2007). *Te Kotahitanga Phase 3 whanaungatanga: Establishing a culturally responsive pedagogy of relations in mainstream secondary school classrooms.* Wellington, New Zealand: Ministry of Education.

Bishop, R., Berryman, M., Wearmouth, J., Peter, M., & Clapham, S. (2011). *Te Kotahitanga: Maintaining, replicating and sustaining change.* Wellington, New Zealand: Ministry of Education.

Bruner, J. (1996). *The culture of education.* Cambridge, MA: Harvard University Press.

Coburn, C. (2003). Rethinking scale: Moving beyond numbers to deep and lasting change. *Educational Researcher, 32*(6), 3–12.

Connelly, F. M., & Clandinin, D. J. (1990). Stories of experience and narrative inquiry. *Educational Researcher, 19*(5), 2–14

Cummins, J. (1996). *Negotiating identities: Education for empowerment in a diverse society.* Los Angeles: California Association for Bilingual Education.

Davies, B., & Harre, R. (1990). Positioning: The discursive production of selves. *Journal of the Theory of Social Behaviour, 20*, 43–65.

Durie, M. (1995). *Principles for the development of Māori policy.* Paper presented at the Māori Policy Development Conference, Wellington, New Zealand.

Durie, M. (1998). *Te mana, te kawanatanga: The politics of Māori self-determination.* Auckland, New Zealand: Oxford University Press.

Foucault, M. (1972). *The archaeology of knowledge.* New York: Pantheon.

Freire, P. (1972). *Pedagogy of the oppressed.* New York: Continuum.

Gay, G. (2010). *Culturally responsive teaching: Theory, research and practice* (2nd ed.). New York: Teachers College Press.

Marzano, R. J., Waters, T., & McNulty, B. A. (2005). *School leadership that works: From research to results.* Alexandria, VA: Association for Supervision and Curriculum Development.

Metge, J. (1990). Te rito o te harakeke: Conceptions of the Whanaau. *Journal of the Polynesian Society, 99*(1), 55–91.

Meyer, L. H., Penetito, W., Hynds, A., Savage, C., Hindle, R., & Sleeter, C. (2010). *Evaluation of Te Kotahitanga: 2004–2008.* Wellington, New Zealand: Ministry of Education.

Ministry of Education. (2009). Statement of intent: 2009–2014. Retrieved from www.minedu.govt.nz/theministry/publicationsandresources/state-mentofintent/soi2009.aspx

Ministry of Education. (2010a). *Participation and attainment of Māori students in National Certification of Educational Achievement.* Wellington, New Zealand: Education Counts, Ministry of Education. Retrieved from www.educationcounts.govt.nz/statistics/schooling/ncea-attainment/ncea-achievement-data-roll-based/participation-and-attainment-of-Māori -students-in-national-certificate-of-educational-achievement

Ministry of Education. (2010b). *Education counts: Teaching staff.* Retrieved from www.educationcounts.govt.nz/statistics/schooling/teaching_staff

Organisation for Economic Co-operation and Development. (2007). *Education at a glance 2007: OECD indicators.* Paris: OECD.

Paris, D., (2012), Culturally sustaining pedagogy: A needed change in stance, terminology, and practice. *Educational Researcher, 41*(3), 93–97.

Ryan, J. (1999). *Race and ethnicity in multi-ethnic schools: A critical case study.* Clevedon, UK: Multilingual Matters.

Salmond, A. (1975). *Hui: A study of Māori ceremonial greetings.* Auckland, New Zealand: Reed & Methuen.

Sidorkin, A. M. (2002). *Learning relations: Impure education, deschooled schools, and dialogue with evil.* New York: Peter Lang.

Sleeter, C. (2005). *Un-standardizing curriculum: Multicultural teaching in the standards-based classroom.* New York: Teachers College Press.

Sleeter, C., (Ed.). (2011). *Professional development for culturally responsive and relationship-based pedagogy* (1ˢᵗ ed.). New York: Peter Lang.

Smith, G. H. (1997). *Kaupapa Māori as transformative praxis.* Unpublished doctoral dissertation, University of Auckland, Auckland, New Zealand.

Smith, G. H. (2003). *Indigenous struggle for the transformation of education and schooling.* Keynote address to the Alaskan Federation of Natives (AFN) Convention. Anchorage, Alaska.

Smith, L. T. (1999). *Decolonizing methodologies: Research and indigenous peoples.* London: Zed Books.

Timperley, H., Wilson, A., Barrar, H., & Fung, I. (2007). *Teacher professional learning and development: Best evidence synthesis iteration (BES).* Wellington, New Zealand: Ministry of Education.

Valencia, R. R. (1997). *The evolution of deficit thinking: Educational thought and practice.* London: Falmer Press.

Villegas, A. M., & Lucas, T. (2002). *Educating culturally responsive teachers: A coherent approach.* New York: State University of New York Press.

Young, I. M. (2004). Two concepts of self determination. In S. May, T. Mahood, & J, Squires (Eds.), *Ethnicity, nationalism and minority rights* (pp. 176–198). Cambridge, UK: Cambridge University Press.

Chapter 8

Indigenous Researchers and Epistemic Violence

César A. Cisneros Puebla

Our knowledge about the social world has been tremendously useless when dealing with the urgency of social justice, social change, and democracy. We have created diverse kinds of sociologies and humanities to analyze and interpret our subjectivity and the miseries that provoke the ambition of power and inequality. As human beings, our 21st century is bringing us a portrait of those negative dimensions of ourselves that never have changed: it looks like our world nowadays is just a globalized way to eternalize poverty, injustice, and inequality. In what ways have the social sciences and humanities contributed to keeping the status quo? In this chapter I will explore what role the current division of scientific labor has played in the construction of the order of our daily activities as researchers. My emphasis will be on Indigenous knowledges and the ways to move to other conceptual coordinates our concerns and questions.

We have learned to do sociology of knowledge and technology (Gouldner, 1976; Latour, 1987), sociology of social movements (Offe, 1985; Touraine, 1985), and sociology of daily life of other people (Schwartz & Jacobs 1979). But a sociology of our own practices as researchers, as scientists, as persons of flesh and blood, is

Qualitative Inquiry Outside the Academy edited by Norman K. Denzin and Michael D. Giardina, 164–178. © 2014 Left Coast Press, Inc. All rights reserved.

still pending. We don't really know too much about ourselves as researchers, and/or as human beings, and how we came to be what we are. But today such a sociology of ourselves is more necessary than ever. Have we become what we are thanks to some educational and scientific institutions? Are we doing what we do having the presumptions and suppositions that we have without doubts? In some ways, the personal pathways of becoming a researcher, scientist, activist, or practitioner of any discipline are mysterious and hidden. Becoming a researcher or scientist and acting in consequence of that is equally a matter of speculation and suspicion in specific scenarios. Sometimes, for opportunistic reasons, as the president of the International Social Science Council says (ISSC, 2010, p. vi), social scientists "did not understand how their own creation worked." With no doubt, our "scientific" concepts are everywhere, and common citizens use them to understand their situation. Also, our social programs, ones based on our "scientific methods," have been around the world for decades, having some real consequences in specific areas. But is our creation what we dreamed?

To do a sociology of ourselves (and our work) is not just necessary, but urgent, from the perspective of creating useful knowledge to change the current situation. Our contribution to global social change is highly valued. We cannot let down the trust that society has in us: knowledge about ourselves and the consequences of our work and actions is the best guarantee for the future of our endeavor. As scientists and/or public intellectuals (Gergen, 2009) we must always know what side we are on. Our personal pathways into social sciences are carved in very specific social, historical, and geopolitical contexts. Obviously, becoming a social scientist in Germany is not comparable to becoming one in Peru. What is more, producing theory and doing social science research along the Rhine River differs from doing so in the Amazon River basin. As social scientists, we live together on a symbolic dimension of words and practices, but we inhabit different worlds. There are not meaningful comparisons between such human realities.

Knowing more about ourselves is not just describing our feelings and desires in a sort of autobiography or autoethnography. This is not what I am writing about. I am talking about putting our critical thought on the historic dimensions of what we are in the context of modernity. As a Latin American scholar, I must say that "my" modernity has a colonial past of its own dating back to the 16th century. Collecting and sharing stories of researchers around the world as to how and why they do what they do would allow us to enhance our awareness about the limits of our methods and approaches, the historical circumstances of our epistemologies, and the geopolitics of our knowledge. Knowing more about ourselves in historical, geopolitical, and epistemological views is our major current challenge. But knowing more about ourselves is also a matter of ethics and responsibilities. Gaining awareness of the historical dimensions of our theories, concepts, approaches, and methods leads us to an insightful moment of recognizing how contested our certitudes and taken-for-granted beliefs are in the encounter with other cultures and knowledges—encounters where the otherness has been eliminated and such process can be shown in critical ways (Dussel, 1995).

Human civilization is shaped by the conjunction of thousands of different trajectories. Such trajectories must be seen from the perspectives of conflict, domination, and inequality. Each society has its own rhythm, pattern, obstacles, problems, solutions, wars, and social memories. As social scientists, we need to find our place in the struggle between dominators and dominated, right and left, past and future, core and peripheries, and superior and inferior perspectives. Certainly, we must recognize that we are dealing with knowledge production in societies that treat humans unequally. After centuries of domination of some countries, people, classes, and races over other countries, people, classes, and races, we are still asking ourselves how such international inequality has been possible and continues to be so. The question about how such a global social order was constructed is still unanswered, although we have several theories about it. Different theories and their associated political and social movements continue to act and look for a new society based on their suppositions and principles.

Nevertheless, the negation of Otherness has been the principal equilibrium. For centuries, our modernity has included much ignorance about Otherness because the only way of knowing was to eliminate, subordinate, and/or oppress our differences from the

Other. Mignolo (1995) has shown how the narrative of modernity needs the notion of "primitives" to create the spatial colonial difference and define the identities of supposed superior and inferior human beings. The colonization of the Americas was based on such terrible assumptions, and the effects of such narratives have been substantial, leading to different ways of producing societies and creating knowledge. And, of course, the coloniality of power also had and still has influence in the ways science is organized and institutionalized in each society.

Core and Peripheries in the Knowledge Divide

Monaterios (2008) has shown that postcolonial primary theoretical sources operate from different historical and cognitive perspectives. The South Asian Subaltern Studies group and scholars such as Fanon, Glissant, Said, Bhabha, and Spivak have framed the origin of modernity in the 18th century. In contrast, based on such Indigenous and non-institutionalized thinkers as Mariátegui and Rivera Cusicanqui, among others, postcolonial Latin American thinkers such as Dussel, Quijano, and Mignolo (to mention but a few) tend to frame the experiences of modernity in the 16th century; the conceptual debates are rooted in our conceptual legacies.

Although it is important to recognize that Spivak (1995) has provided us a way of thinking to deconstruct the legacy of colonialism and show that the subaltern can speak, and Bhabha (1995) has enriched our perspectives with concepts as hybridity to analyze cultural dominance, the postcolonial turn has brought us to other perspectives to analyze our actions regarding cultural products, ethics, conquerors and conquered, knowledge, values, and traditions. Without a doubt, the three "As" (Africa, Asia, and America) are still opposed to the one "E" (Europe) in thinking about subaltern cultures and oppressed groups from a long historical perspective. Among the "As" each "A" is thought to belong to the First Nations, the aboriginal people and civilizations. But we need to think critically about whether to include the islands and the archipelagos in the histories of resistance and struggle against dominion. From Africa, Asia, and America the subaltern voices must be listened so that we can embrace the emerging possibility of new histories and geographies.

The distinction between core and peripheries was first established as a consequence of the colonial world. Such a world of languages, practices, and performances created diverse cognitive processes. According to Quijano (2000), the modern idea of race emerged with the colonization of America: it is a mental category of modernity. It was created as an instrument of basic social and racial classification as "a way of granting legitimacy to the relations of domination imposed by ... conquest" (p. 534). Coloniality of power is a main category that leads us to think in critical ways about how the imposition of the idea of race is and has been an instrument of domination. In a worldwide vision, the narratives of the oppressed must be integrated to let us overcome the accomplice of silence that generates the permanence of the status quo. Believe it or not, the practices linked to the original "modern" idea of race are still everywhere and their subtle presence assures different practices of domination in diverse social, emotional, and cognitive human spheres.

From a Latin American postcolonial perspective and analyzing the global capitalism's dynamics, Quijano (2000) proposes that we include conflict, domination, and exploitation as the basic elements to be considered to study the changes on such social dimensions as work, race, sex, natural resources, authority, governance, and public authority. We can definitely produce very critical approaches to deconstruct the dominant ideas of not just race but also sex, work, nature, authority, and governance, revealing in the process how deeply colonized thoughts and feelings are located in our minds and souls. In such direction, coloniality of power is an important category when thinking about the social geography of capitalism.

The knowledge divide can be seen as a historical consequence of the global dynamics of capitalism, dividing the world into the core and the peripheries. This knowledge divide also classifies social science researchers into core and peripheries. It is possible to think about coloniality of scientific labor as the coloniality that determined the geographic distribution of each one of us in the integrated forms of labor control in global capitalism. Nowadays, the core and peripheries are economically, socially, and technologically obvious when comparing social structures and countries in worldwide perspectives: their differences are apparent from the very first moment. Regardless of their colonial pasts, Africa, Asia, and America—in the sense they are discussed here—share similar processes of creation and institutionalization of knowledge: Indigenous, native voices and beliefs were silenced during colonization. 'Core' is producing theory and methods, and 'peripheries' are consuming and reproducing them. We can think about the postcolonial, decolonizing, and Indigenous knowledge systems discussion (Smith, 1999) as a kind of rebellion against such a distribution. We live together on a planet, but we inhabit different worlds. Global coloniality (Escobar, 2004) is marginalizing and even suppressing the knowledge and culture of subaltern groups; it seems like this oppression will never end. Being social researchers with the marks and traces of ancestral knowledge on the soul allows us to build on the strong shoulders of giants to create new life perspectives. But in the knowledge divide context, the only valid premises and concepts are those based in the dominant, colonial and Western societies. Still today, people from the center are not able to see the peripheries as formed by active actors seeking their own presence and with their own language in the worldwide knowledge production process. Such is natural given the long duration of colonializing ways of seeing, but the opposite is coming very fast: people from the center are changing their minds and souls to see what is coming from the colonized world. And not just listening to the oppressed colonialized voices of "other" researchers as a fake way of being "cool."

Globalized Knowledge and Domination

Coloniality of power is useful to understand how science is organized and institutionalized in each society, but can also be used to understand the current division of scientific labor. If social research methods created by Europeans and North Americans have become a sort of general knowledge (Ryen & Gobo, 2011, p. 411), it is convenient to remind ourselves that there is no context-free knowledge and no power-free interest. In social sciences and humanities, it is a mistake to think in terms of universal knowledge beyond any cultural differences. Nevertheless, questioning the assumed existence of globalized methodology or globalized knowledge leads us to criticize the illusion of homogeneous practices and uniform thinking everywhere around the world. Globalized knowledge means—particularly in social science research—domination of Anglo-American legacies, concepts, and methodologies over the peripheral world with their potentially innovative own conceptual legacies and Indigenous epistemologies.

Using a Mexican example, I would like to illustrate the effects of such ideas on the division of scientific labor in the context of globalized knowledge. In a brief essay, Maerk (2009) discusses what he calls "cover-science" as practiced in social sciences and humanities in Latin America. In his view, scholars in Latin America just copy foreign theories, concepts, and methods. He recalls what the Mexican-Spaniard philosopher Jose Gaos coined as "imperialism of categories," referring to categories that originated from other cultures, especially Europe, and are used to characterize processes of social, economic, and political orders in Latin America with no changes or adaptations. Maerk's analysis is not just based on his epistemological perspective but also in fieldwork he conducted in Mexico when doing empirical research. In his words (p. 186):

> Latin American and other scholars from the "global South" commit the error of "universalizing" the local knowledge of supposedly "great authors": Max Weber analyses and describes the bureaucrat of the "old continent"; Joseph Schumpeter focuses on the innovative European, but mainly British capitalist; Jürgen Habermas directs his attention to the industrialized First World society, in particular to the German society; and Pierre Bordieu studies mainly the French socio-cultural and socio-political condition. Instead of recognizing the singular character of each of these theories, there is a strong tendency in Latin America to believe that any of the resident capitalists is a capitalist in the sense of Schumpeter or Weber, or that the relation between the public and the private in Mexico or Brazil is similar to the one we find in Germany, as assessed by Habermas.

Undoubtedly, there is pendant discussion about globalized knowledge in the sense of validity, reliability, transparency, applicability, replicability, and originality when dealing with concepts and theories in social science and humanities. However, a particular and unique quality of Latin American researchers is the epistemological perspectives we embrace. Such epistemology is full of historical perspectives and political action on the issues researchers are dealing with. From the stance of sociology of science, this uniqueness is due to the differences in the social contexts in which knowledge is produced in each country. But is that quality just singular to Latin America? Are there not similar epistemological perspectives in Asia and Africa? In any case, why are the "great authors" necessary to understand such local, regional, or national circumstances and/or processes when their concepts are not linked to such local, regional, or national circumstances and/or processes?

Hence, the geographical closeness of Mexico and the United States offers an interesting case. Abend (2006) provides an interesting example from Mexican social science that could inspire similar explorations in other countries to create an international debate about practices and uniqueness of doing science and creating knowledge. The more noticeable difference Abend discovered in his analysis by comparing contributions in journals published in the period of 1995–2001 is related to the way Mexican scientists are testing theory or thinking about the dialogue between theory and data. Abend's sample of articles was drawn from the most cited and most prestigious journals in each country: in the United States, the *American Journal of Sociology* and the *American Sociological Review*; in Mexico, *Estudios Sociológicos* and *Revista Mexicana de Sociología*. Based on the social conditioning of scientific knowledge, Abend reminds us that Mexican and American sociologies are epistemologically, semantically, and perceptually incommensurable because of the unique understandings of what theory is, the role of subjectivity, and ethical neutrality. With respect to the differences between Mexican and American approaches to doing sociological research, Abend notes "an empirical sociology of epistemologies would constitute a step forward in the agenda of the sociology of knowledge, as it would further our understanding of the social conditioning of scientific knowledge" (2006, p. 32). Abend's analysis reinforces Maerk's annotation of Mexican sociologists just "copying" theories and concepts.

Let me ask once again but in different words: Is a "Mexican" way of doing sociology particular to just that country or is it also the favorite way of working in other developing countries? Referring to foreign authors' concepts without referring to data collected by native researchers seems to be a general practice to validate inquiry in the academia. "Doing theory" in such a way is just reproducing ideas and arguments in the recreational fiction of "universal" applicability of some sociological concepts, regardless of their historical and cultural situations. Could we reflect and produce some critical stances about what it means to be "doing theory" in different countries and diverse cultural worlds? "Doing theory" in the sense of making quotes of such "great authors" is, here in this chapter and from this desk, and I would assume from other desks and parts of the world, totally unacceptable.

Let me insist: globalized knowledge means, in the field of qualitative research in particular, domination of Anglo-American legacies, concepts, and methodologies over the peripheral world with their own potentially innovative conceptual legacies and Indigenous epistemologies. I must note that it is not the responsibility of any acclaimed and classical "great author" or the contemporary and still alive "great authors" being copied as in the described way of "cover-science" to change this practice. In another context, compare qualitative research and music, to follow the idea on doing "cover-science" as playing "covers": there is a potential dilemma for those musicians who decide to keep their traditional instruments and explore the richness of their own culture versus only playing "covers" of great American or European hits. As with the globalized musical world, the scientific world must be aware of its unity and diversity. It is important to recognize the different narratives we are able to listen to.

As I have elsewhere pointed out (see Cisneros Puebla, 2008), the narratives that are told about the history and development of qualitative research are deeply grounded in the experience of North America, and it is only very recently that the diversity of qualitative research history and experiences has come to light. A rich discussion is emerging regarding our position as global qualitative researchers based on various reflections from different perspectives about the dominance of Anglo-American legacies (Alasuutari, 2004; Cisneros Puebla et al., 2006; Mruck, Cisneros Puebla, & Faux, 2005). Hsiung (2012, p. 5), for example, following Alasuutari (2004), has suggested that the "globalization of qualitative research … is emerging as a subfield where qualitative researchers in the periphery have begun challenging the domination of the Anglo-American core."

Thinking specifically about qualitative research, I believe we need a shift in the current division of scientific labor that sees scholarship in the core producing theory and methods, while those in the peripheries consume and reproduce it. More attention needs to be paid to the indigenization of qualitative research in the peripheral countries. Kathy Charmaz (2012), for instance, is currently leading a query around the ways grounded theory methodologies have been adopted by non-English-speaking researchers, and Gobo (2011) is questioning whether Indigenous methodologies and participatory action research are effective ways to escape methodological colonialism.

Geopolitically speaking, it would be valuable to explore what contributions in the peripheries could be taken in a globalized world of qualitative research to be integrated and practiced in the core. Once again, the music example could be a wonderful analogy to our practices as researchers: is the current division of scientific labor control eternal and non-changeable? It would be interesting to testify about the peripheries producing theory and methods and the core consuming and reproducing it. If qualitative scholars in the core could shift their roles from producers to consumers, the divide would change drastically, and our discussion would be freely moving away from colonial dimensions.

Indigenization and Epistemic Violence

We can assume that indigenization of knowledge consists of creatively adapting concepts, methods, and approaches to a culture different to that where such concepts, methods, and approaches were created. Communication between cultures is a very complex issue, but regarding knowledge production, we can follow the route that recognizes a second-generation indigenization phenomenon that refers to how Indigenous people are being educated in local universities in the peripheries; in previous generations, that took place in the centers. Huntington (1996) asserts that around the globe, education and democracy are leading to indigenization. Discussing cultural backlash, he quotes Roland Dore:

> The first "modernizer" or "post-independence" generation has often received its training in foreign (Western) universities in a Western cosmopolitan language. Partly because they first go

abroad as impressionable teenagers, their absorption of Western values and lifestyles may well be profound. (p. 38)

This second-generation indigenization phenomenon occurred mainly (Maerk 2009, p. 188) in "societies under colonial rule until the twentieth century, e.g., in the Anglophone and Francophone Caribbean, in Africa, in the Middle East, and in parts of Asia." Maerk mentions the case of the Guyanese historian, Walter Rodney, comparing the Trinidadian Eric Williams, the French Martinican Aimé Césaire, and the African American W. E. B. Du Bois to highlight that second-generation members are mainly inclined to produce local knowledge rooted in their own cultural context and benefit and to be masters of what had been done for their predecessors.

But we need to identify that this is just one side of the phenomenon! Given the asymmetrical hierarchy Indigenous persons maintain with the non-Indigenous, the complex world of unfair subordination is reproduced and the dominion the colonizer performs to the colonized, or the power the conqueror executes to the conquered, appears as eternal "naturalized" social relationships difficult to be destroyed.

Developing autochthonous research methods is decisive to overcome the epistemic—and I would add racial—violence. Walker (2013, p. 302) has recognized such violence when Indigenous peoples in colonized countries "are told that scholarly research must focus primarily on 'linear intellectual analysis.'" But it is also crucial to enrich our practices as researchers by getting into new ways of experiencing relationships and human interactions. Ancestral knowledge around the world is still waiting to be listened to in the horizon to change our presence on the planet. As in the case of the music, just to follow the analogy once again, any ethno-musicologist would be able to testify how some rhythms, sounds, instruments, scales, and tunes have been provided to the "globalized musical sphere" because they have been produced in the very marginal societal areas or in the deep subaltern social structure. Yet why have colonized qualitative researchers not been listened to by their colleagues when producing their own approaches or Indigenous methods? Is it just a consequence of the quality of their products? Or is it a result of the lack of integrity, validity, reliability, transparency, applicability, and/or replicability accorded to the dominant Western epistemology? Such questions must to be answered by all people involved in the field: experts, students, novices, senior researchers, funding agencies, practitioners, "great authors" and "small authors," from the core and from the peripheries, from the North and South and from the West and East.

The personal pathways of becoming researcher, scientist, activist, or practitioner of any discipline will no longer be mysterious and hidden if we develop efforts to create a movement to emphasize the multiple and complex connection between the self and the social. Such a complex connection should be analyzed even if hurts. Recently, Garot (2013) has questioned himself in his role as white male ethnographer in the context of how he is acting the colonialized self of some clandestine actors by using some of Fanon's ideas. And his example will hopefully call attention to how it will be possible to do research after the postcolonial turn if we are able to bring the discussion to final consequences. What are such lasting consequences?

- Understand that the current division of scientific labor can't be eternal
- Deconstruct the very basic concepts of our certitude, certainty, evidence, and truth
- Destroy the asymmetrical hierarchy of knowledge and practices
- Recognize that epistemic violence has silenced other ways of knowing
- Re-examine the role of Indigenous and native methods in knowledge production
- Transform the relationship between core and peripheries
- Integrate the Asian and Latin American postcolonial thoughts
- Produce a critical sociology of knowledge
- Create a network of critical and Indigenous methodology
- Create and perform the decolonized self in daily life

'Indigenize' has different meanings depending on what area of the world we are located in. Rivera Cusicanqui (2010) has a powerful and meaningful voice from Aymara culture and legacies. She argues for a political economy of knowledge instead of a geopolitics of knowledge—the prevailing thread in postcolonial literature—because such discussion is not leading to social justice or human rights. As a non-institutionalized Bolivian thinker, her interesting approach should be considered by others. However, for me, doing science as Indigenous is not just related to *indigeneity*: it is a kind of critical awareness about our own beliefs' and thoughts' limits in the realm of a decolonized geopolitics of knowledge and language. I am not as Indigenous as Rivera Cusicanqui, but I can't accept being mestizo because of the accumulated violence such words contain. In colonialism, as our Aymara non-institutionalized thinker has told us, the words do not express anything—the words hide. As a colonial word, "mestizo" hides multiple processes.

In this last part I am talking about myself through dialogue with postcolonial thinkers. In the end, we need to define ourselves within the globalization of qualitative research to acknowledge we are persons of flesh and blood, with culture, history, and language. Other voices from Asia and Africa are necessary to go beyond any limitation—to cultivate our analysis of the hidden and deep epistemic violence nested in the current division of scientific labor worldwide.

Acknowledgments

A previous and preliminary version was presented as a paper at the 2013 International Congress of Qualitative Research, hosted by the University of Illinois, Urbana-Champaign in May 2013, and was published as "The Journey Ends: An Epilogue" in: D. Mertens, F. Cram, & B. Chilisa (Eds.), *Indigenous pathways into social research. Voices of a new generation* (pp. 395–402). Walnut Creek, CA: Left Coast Press, Inc.

References

Abend, G. (2006). Styles of sociological thought: Sociologies, epistemologies, and the Mexican and U.S. quests for truth. *Sociological Theory, 24*, 141.

Alasuutari, P. (2004). The globalization of qualitative research. In G. Gobo, C. Seale, J. F. Gubrium, & David Silverman (Eds.), *Qualitative research practice* (pp. 595–608). Thousand Oaks, CA: Sage.

Bhabha, H. (1995) Interview with cultural theorist Homi Bhabha by W.J.T. Mitchell. (1995). *Artforum*, *33*(7), 80–84.

Charmaz, K. (2012). Grounded theory in global perspective. Paper presented as part of the panel Challenges for Qualitative Inquiry as a Global Endeavor I: Methodological Issues, at the Eighth International Congress on Qualitative Inquiry, University of Illinois, Urbana-Champaign, May 18, 2012.

Cisneros Puebla, C. (2008). On the roots of qualitative research. In J. Zelger, M. Raich, & P. Schober (Eds.), *GABEK III. Organisationen und ihre wissensnetze* (pp. 53–75). Innsbruck, Austria: Studien Verlag.

Cisneros Puebla, C. A., Figaredo, D. D., Faux, R., Kölbl, C., & Packer, M. (2006). About qualitative research epistemologies and peripheries. *Forum Qualitative Sozialforschung/ Forum: Qualitative Social Research*, 7, Art. 44. nbn-resolving.de/urn:nbn:de:0114-fqs060444 (accessed January 13, 2012).

Dussel, E. (1995). *The invention of the Americas: Eclipse of "the Other" and the myth of modernity*. New York: Continuum.

Escobar, A. (2004). Beyond the Third World: Imperial globality, global coloniality, and antiglobalization social movements. *Third World Quarterly, 25*, 207–230.

Garot, R. (2013). The psycho affective echoes of colonialism in fieldwork relations [21 paragraphs]. *Forum Qualitative Sozialforschung/Forum: Qualitative Social Research, 15*(1), Art. 12. www.qualitative-research.net/index.php/fqs/article/view/2102/3624 (accessed December 3, 2013).

Gergen, K. (2009). *Relational being: Beyond self and community*, New York: Oxford University Press.

Gobo, G. (2011). Globalizing methodology? The encounter between local methodologies. *International Journal of Social Research Methodology, 14*, 417–437.

Gouldner, A. W. (1976). *The dialectic of ideology and technology: The origins, grammar, and future of ideology*. London: Macmillan Press.

Hsiung, P-C. (2012). The globalization of qualitative research: Challenging Anglo-American domination and local hegemonic discourse. *Forum Qualitative Sozialforschung (Forum: Qualitative Social Research), 13*, Art. 21. nbn-resolving.de/urn:nbn:de:0114-fqs1201216 (accessed February 23, 2012).

Huntington, S. P. (1996). The West: Unique, not universal. *Foreign Affairs, 6*, 28–46.

ISSC Report. (2010). *World social science report. Knowledge divide*. Paris: ISSC, UNESCO.

Latour, B. (1987). *Science in action: How to follow scientists and engineers through society*. Cambridge, MA: Harvard University Press.

Maerk, J. (2009). Overcoming cover-science in Latin American social sciences and humanities—An intervention. In M-L. Frick & A. Oberprantacher (Eds.), *Power and justice in international relations: Interdisciplinary approaches to global challenges. Essays in honor of Hans Köchler* (pp. 185–192). Farnham, UK: Ashgate.

Mignolo, W. D. (1995). *The darker side of the renaissance: Literacy, territoriality and colonization.* Ann Arbor: University of Michigan Press.

Monaterios, E. (2008). Uncertain modernities: Amerindian epistemologies and the reorienting of culture. In S. Castro-Klaren (Ed.), *A companion to Latin American literature and culture* (pp. 553–570). Malden, MA: Wiley-Blackwell.

Mruck, K., Cisneros Puebla, C. A., & Faux, R. (2005). Editorial: About qualitative research centers and peripheries. *Forum Qualitative Sozialforschung (Forum: Qualitative Social Research),* 6, Art. 49. nbn-resolving.de/urn:nbn:de:0114-fqs0503491 (accessed February 23, 2012).

Offe, C. (1985). New social movements: Challenging the boundaries of institutional politics. *Social Research, 52,* 817–868.

Quijano, A. (2000). Coloniality of power, Eurocentrism and Latin America. *Nepantla, 3,* 533–580.

Rivera Cusicanqui, S. (2010). *Ch'ixinakax utxiwa : Una reflexión sobre prácticas y discursos descolonizadores.* Buenos Aires: Tinta Limón.

Ryen, A., & Gobo, G. (2011). Managing the decline of globalized methodology. *International Journal of Social Research Methodology, 14,* 411–415.

Schwartz, H., & Jacobs, J. (1979). *Qualitative sociology: A method to the madness.* New York: Free Press.

Smith, L. T. (1999). *Decolonising methodologies: Research and Indigenous peoples.* New York: Zed Books.

Spivak, G. C. (1995). Can the subaltern speak? In B. Ashcroft, G. Griffiths, and H. Tiffen (Eds.), *Post-colonial studies reader* (pp. 24–28). London: Routledge.

Touraine, A. (1985). An introduction to the study of new social movements. *Social Research, 52,* 749–487.

Walker, P. (2013). Research in relationship with humans, the spirit world, and the natural world. In D. Mertens, F. Cram, & B. Chilisa (Eds.), *Indigenous pathways into social research. Voices of a New Generation* (pp. 299–315). Walnut Creek, CA: Left Coast Press, Inc.

Part III
Outside

Chapter 9

Episodic and Expert Interviews beyond Academia

Health Service Research in the Context of Migration

Uwe Flick and Gundula Röhnsch

Introduction

Interviews continue to be one of the most prominent methods in qualitative inquiry. They are particularly relevant when it comes to taking our research activities outside academic circles for studying issues of professional practices or specific experiences of client groups. Interviews are used for analyzing the needs of hard-to-reach marginal groups, clients' experiences, professional experiential knowledge, or service evaluation, for example. This shows the particular relevance of interviewing and is the starting point for analyzing this research practice from several angles: What kind of interviewing may be adequate for research outside Academia—e.g., services for and their utilization by marginalized groups? Which are ethical issues of interviewing marginalized groups outside academia (see Mertens, Chapter 10 this volume)? Using qualitative inquiry for analyzing social problems outside academia often asks for specific methodological approaches. Sometimes, we face simple time problems, such as if we want to interview experts in the healthcare system. Or we have to do some of the interviews in different languages. In health services research, it has been useful to use expert interviews for analyzing

Qualitative Inquiry Outside the Academy edited by Norman K. Denzin and Michael D. Giardina, 181–196. © 2014 Left Coast Press, Inc. All rights reserved.

the professionals' views on health problems, with the clients who have these problems and use professional services (or don't), and for analyzing institutional routines. Also, it has been helpful to use small-scale narratives and question/answer formats for analyzing the clients' own perspectives. The episodic interview was developed for combining small-scale narratives and question/answer approaches for analyzing clients' experiences in the health service system. In this chapter, examples of using these methods for studying a group of migrants' experiences and access to the health care system will be discussed embedded in outlining the methodological principles behind them.

Types of Interviews for Use Outside Academia

In general, we can use four kinds of interviews for studying issues outside academia (Flick, 2014): *semi-structured* interviews are based for preparing more or less open questions in an interview schedule—questions which should be applied in a flexible way with the interviewee. *Narrative* interviews focus on biographical narratives and are based on the interviewees' storytelling as an approach in data collection. In its most consequent form, this kind of interviewing refrains from asking questions in order to not interrupt the interviewee's narrative (Riemann & Schütze, 1987). We can also use combinations of both approaches—narratives and questions, for example—in the *episodic* interview (Flick, 2014). And we can use *expert* interviews in the study of social problems.

The Social Problem Studied Outside Academia Used as an Example

Alcohol and drug abuse is widespread among migrants in Germany. In particular, migrants coming from Russian speaking countries to Germany often have particularly risky (i.e., intravenous) consumption patterns. Their awareness of risks linked to such consumption patterns is reported as being rather low. As international studies show, this target group is very vulnerable to becoming addicted to alcohol and drugs and to chronic infectious diseases like Hepatitis C (Isralowitz, Resnik, Spear, Brecht, & Rawson, 2007; Weiss, 2012). Such health-related consequences of alcohol and drug abuse indicate a strong need for care and support in this target group. However, its members often do not accept existing services or use them with much delay and are not reached by the care system in an adequate way. As a reason for this reluctance, a specific understanding of addiction in Russian speaking countries is discussed—an understanding which is different from the discourse in Germany that informs the working concept of the health care system.

In Germany and many other Western countries, being addicted to alcohol or drugs is seen as a disease, which progresses in a relapsing way. Relapses into a stronger pattern of consumption are seen as imminent to this disease (Saitz, Larson, Labelle, Richardson, & Samet, 2008; White, Boyle, & Loveland, 2003). Addiction to alcohol or drugs affects the whole person and has physical, mental, and social dimensions. In contrast to this understanding, in Russian speaking countries the addiction to illegal drugs in particular is strongly moralized (Mendelevich, 2011). It is seen as a disgrace and individual failure. Drug addicts are seen as perverted, hedonistic, and egoistic, and, thus, as people who should have no rights. Such a stigma makes many of the addicted persons refrain from utilizing help in their countries of origin (Bobrova et al., 2006; Grund, Latypov, & Harris, 2013), but also in host countries like Germany. How do the migrants themselves see their needs and demands for care and help when they arrive in Germany, and what does that look like from the viewpoint of the health care system? What makes immigrants, beyond their differing drug specific illness concepts, refrain from utilizing professional support? These questions are pursued in an ongoing project focusing on the help seeking behavior of Russian speaking migrants with intensive alcohol or drug abuse and a high risk for secondary diseases like Hepatitis C following the addiction.

Our Study

The example we refer to is a study funded by the German Ministry of Education and Research for three years in the context of the program health care research (FKZ: 01GY1121). It focuses on two perspectives—that of the migrants and that of providers of the health social care—and compares them. The interviews with the migrants are still in progress. So far 43 migrants (age 17–40; 28.4 years on average) coming from various Russian-speaking countries (Kazakhstan, Russia, Ukraine, Latvia, Lithuania) have been interviewed (see table 1).

Table 1: Sample of the Russian Speaking Migrants

Age	Male N=33	Female N=10	Total N=43
17–20 years	5	2	7
21–30 years	14	4	18
31–40 years	14	4	18

Access to the interviewees is mostly achieved via the professionals working at the service providers migrants with addiction problems utilize. The professionals are informed about the research beforehand and try to find interviewees among the migrants and convince them to work with the researchers.

The migrants are interviewed with episodic interviews (Flick, 2014). The starting point for these interviews is that individual experiences concerning a specific issue are stored and remembered in the form of narrative-episodic knowledge on the one hand and as semantic knowledge on the other. Narrative-episodic knowledge is close to experience and refers to concrete situations and circumstances (e.g., professionals' behavior in counseling or therapy processes). Semantic knowledge includes more abstract and generalized assumptions and relations—for example, about what causes an infection with hepatitis and how the disease develops. In order to capture both forms of knowledge in the interview situation, the interviewees are invited to recount concrete events or situations relevant for the issue of the study. At the same time they are asked more general questions leading to more abstracted answers and thematically relevant definitions or argumentations.

The interviews with the migrants last 60 minutes in average and mainly are conducted in German, although quite a number of interviews are done in Russian. Central issues of the interview guide are: addiction and hepatitis related disease experiences and practices; protection and risk awareness; help seeking behavior; experiences with the help system and expectations to help.

The interviews with the migrants are analyzed with thematic coding (Flick, 2014). First, all statements about an issue or an area are categorized in a case-specific way. Across cases, comparative dimensions are defined, which allow researchers to group cases and to analyze them for specific combinations of features.

Contrasting cases allows first comparing cases in a group for their similarities. Comparing cases across groups aims at elaborating existing differences between them. Typologies of interpretive and practice patterns resulting from these steps are analyzed and interpreted for their meanings.

It can be assumed that the necessity to utilize (addiction specific) help and the possible barriers against this utilization in the view of the migrants look different from external, 'objectified' criteria. Therefore, our study confronts the migrants' subjective views with the experiences of professionals working in the health care service system. The professionals are interviewed in expert interviews (Bogner, Littig, & Menz, 2009; Meuser & Nagel, 2009). These interviews are used in the study for collecting additional information for analyzing and embedding the migrants' statements. In the course of the study, expert interviews first have an explorative function. They support the researchers' sensitization of the study's target group's specific situation less from a theoretical than from a practice oriented point of view. This also allowed the interview guide for the migrants to be reworked and finalized. Later on, the expert interviews were also used for collecting comparable information about the issues of the study, so that they had more and more a systematizing function.

The interviews with the experts are completed. All in all, we were able to include 33 experts aged between 28 and 71. The interviewees—social workers, psychologists, and physicians in private practices—work in various areas of the psychosocial and health-related care system (see table 2).

Table 2: Sample of the Experts: Service Providers (Gender and Area of Work)

Area of work	Male N=18	Female N=15	Total N=33
Health	8	7	15
Social work	7	2	9
Migration	1	2	3
Justice	—	3	3
Administration	1	1	2
Education	1	—	1

Main focuses of the expert interviews were on the perception of the clients in therapy and counseling, on how the target group deals with hepatitis, on representations of good care, and on conditions of a good collaboration in working with the target group.

The analysis of the expert interviews is based on working through thematic units of each interview in a sequential way. Paraphrases are formulated and coded. This is followed by a thematic comparison aimed at building categories. Finally, the theoretical generalization follows, which is based on a sociological conceptualization of the statements (Meuser & Nagel, 2009).

Some Results

For illustrating the relevance of the two approaches discussed in this chapter, first some experts' experiences of why many Russian-speaking migrants refrain from using help from (existing) services will be discussed. Later in this chapter, we will confront these professionals' view with the migrants' subjective views of barriers against utilization. However, in this chapter, the migrants' views can only be discussed in a summarizing and exemplary way because otherwise we would exceed the limits of this chapter. A deepening analysis of the migrants' views of barriers of utilization will be presented elsewhere.

Barriers against the Migrants' Utilization of Services: Service Providers' Views

Which barriers do the service providers see as preventing the Russian-speaking migrants from seeking professional help and from accepting it on a long-term basis? The following questions were asked in the expert interviews:

- How do Russian-speaking migrants deal with their alcohol and drug problems? Can you illustrate this with an example?
- Which factors prevent Russian-speaking migrants with alcohol and drug problems from seeking and accepting help?
- What could be obstacles for really receiving professional help? Could you please illustrate this with a situation from your professional practice?

According to the experts we interviewed, barriers against utilization can be identified on three levels: barriers rooted in the health system, in the migrants' behavior, or in socio-structural causes. Most of the interviewees refer to several kinds of barriers the migrants are confronted with.

Barriers on the Level of the Health System

That immigrants are prevented from utilizing services due to institutional factors is highlighted by 16 of our interviewees. If migrants are used to a not very differentiated health care system in their countries of origin, they have problems of finding an orientation facing the variety of potential forms of help in Germany. Which service covers which needs for care and who might be the responsible contact person in case of health problems remains often obscure for these migrants. Facing a highly differentiated and at the same time very fragmented help system, finding efficient support becomes a tedious endeavor, including trial and error learning, for the migrants.

For these experts, another reason why migrants often refrain at first from seeking addiction specific help is that many services wait for the clients to come and address them. To seek help, the migrants needed first to be aware of their own problems with alcohol or drugs, which is often not the case.

The concentration of services on the problem of addiction prevents many clients from seeking help in time, according to these interviewees. They see that every day and, for the clients, more urgent challenges are hardly addressed in what the services offer. Such problems—for example, maintaining satisfying relations with parents and friends—make the use of alcohol and drugs more likely. The interviewees also complain that services working with drug users are lacking a holistic concept of addiction diseases.

They also highlight that migrants often shrink back from using professional help because the professionals in the care system are not very empathic in working with people from other cultures. Often they are not familiar enough with tabooed topics or culture specific representations of health and illness. They do not adequately understand the relevance of certain problems and thus cannot cover their clients' specific needs for care:

> *There are still people who still don't know how Russian adolescents or young adults have a concept of healing, of addiction and so on...*

If they have a problem, then they will come, and if they do not come, they just don't have a problem. So easily the world goes. [Mr. Stoll, social work[1]]

Barriers on the Political-Administrative Level

In the view of 15 experts the migrants' help seeking behavior is confronted with several political and administrative barriers, which are beyond the experts' influence and rather call for solutions on a socio-political level.

These interviewees talk about their experiences with how the migrants' living conditions contribute to making the migrants seek help rather late in the case of alcohol or drug problems. These living conditions are characterized by a far-reaching lack of perspective and by stressful insecurities. If the migrants come from instable family backgrounds, have hardly any friends, and have no steady work, they also lack the motivation for moderating their use of alcohol or drugs. If the migrants' life situation is determined by a stressful insecurity, they also lack the resources for seeking help in the case of alcohol or drug problems. Fugitives in particular suffer from a severe everyday stress, as they continuously have to fight to secure further permission to stay in Germany. In addition, they are often confronted with worrying news from their home countries. Such news also comes with worries about their relatives who stayed in the home countries. Alcohol and drugs serve to help endure such uncertainties:

> *[There is an] appointment at the Federal Agency, there is a court date at the administrative court. … [T]here are new information from the home country, that relatives, brother, are imprisoned, in particular for the Chechen fugitives … who were actually active for managing their addiction problems for example, and who then crash again.* [Mrs. Mylius, migration service]

Another political-administrative barrier is the stigmatization and tabooing of illegal drug consumption in the migrants' countries of origin, which contributes to a circle of not very adequate reactions in the family. For many families socialized in Russia, one of the worst things that can happen is for the children to use drugs and even become addicted. Drawing on the background of their own education and of real experiences in their home country, parents see illegal consumption of drugs as leading to an inevitable decline, a successive impoverishment, and to dying in agony. Driven by such fears, they are no longer accessible for rational argumentation. A consequence of this process is that young migrants with drug problems have no one to talk to about their drug consumption except friends who also take drugs. Thus they are not motivated to look for professional help if they need it:

In our mind, drugs are the death. If some contact with drugs, that—; no more future for this person. ... [The] kids basically have no chance to talk with their parents about drugs.... [The] father might beat the children.... [T]he mother always has a hysterical reaction. She cries day by day. [Mr. Grunow, health]

These experts also refer to the problem that many migrants from Russian speaking EU-countries have no health insurance, so that they have no access to addiction services of the regular care system.

Barriers in the Young Migrants' Behaviors

A third kind of barrier obstructing the timely use of addiction specific help is mentioned by 19 experts, who refer to barriers on the side of the migrants. They highlight that migrants tend to deny problems with alcohol and drugs much longer than their clients without a migration background. Migrants often do not turn to counseling or therapy services before a manifest addiction is established or secondary diseases have already begun. One cause for such a delay in searching for help is subjective understandings of health or treatment that differ from Western oriented concepts. The migrants' health and help seeking behavior often consists of emergency activities in case of the worst health problems. Such a practice often is rooted in the life conditions in the home countries, which are determined by deep poverty:

They turn to seeking help, if it is bleeding or if it is really serious. That means help is understood as emergency help ... there is no help that is preventive, as this is not seen as help. That is some kind of provision, luxuries. [Mr. Grodno, health]

Russian-speaking migrants, according to these experts' views, address the help system very late because they lack the awareness that addiction to alcohol or drugs is a disease. Also, alcohol is much more a part of everyday life in the migrants' home countries than it is in Germany. It is felt that intensive consumption of alcohol proves toughness, physical strength, and masculinity. That it could be problematic is for the migrants hardly an issue, according to these interviewees.

Many migrants or their relatives have expectations of (addiction specific) help that the German health care system can hardly fulfill. Thus, the migrants feel over-challenged by (long-term) drug therapy based on an extensive readiness for reflection, collaboration, and pro-activeness. A relationship between therapist and client that is hardly formalized and that is characterized by flat hierarchies contributes to uncertainty and irritation on the side of the migrants. Based on their background of socialization they are rather used to receiving definitive instructions of how to behave in various situations in the help process:

> *Really jagged hard methods, for them this seems more adequate. Something slightly military, clear lines, clear solutions, clear announcements. ... [T]hey really want a bit the exercise ... that is a bit what they know from their socialization.* [Mrs. Jordan, justice]

Many migrants' attitudes towards substitution therapy are inadequate and irrational, according to these interviewees. Many migrants see a treatment with methadone, for example, as a medically tolerated form of addiction and not as an effective help. Such views result from the far-reaching proscription of opiate substitution in their home countries or from its prohibition, as in Russia. According to the experts' experiences, these migrants are hardly aware that a substitution treatment might protect them—for example, from being infected with HI-viruses.

For these interviewees, the migrants' strong reference to the values, norms, and habits in their home countries often contributes to making them refrain from seeking professional help. Many migrants would rather trust in traditional forms of self-help or the help system in Russian-speaking countries than the local services in Germany. Confident that they can find the kind of help that is adequate for them in their home countries, migrants get involved with cost intensive programs that are more than suspect from a professional point of view. The migrants become victims of 'bad seeds' who purposefully abuse their vulnerability:

Try to search for the people and to send them to expensive treatments to Russia, which meet our addiction treatment standards in no way but are very dubious. Vomiting cures and the like, that you drench so much saline solution, that they vomit ...advertised in Russian speaking journals. [Mr. Vester, administration]

According to these interviewees, many migrants are more than ready to follow such massively advertised treatments, which are often based on false promises of a 'quick' healing. German help system treatments, which propagate a time-consuming exit from addiction, seem not very attractive compared with those promises.

For these interviewees, many migrants are too proud to confess their own need for help to themselves and to their environment—not only in the case of alcohol and drug problems. They fear to be seen as weak and to lose their social reputation if they use professional help. In particular, younger migrants feel strong and invulnerable if they cope with their (health) problems by themselves and endure their troubles without complaining.

A few experts assume that the migrants refrain from utilizing help because they understand only a little German. It is difficult for these migrants to talk about issues beyond the normal everyday communication. This is mainly a problem in the therapy process, if inner states and deeper conflicts have to be addressed.

All in all, the experts we interviewed see Russian-speaking migrants with alcohol or drug problems as a very mistrustful and closed target group who often seek help too late. In many cases the migrants turn to professional help only after a stabilization of social and health problems. They also see that the migrants are prevented from utilizing help by a complex of internal and external barriers. Such barriers on the one hand are specific for drug users in general, like the neglect of problems or that drug services just wait for the clients to come to them, for example. On the other hand, our experts refer to barriers that are specific for (Russian speaking) migrants. Here they mention their feelings of shame and guilt about their drug consumption or expectations towards help that can hardly be fulfilled in Germany.

The professionals' experiences about barriers against utilization are confronted with migrants' views in an exemplary and summarizing way in the next step.

Selected Barriers against Utilization of Help: The Migrants' Views

When we interviewed the migrants about why they refrain from using addiction specific help, we used questions like the following ones:

- Before you came to this institution, did you use other forms of help in the context of taking [the drugs mentioned before]? Which experiences have you made with such help, could you please tell me a situation for this?

- How far are you satisfied with the [help, the counseling, treatment] you receive? What do you like less? Could you please tell me a situation for this?

- What in particular prevents you from seeking help by a doctor, social worker, or other people? Is there a situation, which illustrates that for me?

Our interview partners mostly refer to the negative experiences they had with the healthcare system or to negative expectations as reasons why they do not turn to the existing services with their problems. If we summarize their answers, it becomes evident that many of the migrants we interviewed experience the demands and expectations put on them in the help process as over-challenging, which makes them refrain from further using professional help. They have problems discussing their addiction to alcohol or drugs and talking about personal feelings and mental states. For them, these are the business of nobody beyond their closest circle of friends and relatives:

> *In front of sixty people I had to present myself, I got attacks of sweating. That was awful for me ... and all have come up to me saying: 'Hey, hello, how are you, how are you, how do you feel' and I think, 'oh boy, why is everybody asking you that?'* [Arkadij, 22 years]

These interviewees see as particularly embarrassing therapists' attempts to reprocess their history of addiction by identifying and resurfacing complicated family situations. They fear that they might betray their family—who is 'sacrosanct' in the Russian-speaking areas and whose integrity must not be openly doubted (Rau, 2009)—once they admit possible conflicts. Many of our interviewees see it as meaningless to talk about their own consumption of alcohol and drugs to other affected people in a therapeutically guided way. They are not interested in the situation of other people with addiction problems. At the same time they think in reverse that the others could not understand their own problems because they have completely different problems.

Counseling and therapy are seen as something coming with high 'costs' in the form of unfamiliar efforts and demands without any profit for our interviewees. The offered help seems to be deficient in several respects. Therapy does include any options to work (for their living) that meet their own interests and skills, so that they could combine business with pleasure. In addition, many interviewees complain that, for lack of time, physicians and therapists are not available for them for conversations when the migrants subjectively feel that they need help most strongly. As a consequence, the migrants feel left alone with their problems. They also lack opportunities to build intense and personal relationships with the professionals. According to an understanding in Russian contexts, such relationships would be necessary for revealing (alcohol or drug related) problems.

Comparing Both Perspectives

If we compare the migrants' and the professionals' views of what makes the utilization of (addiction specific) help difficult, we see that the potential clients focus mainly on system-immanent barriers. They complain that reliable, always available contact persons, who engage as 'human beings' in the process of care, are missing. In contrast, the experts we interviewed see the reasons for the non-utilization of addiction specific help primarily on the migrants' side as they do not seem to 'fit' into the existing health care system. The experts have a limited awareness of which barriers are decisive in the migrants' view as causing them to refrain from using help. Service providers' excluding behavioral patterns or structural factors are hardly mentioned by the experts as barriers for the migrants. That the non-utilization of health care services is the result of an interaction process, in which more than one side is involved, remains rather obscure for the experts.

Challenges of Interviewing Outside Academia

If we take examples like our study, we can identify a number of challenges in the use of interviews for our research outside academia. The first is how to reach the actual target groups. This is sometimes a problem if we work with experts—to identify the 'right' experts, i.e., those who are most familiar with the issue of the study and able to give the most of insights into the field and its practices. If we work with marginalized, vulnerable, or hard-to-reach groups, access to interviewees can become an issue in particular. Sometimes it is helpful to take several routes—for example, to get in touch with the potential clients of services by asking service providers to establish the contact and to support the access. In the case of the study about the alcohol and drug problems of Russian-speaking migrants reported here, a specific problem of access was that we had to assume that the target group was hardly familiar with qualitative research. Against the background of Russian history, in particular, the researchers' neutral attitude in qualitative interviews and the principle of non-directed interviewing are often the cause for big mistrust (Weaver, 2011). To work against the interviewees' fears of being 'sounded out,' the interviewers often gave reflections of what the interviewee had said over the course of the interview. In addition, we emphasized for every interviewee that there are no 'right' or 'wrong' answers.

The second problem is to find the right way to do the interviews. Issues of time and flexibility in using interview formats are much more relevant in doing research outside than inside academia—experts do not have much time they can offer for being interviewed, and clients have to be identified in the field and sometimes interviewed 'out there' and not in university offices, for example. Working with several kinds of interviews in a study—as in our example—produces new challenges for how to analyse the interviews in a meaningful way (Roulston, 2014, for more details) and to take the specific features of the interview type into account. Starting from the analysis, how do we transform our results into relevant insights? That means insights which are theoretically relevant (Thornberg & Charmaz, 2014) but also relevant and meaningful for the fields outside academia (Murray, 2014). In our case a particular challenge resulted from using interpreters and translators, as some of the interviews had to be done in

Russian. This led to a number of issues in assuring the quality of the interviews (Williamson et al., 2011; Jones & Boyle, 2011), which cannot be addressed here in detail. These issues also relate to the necessary inclusion of interpreters and translators in the process of analysing the data (see also Flick & Röhnsch, 2014). And finally, what are ethical issues about interviewing marginalized or vulnerable groups in our studies (see Mertens, this volume, Chapter 10)? These are challenges which we should consider how-to-do issues rather than seeing them as reasons for refraining from using interviews in our research outside academia.

Acknowledgments

This chapter was developed in the context of the spotlight session "Interviewing Inside and Outside Academia—Chances and Challenges" during the 9th International Congress of Qualitative Inquiry, May 2013. We want to thank the presenters in the session, Kathy Charmaz, Donna M. Mertens, and Kathy Roulston, and the audience for their helpful comments and questions. The research used as an example here is funded by the German Ministry of Education and Research (FKZ: 01GY1121).

Note

1 All names of interviewees are pseudonyms.

References

Bobrova, N., Rhodes, T., Power, R., Alcorn, R., Neifeld, E., Krasiukov, N., Latyshevskaia, N., & Maksimova, S. (2006). Barriers to accessing drug treatment in Russia: A qualitative study among injecting drug users in two cities. *Drug and Alcohol Dependence, 82*, 57–63.

Bogner, A., Littig, B., & Menz, W. (Eds.). (2009). *Interviewing experts*. Basingstoke, UK: Palgrave McMillan.

Flick, U. (2014). *An introduction to qualitative research* (5th ed.). Thousand Oaks, CA: Sage.

Flick, U., & Röhnsch, G. (in press). *Migrating diseases, triangulating approaches: Challenges for qualitative inquiry as a global endeavor.*

Grund, J. P., Latypov, A., & Harris, M. (2013). Breaking worse: The emergence of krokodil and excessive injuries among people who inject drugs in Eurasia. *The International Journal on Drug Policy, 24*, 265–274.

Isralowitz, R., Reznik, A., Spear, S. E., Brecht, M. L., & Rawson, R. A. (2007). Severity of heroin use in Israel: Comparisons between native Israelis and former Soviet Union immigrants. *Addiction, 102*, 630–637.

Jones, E. G., & Boyle, J. S. (2011). Working with translators and interpreters in research: Lessons learned. *Journal of Transcultural Nursing, 22*, 109–115.

Mendelevich, V. D. (2011). Bioethical differences between drug addiction treatment professionals inside and outside the Russian Federation. *Harm Reduction Journal, 8*, 15.

Mertens, D. M. (2014). Ethical use of qualitative data and findings. In U. Flick (Ed.), *The SAGE handbook of qualitative data analysis* (pp. 510–523). Thousand Oaks, CA: Sage.

Meuser, M., & Nagel, U. (2009). The expert interview and challenges in knowledge production. In A. Bogner, B. Littig, & W. Menz (Eds.), *Interviewing experts* (pp. 17–42). Basingstoke, UK: Palgrave MacMillan.

Murray, M. (2014). Implementation: Putting analyses into practice. In U. Flick (Ed.), *The SAGE handbook of qualitative data analysis* (pp. 585–599). Thousand Oaks, CA: Sage.

Rau, H. (2009). *Kultursensible rehabilitation—Suchtbehandlung und integration von migranten* [PowerPoint slides]. Retrieved from suchthilfe.de/veranstaltung /jt/2009/vortrag_rau.pdf

Riemann, G., & Schütze, F. (1987). Trajectory as a basic theoretical concept for analyzing suffering and disorderly social processes. In D. Maines (Ed.), *Social organization and social process: Essays in honor of Anselm Strauss* (pp. 333–357). New York: Aldine de Gruyter.

Roulston, K. (2014). Analyzing interviews. In U. Flick (Ed.), *The SAGE handbook of qualitative data analysis* (pp. 297–312). Thousand Oaks, CA: Sage.

Saitz, R., Larson, M. J., Labelle, C., Richardson, J., & Samet, J. H. (2008). The case for chronic disease management for addiction. *Journal of Addiction Medicine, 2*, 55–65.

Thornberg, R., & Charmaz, K. (2014). Grounded theory and theoretical coding. In U. Flick (Ed.), *The SAGE handbook of qualitative data analysis* (pp. 153–169). Thousand Oaks, CA: Sage.

Weaver, D. (2011). Neither too scientific nor a spy: Negotiating the ethnographic interview in Russia. *Comparative Sociology, 10*, 145–157.

Weiss, S. (2012). Alcohol use and treatment among former Soviet Union immigrants in Israel: review of publications July 2009–December 2011. *Journal of Addictive Diseases, 31*, 397–406.

White, W. L., Boyle, M., & Loveland, D. (2003). Alcoholism/addiction as a chronic disease: From rhetoric to clinical reality. *Alcoholism Treatment Quarterly, 3/4*, 107–130.

Williamson, D. L., Choi, J., Charchuk, M., Rempel, G. R., Pitre, N., Breitkreuz, R., & Kushner, K. E. (2011). Interpreter-facilitated cross-language interviews: A research note. *Qualitative Research 11*, 381–394.

Chapter 10

Ethical Issues of Interviewing Members of Marginalized Communities Outside Academic Contexts

Donna M. Mertens

Interviewing is either one of the simplest ways of collecting data or one of the most complex. Conceived as conversational data collection, interviewing seems to be quite simple. However, the wonderful issues of cultural diversity and power relations arise in unique ways when interviewing members of marginalized communities. With these populations, complexities arise from a number of sources, including the identification of community members, inclusion/exclusion criteria, diversity within communities, appropriate invitational strategies, support in terms of communication and other logistical issues, strategies for addressing power inequities to insure accuracy and comprehensive representation, and responsiveness to cultural issues in terms of confidentiality and protection or revelation of identity. These issues are illustrated based on an example from research with the American Deaf community.

The Researcher as Instrument

As a way of setting the context for this discussion of ethical issues that arise in interviewing outside of the academy, I begin with an

Qualitative Inquiry Outside the Academy edited by Norman K. Denzin and Michael D. Giardina, 197–203. © 2014 Left Coast Press, Inc. All rights reserved.

introduction of myself as a researcher who comes from a privileged group but conducts the majority of my research with marginalized communities. I am a hearing person who has worked with the Deaf community for more than 30 years as a professor at Gallaudet University, the only university in the world with a mission to serve the Deaf community. When I arrived at Gallaudet to teach research, I had never met a deaf person, nor did I know how to sign or anything about Deaf cultures. My first two semesters, I had an interpreter in my classroom who signed for me as I spoke. During that time, I concentrated on learning American Sign Language, the language of the culturally Deaf community, as well as learning about Deaf culture. After more than 30 years in that context, I still consider myself a learner as I am not yet deaf and am not a native ASL user.

In my teaching at Gallaudet, I was immersed in Deaf culture, meaning that I did not use my voice; I communicated visually through the air and used English for print communication. That was appropriate in the academic context. However, there is great diversity in the deaf and hard of hearing communities; some deaf people sign ASL; others use pidgin signed English; sign language users from other countries use their own countries' sign language; and others rely on lip reading, speaking, and/or assistive listening support systems such as cochlear implants or hearing aids.

Prior to my arrival at Gallaudet, I had concentrated on doing research in marginalized populations, such as high school dropouts, students in isolated rural or decaying urban areas, women in the workforce, and people with disabilities. However, I sensed there was something amiss, because I was not involved with these communities; I was doing research *on* them, but not *with* them. So I deliberately sought an opportunity to enter a marginalized community to determine what was required to enter that community respectfully and build the relationships that were necessary to do this type of research. Gallaudet represented that opportunity.

My first two semesters at Gallaudet were very rough, not only because I did not know the culture or the language, but because what I was teaching in my research courses did not reflect the experiences of my students. They did not see themselves in any of the methods or prior research that I had at my disposal to share with them. This sense of disconnect and my desire to do research with the Deaf community led me to develop a framing for research in the form of the transformative paradigm that provides a philosophical lens for conducting research with diverse marginalized communities (Mertens, 2009; Mertens, 2014; Mertens & Wilson, 2012). The added benefit of working with the Deaf community was that it represents a microcosm of the world, including issues of disability, language, gender, sexual identity, race, ethnicity, indigeneity, country of origin, etc. Hence, the transformative paradigm is a framework that encompasses theoretical stances associated with marginalized communities such as critical theory, feminist theory, queer theory, Indigenous theory, disability rights theory, and deafness rights theory.

The transformative paradigm includes assumptions related to use of ethical lenses developed by members of marginalized communities, e.g., Te Ara Tika Maori Ethical Guidelines (Te Putaiora Writing Group, 2010), the Indigenous Framework by the American Indian Higher Education Consortium (LaFrance & Nichols, 2010), and Terms of Reference for Research in the Sign Language Community (Harris, Holmes, & Mertens, 2009). What these guidelines have in common is the need to be respectful of the cultures and practices of those communities.

Outside the Academy: Example from Deaf and Hard of Hearing Populations

Based on my immersion in the ASL community in an academic context, I accepted the value of ASL as a visual language and associated cultural imperatives in terms of effective communication and respectful relationships. However, an invitation to conduct research with the deaf and hard of hearing communities across the United States required me to expand my skills and understandings to be able to conduct interviews in an ethical manner. I was invited to work on a project designed to determine the accessibility of courts for deaf and hard of hearing people throughout the United States. It was in that context that I learned of the diversity within that community and the need to adapt interviewing strategies to be responsive to that diversity. The program and research teams were guided by an advisory board made up of people who worked in the court system and were inclusive of the diversity of language and communication systems that were present outside the academy.

The court access study required that we develop strategies for being responsive to the diversity within the deaf and hard of hearing communities, especially with regard to language and cultural practices. The project advisory board indicated that the most important dimensions to consider in working with diverse deaf and hard of hearing people were the language and mode of communication. Deaf people who use American Sign Language effectively as a language constitute one group that can be supported either by direct communication with a Deaf researcher or by having a skilled ASL interpreter in the interview setting. This was the segment of the Deaf population with which I was familiar from my experience at Gallaudet. However, if we had stayed in our comfort zone, we would have missed many of the important issues related to court access by other segments of the deaf and hard of hearing populations.

The advisory board provided suggestions of other sub-groups in the deaf and hard of hearing communities who showed up in courts in the United States. These included: 1) deaf people with limited signing ability who relied on gestures, pantomimes, and some signs (effective communication with this segment required the services of a deaf interpreter who watched the hearing ASL interpreter and then acted out the interview questions in a more visual and gestural way); 2) deaf blind individuals who needed to have tactile interpreters that signed into their hands so they could feel the signs; 3) hard of hearing people who used assistive listening devices such as hearing aids or cochlear implants (the support of a loop system that amplified sounds for their listening devices aided communication); 4) oral deaf adults who lost their hearing, did not benefit from assistive listening devices, and did not know sign language(they needed an oral interpreter who carefully enunciated the interview questions); and, 5) Mexican Sign Language users who conveyed their experiences by having a Mexican Sign Language interpreter who also understood ASL.

The importance of understanding the diversity and complexity of this population is critical for obtaining results that represent the experiences of a wide range of deaf and hard of hearing people in the courts. For example, a deaf blind woman was raped by a co-worker. She went to the police station to report the crime, but they did not have an appropriate interpreter. The police sent her to social services that did have the appropriate type of interpreter support; however, the lawyer for the accused came into the social services office and did not work appropriately with the interpreter. Rather than allowing for the necessary wait time for the translations to happen, he spoke quickly and left quickly. When the young woman went to court, she was told that her case was dismissed. To this day, she does not know the grounds for dismissal; she was told it had something to do with the way she reported the crime.

Contrast this with the experience of an oral deaf person who could use his voice but could not benefit from assistive listening devices. When he went into court, the judge asked him if he was really deaf. The man had to get a hearing test to prove that he was deaf. Upon returning to court, the judge told the man, "If you can speak that well, you don't need any accommodations" (Mertens, 2009).

A third example illustrates the implications of a lack of knowledge when a court system does not know about sign languages other than ASL. A deaf young man from Mexico got a ticket because he did not have on his seatbelt. He did not know English or Spanish or American Sign Language; he communicated using Mexican Sign Language. He went to the courthouse to pay the ticket, but he could not find someone who could communicate with him effectively in Mexican Sign Language. So he got frustrated and left. A few days later, he did not have money for the subway train, so he jumped over the pay still. The police caught him, ran a check with his driver's license, and found that there was a bench warrant out for his arrest because he had not paid the traffic ticket. The police tried to arraign him, but given their inability to communicate with him, they put him in a holding cell. The young man sat in the cell for a few days until someone who knew him happened to be walking past the cell. Their ability to communicate in Mexican Sign Language resulted in his being able to contact his family to tell them where he was and to resolving his problems with the court.

These diverse experiences came to light because we designed the study in a way that could reveal different versions of reality and interrogated those versions of reality to determine which support an oppressive status quo and which have the potential of supporting human rights and furthering social justice. As a way of formalizing terms of reference for ethical research in the American Sign Language community, Harris et al. (2009) developed these guidelines: the ASL community has the authority to construct meanings, the values of the SLC are given priority, the SLC judges if the research is appropriate and what type of impact it will have on its members, and the researchers need to understand and support the diversity found in the ASL community. Researchers should also negotiate criteria for meeting the cultural and social needs of the community in which they are working.

The possibility of meeting these ethical terms is enhanced by consideration of universal design when considering interviewing with diverse marginalized communities outside of the academy. Kohler, Gothberg, and Coyle (2012) provide the following guidance with regard to interviewing members of marginalized populations using the principles of universal design:

• All people are included; location is accessible
• Informed consent is accessible
• Appropriate communication options are supported
• Variety of strategies (more time for participants with slower cognition or language barriers)
• Consider multi-media formats
• Share transcripts/findings in appropriate ways
• Conduct pilot tests

They provide practical advice about how to make interviewing outside the academy more ethical and to increase the potential that researchers will report an accurate picture of the realities experienced by members of marginalized communities.

Conclusion

Each researcher who interviews inside or outside of the academy carries the responsibility of identifying the dimensions of diversity that are relevant within their research context. When we move outside of our comfort zone, i.e., outside the academy, we are more likely to need the help of members of the community who have experience in those settings. Lack of attention to this issue can lead to an overly simplistic picture being presented about marginalized communities. Inaccurate conclusions can be viewed as unethical conclusions because the implications for actions to address issues of social justice and human rights might not be accurately conveyed.

This leaves us with questions on which to reflect, such as: How can you adapt your interviewing strategies to enhance your understanding of the cultural diversity in your research context? How can you engage with members of the communities in which you work to improve the accuracy of your understandings about who needs to be included and strategies that can be used to appropriately interview the diverse members of the communities? If we ignore these issues, what are the ethical implications? If we address these issues, how can that enhance our ability to link our improved understandings to furthering social justice and human rights?

References

Harris, R., Holmes, H., & Mertens, D. M. (2009). Research ethics in sign language communities. *Sign Language Studies, 9*(2), 104–131.

Kohler, P. D., Gothberg, J., & Coyle, J. L. (2012) *Evaluation toolkit.* 2nd ed. Kalamazoo, MI: National Secondary Transition Technical Assistance Center, Western Michigan University.

LaFrance, J. & Nichols, R. (2010). Reframing evaluation: Defining an indigenous evaluation framework. *Canadian Journal of Evaluation, 23*, 13–31.

Mertens, D. M. (2009). *Transformative research and evaluation.* New York: Guilford.

Mertens, D. M. (2014). *Research and evaluation in education and psychology: Integrating diversity with quantitative, qualitative, and mixed methods.* 4th ed. Thousand Oaks, CA: Sage.

Mertens, D. M., & Wilson, A. T. (2012). *Program evaluation theory and practice.* New York: Guilford.

Te Putaiora Writing Group (2010). *Te Ara Tika: Guildelines for Maori research ethics: A framework.* Auckland: Health Research Council of New Zealand.

Chapter 11

Closing the Qualitative Practice/Application Gaps in Health Care Research

The Role of Qualitative Inquiry

Janice Morse, Kim Martz, Lory J. Maddox,
and Terrie Vann-Ward

We are interested in the applied contribution of qualitative research, especially in health care, and the essential—yet unacknowledged—role it plays. At one time, Mike Agar was collecting instances of the most significant contributions of qualitative inquiry. The example that most impressed him was the *Hawthorne Effect* (Landsberger, 1958). Jan took up Agar's challenge, and added Piaget's work in infant development (Piaget & Cook, 1952), Bowlby's attachment theory (Bowlby, 1973), and Goffman's research (in particular that of delineating the concept of stigma [Goffman, 1986/2009]). All of this work may be considered "old," for it is necessary that significant contributions stand the test of time—and important basic work in social science does not expire (Morse, 2003).

Agar's challenge is an important one, for too often those in academia are constantly devaluing both the role and the "products" of qualitative inquiry. We read that qualitative inquiry can be used as a "preliminary" to quantitative inquiry, such as a foundation to instrument development; or that, in mixed methods, qualitative *adds* content, such as the patient's voice, and dimensions that are not accessible to measurement. But we believe that qualitative researchers do not adequately attend to basic work in

Qualitative Inquiry Outside the Academy edited by Norman K. Denzin and Michael D. Giardina, 204–232. © 2014 Left Coast Press, Inc. All rights reserved.

concept and theory development, such as recognizing processes in interactions, identifying the microanalytic processes and models of causation. Additionally, we do not consider qualitative research to be solid evidence, until we have moved the results to the level of quantification, and at that point ignore the highly significant contribution of the *qualitative*. Qualitative inquiry brings the problem to the forefront, identifies all the "variables," and creates a solid theoretical model amenable to quantitative testing. Alternatively, the results may stand on their own as solid evidence.

Yet qualitative researchers have not pushed back and demanded the recognition and funding that our research deserves in order to be conducted at a scale that will have impact and acknowledgment. We argue that qualitative research has an essential role in health care, *but*, at the same time, we are unclear exactly what that role is. Without this support and funding, the development of qualitative research is impeded. Further, all qualitative research is not the panacea to health research. Qualitative research is often misused and oversteps crucial aspects in logic, so that criticism of qualitative research is sometimes warranted. For example, we see studies of "nurse's *perceptions* of causes of patient falls." The results of such qualitative interview research is that nurses perceive that drugs (medications) contribute to falls (Roig & Reid, 2009). Now, are these findings true or false, helpful or not helpful, in the provision of care and the prevention of patient falls? *This is not the way to research fall causation*: the investigation of the interaction of medication and falls requires pharmaceutical research, large RCTs (randomized control trials), or some other experimental design. By using qualitative perceptions, *qualitative research loses credibility*. Qualitative researchers need to clearly identify appropriate and inappropriate use of qualitative inquiry, and the appropriate methods for investigating qualitative topics. Such a discussion is long overdue in qualitative health research methods.

What happens when quantitative researchers ignore qualitative inquiry? In the next example, quantitative researchers have tried to apply qualitative phenomena that they do not understand. For the past decade, health care practitioners have tried to quantify pain research using a uni-dimensional *pain rating scale* (Bijur, Latimer, & Gallagher, 2003). Briefly, the patient is asked to rate his or her pain on a scale of 0 (no pain) to 10 (worst possible pain). Such a scale provides the practitioners with a score that may justify administering an analgesia, and may also permit them to quantify the increasing (in severity) and decreasing (relief) level of pain. But researchers have now applied this scale to measure "distress," in particular the distress associated with cancer treatment, using the same 0–10 scale and labeling it the "distress thermometer." Researchers studying distress associated with breast cancer diagnosis and treatment noticed that some patients were stoic, without emotion, and others were distressed, depressed, and crying. Had these researchers understood the qualitative research regarding suffering, and the states of enduring and emotional suffering, the invalidity and inappropriateness of the use of the distress thermometer in this context would have been evident. The distress thermometer's supposed ability to quantify distress and enable billing *overrides qualitative sensitivity.* We do not trust ourselves (and demand the right) to evaluate a patient's state as clinicians, and to use qualitative empathetic understanding. It is an issue of qualitative understanding and validity versus the convenience of administration. We have denigrated qualitative knowledge as clumsy, individualistic, nonstandard, and not linked to therapy or, most of all, calculating costs of health care.

In this chapter, we argue that the most common "use" of qualitative inquiry is as a foundation for instrument development. We have research using only a "few" focus groups, or preliminary interviews. We list the perceived clinical benefits of qualitative inquiry as:

- Providing an understanding of the experience of health and illness;
- Developing experiential models/theories of illness causation, responses to illness, recuperation, health behaviors; and
- Providing a foundation for quantitative measures.

We are often told that qualitative inquiry "does not go anywhere." We finish, publish, and then move on. We do not differentiate between the incremental aspects of quantitative inquiry (that replaces previous studies as "out of date" and no longer useful) and the enduring merits of qualitative inquiry.[1]

There are significant gaps in our understanding of health care and health care research. Researchers tend to ignore the qualitative studies we publish, and the perception that it is "only a qualitative study," misconstruing and misunderstanding sampling techniques, sample size, and rigor. We consider the establishment of our own journals, such as *Qualitative Health Research*, as a step forward, but it places our work out of sight of the policy folks and, by default, makes the other journals quantitative. Moreover, it seems that it takes many articles to make a critical mass in order to come to the attention of the clinicians, and an even greater number to be established in students' texts—one indicator of formal acceptance as knowledge. And qualitative researchers value uniqueness. In fact, one of the publication criteria for *Qualitative Health Research* is that the submission must offer new findings. Qualitative researchers do not replicate, unless they explore the original findings in a new population, age group, ethnicity, or condition (Morse, 2012).

Researchers have examined the delay from publication to application for quantitative research to be 17 years (Green, Ottoson, Garcia, & Hiatt, 2009). But this delay has not been examined for *qualitative* findings, and we suggest that most qualitative research does not even make it to the bedside. We contend that the field lacks methods of translation to move inquiry beyond the theoretical models that "provide understanding." Which is to say, we need to develop modes of implementation and tools for application. Qualitative inquiry has much to offer, such as:

- To identify and develop the most salient concepts to be studied, for assessment, for providing safe care;
- To examine alternative environments for healthcare delivery, for reducing health care costs, and for saving lives.

In what follows, we provide three examples of qualitative research that will fill huge gaps in health care. In the first example, Terrie Vann-Ward dives head first into uncharted waters, examining how people with a chronic and increasingly disabling condition, in this case Parkinson's syndrome, maintain their sense of self. She uses a new concept, *preserving self*, to explore these changes. Next, Lory Maddox explores workarounds: ways that nurses circumvent drug administration policies and procedures in order to provide safe care for patients. Rules and policies that are in place to ensure safe drug administration—that the right drug is given to the right person, by the right route, at the right time, and in the right amount—also preempt a nurse from obtaining a drug that is needed in an urgent situation. Paradoxically, in these cases the rules must be bent or broken in order to provide safe, effective care. In the third example, Kim Martz reveals the paradox of providing safe care for the dying. Attempting to provide appropriate care to the elderly, we have "leveled" care by standards required according to the increasing needs of the elderly. We have leveled assisted care (for the semi-independent), nursing homes (for those unable to care for themselves), and hospice or inpatient hospital care for those who have serious medical needs and complications. The result is that the *person*, the dying person, is moved from institution to institution, at the most critical and fragile time of their lives. These transitions, moving them from their semi-permanent, familiar, home, to new caregivers who do not know them or their families, are extremely disorienting and stressful for both the resident/patient and his or her family.

Times of Change, Aging, and Illness
Advancing Understanding by Developing Concepts

Terrie Vann-Ward

Here I describe the development of a concept, *preserving self,* as it increases the depth of our understandings of chronic illness to a level of realistic clinical application. The relationship of *preserving self* to self-identity is discussed through its application to an exemplar chronic illness, Parkinson's disease. Data from participant interviews are used to highlight attributes of *preserving self.* The interviews are from my constructivist grounded theory research-in-progress, which examines the challenges and strategies for people with Parkinson's.

The Losses of Parkinson's Disease

Parkinson's disease (PD) is a movement disorder with strong associations with intellectual and emotional deterioration. As a chronic illness, PD has a progressive nature with unpredictable individual-ized processes of symptom development. The inhibiting effects of the physical changes limit movement and mobility, inhibit speech, and alter expression—all of which silences the personality and increasingly prohibits the person from participating in everyday life. The physical, social, and psychological losses contribute to a state of frailty. People with PD can no longer walk without assis-tance, perform the simplest of self-care activities, or participate in conversations. Through this insidious process of repetitive multiple losses, the sense of self may become distorted, diminished, or lost (Charmaz, 1983, 1990, 1991, 1995, 2002).

Parkinson's disease is a lifelong and life-ending condition. Treatments provide limited remedy, often cause a worsening of symptoms, and do not slow illness progression. As a chronic ill-ness, people with PD strive to retain the familiarity of daily life in the midst of challenging symptom control. A current public health focus is the prevention of chronic illness (Halpin, Morales-Suárez-Varela, & Martin-Moreno, 2010); a distinctly unhelpful perspective for an illness without a known cause. PD has not been widely understood or accepted as a life-ending condition. Yet, upon receipt of this diagnosis, many people report feeling they have received a death sentence; others hope for a cure in the reachable future. Living between dichotomous perspectives of life or death repre-sents a struggle for day-to-day continuity. Valued relationships lose closeness due, in part, to increasing depression, deteriorating communication, and the lonely nature of the illness. Social isola-tion may become a strategy to avoid public display and humiliation (Nijhof, 1995). Coupled with the potential for feeling unworthy of respect or becoming a target of intentional disregard creates a perpetual cycle for a growing loss of one's dignity (Lucke, 2009).

We Know So Very Little of the PD Lifestyle

Parkinson's disease is frighteningly common, comprising approxi-mately 80% of all cases of the major movement disorder category of Parkinsonian syndromes (Dickson, 2012). PD affects approxi-mately 1 of 250 people older than age 40, about 1 of 100 people older than 65, and about 1 of 10 people older than 80 (Eidelberg & Pourfar, 2007). It has been speculated that within 20 years, this prevalence will minimally double. This increasing prevalence has been attributed to an aging population, extending life expectancies, and a growing burden of chronic disease (Dorsey et al. 2007; Dorsey, George, Leff, & Willis, 2013). The risk of experiencing the diagnosis of PD with devastation, loss, and suffering for the remainder of one's life is high.

How do people face the challenges brought on by PD? Who do people turn to in these times of change, illness, and aging? These questions are relevant and timely. Access to primary and specialty care physicians is limited, for example, due to issues of transportation and decreasing numbers of providers (Dall et al., 2013), while professional homecare services have restrictive guidelines for restorative services. Community-based programs for older adults have experienced drastic service reductions (see, e.g., Senger, 2013). Although the Affordable Care Act (in the United States) represents a comprehensive approach to healthcare reform, it is complex and, at this time, in the infancy of its implementation (James & Levine, 2012); this has caused growing levels of frustration and anxiety, especially for people with long-term illnesses such as PD (see, e.g., the work being done by the Parkinson's Action Network).

Most people with a chronic illness, such as PD, want to live in their own homes and communities as they grow older (see Keenan, 2010). Because of this, it has become increasingly common for the familiar home environment to become the setting for long-term care (Gitlin, 2003). Subsequently, family members and friends perform personal care, household chores, and complex medical or nursing tasks formerly conducted only in hospitals and formerly confined only to hospital care. Many of my participants report seeing a PD specialist approximately once per year, do not attend educational support groups, and describe the internet as a source of worrisome, depressing, and unreliable information. Others report seeing a neighborhood medical doctor for a sudden illness (especially those people with PD and additional chronic conditions), receive prescriptions, and subsequently experience dire drug interactions. People with PD and their families are consequently left on their own to handle whatever comes their way and to plan for a future with little guidance about the usual or expected outcomes of PD.

How do people handle the multitude of daily concerns while living with the knowledge that they will, eventually, be unable to walk, be unable to communicate, and suffer from emotional pain and intellectual deterioration? Living in the community and primarily receiving care from family members, the parkinsonian life is shielded through isolating privacy. Because of this, we know little of the day-to-day workings of how families live, and about the experiences of people facing the challenges of living with PD. Take, for example, one older gentleman who no longer works and faces the personal hardship of losing his home to foreclosure. He is the sole support for his wife, his adult daughter, and his four grandchildren. This man has considered stopping his PD medications; this money would help with household finances. But, he drives 100 miles round trip to serve as a volunteer four days per week, just as he has done for many years, and does not consider it reasonable to stop this activity. He has not disclosed any of this information to his health providers. The literature does not sufficiently address how people with PD continue to strive to maintain daily life. Appreciating how people face the challenges of life and the strategies they use provides an opportunity for healthcare providers to learn, offer guidance, and become fundamentally effective in working with people.

The Contribution of Quantitative Research

There are no pre-illness indicators or definitive testing to confirm the presence of this insidious progressive illness. A diagnosis of PD relies on the clinical judgment of a healthcare professional. This process of reasoning depends largely on quantitatively devised scales for comparing, generalizing, and (subsequently) identifying the nature of an individual's movement disorder. Two such scales are the Hoehn & Yahr Disease Staging Scale (H & Y) (Goetz et al., 2004; Hoehn & Yahr, 1967) and the Schwab & England Activities of Daily Living Scale (ADL) (Perlmutter, 2009). The H & Y uses observation to rank the presence of motor disability, impairments, and balance; it does not measure function. The ADL scale measures functional abilities, such as bathing, dressing, and eating, but does not measure motor dysfunction.

But Wait… There Are Problems with Symptom Ranking

Although self-care abilities and movement limitations might be helpful for describing and predicting the illness stages, we are presented with numerical conclusions that seem blatantly obvious. For example, people who are in the later stages of PD, with greater immobility and increasing falls, are reported to have greater depression than those who are in the beginning stages of illness, who don't fall (Bryant et al., 2012; Farabaugh et al., 2011). Scales of measurement contributed no new findings to this common-sense conclusion. Depression becomes identified through self-awareness or in the sharing and acknowledgment of one's feelings with another person. Overwhelming sadness, despair, and tremendous loss contribute to a very personal suffering, which is not measureable on a ranking scale. Even with the availability of multiple depression scales, more than 40% of people with PD have symptoms of depression not recognized by the HCP (Shulman, Taback, Rabinstein, & Weiner, 2002). This seems to suggest that numbers cannot measure the depth of human feelings.

Relying on theoretical models for an "understanding of the experience" may have genuinely good intentions, but this is simply an intellectual exercise for the researcher. The ranking of personal situations and feelings do not measure a person's psychological reality, the depth of feelings, or offer a glimpse into their understanding of the experience. For example, when a PD participant was asked to describe his pain, he adamantly stated, "My pain is not measureable on a scale of 0 to 10. My pain is 12. It is how I feel and it is *my* pain."

The Contribution of Qualitative Research

The work of Strauss et al. (1975, 1984) propelled living with chronic illness into the social science arena; followed by entry into public health policy (Strauss & Corbin, 1988), and subsequently practice (Corbin, 1998; Corbin & Strauss, 1993). A major contribution to our understandings of chronic illness and self-concepts was provided by Charmaz (1983, 1991, 1995, 1999, 2002) through descriptions of the struggles and losses with chronic illness. Research on PD has derived benefit from these understandings; however, while the chronic illness literature provides insight into general concerns of long-term conditions, it does not encompass the simultaneous multiple complexities occurring with PD. Both healthcare professionals and people with PD use medical knowledge to understand and manage the progressive complex symptoms, yet these understandings are quite different (Bury, 1982; Pinder, 1992). As diagnostic specialists, physicians are trained to view the human body as classified into organs, functions, and related systems (Goldman & Schafer, 2012). Considering the unknown factors of causation, the limited treatment options available, a continuing search for the next new drug, and the current research priority on neurotechnologies (National Institutes of Health, 2013), PD has become a concern of contrasts for the afflicted individual, his or her family, diagnosticians, and researchers. A diagnosis of PD brings chaos and an incomprehensible life path for the person with PD and a sense of intellectual logic and certainty for the diagnostician (Pinder, 1992).

People with PD Seek Useful Explanations

The lifestyles of people with PD portray a desire to complete responsibilities, satisfy obligations, and share fulfilling relationships. People seek meaningful explanations and perspectives of their situations relying on family, friends, and HCPs as they struggle through day-to-day living with a long-term illness. Without thoughtful explanations or guidance, people are left on their own to devise ways of making sense of their lot, creating a new self, new forms of relationships, and a new future. In order to be helpful, we need to appreciate how illness is understood by those who experience it. How do people persevere when faced with unknown but perpetual deterioration in their physical, intellectual, and emotional capabilities? What are the strategies used? How do family members maintain and then recreate their roles to care for this family member with PD? Without an appreciation of the depth of daily suffering, health care providers have little opportunity to wield their skills in meaningful ways.

One married couple, both with forms of PD, live a quiet life. They suffered a tremendous loss with the sudden death of their son. Now, wanting to be closer with their adult daughter, the couple has recently moved across the country. The husband has been experiencing a rapid deterioration with falls, personal care difficulties, and memory changes. Both husband and wife have received treatment for major depression. They have relied on their family medical doctor for supervision of their multiple illnesses. They have seen a neurologist once but do not believe that he can help them remain living independently. Appreciating the circumstances of a person who suffers from PD requires the translation of qualitative research into actual, usable tools for implementation.

The Patterns of Yesterday Are Templates of Action

Knowing who we are as a person propels each of us into action—establishing connections to communities, developing a career, forming family relationships, and envisioning a future for a personal lifestyle. The loss of capabilities and potentials is not only a futuristic worry for many but is a current reality of suffering for many others. The American cultural values of independence and self-reliance strongly suggest that the potential loss of one's self through the gradual erosion of capabilities might be considered the greatest fear. The well-worn patterns of many yesterdays are relied upon as templates of action (Blumer, 1969; Mead, 1934; Mills, 1959) during times of change, aging, and illness as people, consciously or unconsciously, strive to relate and function.

Our ability to make decisions and to effectively act in the world is directly associated with our self-identity. "What should I do?" "How should I act in this situation?" To participate meaningfully in daily life requires these questions be answered; we need to make sense of the circumstances in front of us in order to act accordingly. When presented with a situation, an individual may choose a response from several options, ultimately choosing the one which seems most 'normal.' The option selected relies on habit, or inner templates of action, created through context, socialization, and language experiences (Blumer, 1969; Mead, 1934; Mills, 1959; Schwalbe, 1983). The person with PD experiences multiple physical, social, and psychological losses that must be interpreted and reinterpreted within the social context of his or her daily life to understand who he or she is, what to do, and how to act. One gentleman tells me that he does not and will not ever use a cane or walker; "I would rather crawl on the ground. That is not me … I don't want anyone to see me like that because that is not who I am." It is this environment of increasing losses that presents as opportunities for the researcher. It enables 'seeing' the strategies used by the person with PD and his or her support persons to reverse the process of losing the self.

Advancing Understanding through Concept Development

The theory of the loss of self (Charmaz, 1983, 1990, 1991, 1995, 2002) recognizes antecedents occurring through the process of chronic illness. These antecedents represent multiple and repeated losses of valued physical, social, and psychological functioning, changing relationships, and instances of devaluation. This loss of personal identity is continuum-based with varying levels of vulnerability, sensitivity, and loss. It is demonstrated through passivity, lowered self-worth, and social withdrawal. Although general implications have been presented by Charmaz (1983, 1990, 1991), these generalities can be heightened through increasing specification of chronic illnesses that includes PD. Discovering the loss of self for individuals with PD represents enormous potential for health professionals to work with people for the reduction of this invasive and devastating suffering. 'Reversing this process' of the loss of self refers to recognizing the loss of self through the challenges people face and identifying protective strategies to maintain normal behaviors and habits associated with the person, while these very abilities to maintain normal identity diminish. *Preserving self* is a social process of making new meanings and understandings (in this case, for people with PD and their support persons) and then taking action based on these meanings and understandings.

Preserving self is an emerging concept and, although mentioned several times in the literature, is currently at a descriptive level of development. Therefore, a working definition can be understood through the contextual descriptions of prior research. The concept of preserving self was initially identified by Johnson (see Morse & Johnson, 1991) as an element of the recovery process for women who had experienced a myocardial infarction. Becoming a heart attack victim meant physical restrictions and beliefs that she was "less than" and could never be as she was before. The women experienced changes in self-confidence, worth, and independence. It was difficult for the women to watch others do "their work." They managed the role transition by "bending the rules" to participate in restricted activities, rather than watching and feeling dependent. These women preserved self by working to gain control by asserting themselves.

Since this conceptual introduction of preserving self, other authors have described preserving self within the context of physical or psychological threats; for example, after surviving serious traumatic injury (Morse & O'Brien, 1995); women and cardiac surgery (King & Jensen, 1994); hereditary breast cancer; and ovarian cancer risk reduction (Howard, Balneaves, Bottorff, & Rodney, 2011). Common conceptual attributes are: striving, asserting, protecting, defending, and engaging. Additionally, preserving self can be viewed as sharing a continuum with Charmaz's theories of the Loss of Self (1983, 1990, 1991, 1995) and Regaining a Valued Self (2005). Preserving self describes a way of being that constitutes self-identity through everyday activities and attitudes. Sharing holidays with family, seeing friends, going to work, and the seemingly mundane tasks of dressing or having breakfast all represent a portion of what an individual sees as being his or her own self.

Through an understanding of who people are and who they strive to be, strategies to preserve can be understood. Preserving self is a process representing the struggles, transitions, and strategies for an affected person within the context of familiar roles and interpersonal relationships. The concept of preserving self has implications for practical bedside application for potentially reversing or halting the loss of self. The protection and preserving of one's self-identity is a natural advancement in the world of qualitative research, building on the unending work in regard to chronic illness (Corbin & Strauss, 1985, 1988) and the loss of self (Charmaz, 1983, 1990, 1991, 1995). Preserving self is a concept warranting acknowledgment and application during times of aging, emotional devastation, physical trauma, and, in this example, a specific chronic illness: Parkinson's. This application of preserving self is still in the building stages of concept and theory development. These are necessary steps in the translation of experiential and interpretative findings into healthcare programs and evidence-based practice (Morse, 2012). Qualitative research provides a basis for developing methods of guidance for professionals and, importantly, for the people themselves.

Working Around Technology

Lory J. Maddox

The necessity to provide safe, effective, and efficient healthcare has produced a healthcare system that by necessity is filled with regulations, policies, and procedure manuals. Healthcare delivery relies upon expert consensus, evidence-based practice, and randomized control trials for best practices to treat patients for optimal outcomes. Further, it is comprised of legal, regulatory, administrative, and technological controls designed to protect both patients and healthcare providers from accidents, injury, or harm. The enormity of these social, political, organizational, and technological forces weighs heavily upon the day-to-day interactions between patients and nurses. A microanalysis of technologically driven medication administration process provides an example of how technology and organizational controls intended to improve safety can impede patient centered care.

Reducing Medication Administration Errors

Medication ordering, dispensing, and administering processes are key areas highlighted in the 1999 report in the Institute of Medicine (IOM) report, "To Err Is Human," with subsequent funding for technology and software research. In 2006, the IOM promoted bar code scanning technology and computerized medication administration records as tools to prevent medication errors (Preventing Medication Errors, 2006). The Health Information Technology for Economic and Clinical Health (HITECH) Act on February 17, 2009, provided significant funding for healthcare information technology (HIT) development and information exchange. One of the goals of HIT is to improve safety by preventing and detecting errors before reaching the patient.

Medication administration practices mediated by HIT require that a name band containing individual unique identifying information encircle each patient's wrist. The processes of scanning patient wristband, medication, and computerized verification have been coined *bar code medication administration*, or BCMA. A scanning device reads this band, much like stickers and scanning devices used in retail markets. Medications are dispensed with scanning codes from the pharmacy and when administered to the patient, both patient and medication codes are scanned to electronically verify medication administration.

Nurses, at the sharp point of medication error, have long used the five rights of medication administration upon which BCMA was developed. BCMA does prevent certain types of medication errors that result in a safer hospital environment; however, BCMA technology and workflows assumed that medications are delivered and administered in a logical, sequential order and did not anticipate the adaptive responses used by nurses delivering direct patient care. Nurses do adapt, but in ways that surprise HIT designers. Nurses are adept problem solvers and manage to deliver care in the fast paced, fluid environment of acute care hospitals, and will use workarounds that bypass technical controls intended to increase patient safety.

However, the goals of HIT are not only safety, but to increase efficiency. Current HIT designs have technological and administrative controls that provide safe and efficient healthcare delivery processes. Standardized approaches are associated with greater efficiency and reproducibility that maximize value and spread the cost of large capital investments in health care technology across multiple divisions. Both clinical and financial stakeholders will have spearheaded efforts to implement HIT at high cost to organizations. When discrepancies between clinical workflow and technology controls are identified, organizations must respond. Given the high cost of implementing HIT, organizations often respond by exerting administrative controls upon end users, rather than changing the technology.

Despite technology being promoted as a way of increasing patient safety, mitigating technologic deficiencies at the bedside have been selectively implemented. As hospital administrators implement technology in their hospitals, they use a return on investment (ROI) financial model that assumes decision criteria different from those of other stakeholders, e.g., nurses, physicians, and pharmacists. Early adopters of BCMA calculated the cost of avoided medication errors when making a financial case for technology investment. As medication errors continued despite the investment in technology, initial ROI assumptions had to be revisited. The cost to an organization can be significant if an organizational approach to reducing technology induced medication errors is to be taken seriously. Often it is more cost effective and expedient in the short term to provide re-education and training to mandatory users than to invest in further technology (Maddox, Danello, Williams, & Fields, 2008)

Nurses, mandatory users of HIT, are frequently the workforce upon which administrative controls are concentrated. Patient safety is touted to nurses as the reason for technological controls—a message to which nurses respond. An examination of BCMA research reveals that tension between nurses and organizational goals often arises, and administrators choose to change the practices of users, not the implementation of HIT, to meet organizational goals.

Challenges of Bar Code Medication Administration

Information system engineers envision nurses following sequential processes when delivering direct patient care. Unlike the work of a production worker, the work of an acute care nurse is rarely linear and methodical, nor is it easily reproduced in a computerized system (Potter et al., 2005). Intense focus upon medication administration, such as time of administration, once difficult to capture in the era of the handwritten records, is now conveniently summarized and amenable to data mining, discovery of patterns, and intensive research. A computer generated reporting tool to assess medication administration and user compliance with prescriptive processes is now in place.

Patterson, Cook, and Render (2002) are human factors researchers and medical specialists that studied nurses' administration of medication at VA hospitals pre and post BCMA implementation. They identified a myriad of ways in which nurses used BCMA differently than intended and coined these activities 'workarounds,' a term borrowed from computer scientists. These so-called workarounds were captured through observational techniques and computer generated reports. Patterson et al.'s (2002) research is observation based and intended to evaluate the effectiveness of BCMA systems. This research describes at least five unintended consequences from BCMA and advocates for organizational responses to address these process weaknesses and deficiencies, such as replacing patients' bar coded wristbands on a weekly basis, hospital sponsored continuous quality improvement initiatives, and staff training. Patterson and colleagues then shift focus to end users—nurses—and their compliance with scanning patient wristbands between acute care and long term settings (Patterson, Rogers, Chapman, & Render, 2006).

Over a four year period, failing to scan a patient's wristband has gone from a "new pathway to an adverse drug event" (Patterson et al., 2002) to an end user compliance issue (Patterson et al., 2006). This represents a critical shift in the focus of research, from describing a new process that can lead to medication errors to examining nurses as BCMA end users and recording the frequency and type of workarounds employed. The emphasis shifts from developing a technological solution to improve medication safety to a focus on employing managerial controls on mandatory users.

Deficiencies and system weaknesses in health care technology such as BCMA were documented early. Nurses were expected *to adapt to the new technology versus technology adapting to nursing work*. Unbeknownst to many staff nurses, workaround strategies can have a multiplying effect, as demonstrated in various risk models and safety reports (Henriksen & United States Agency for Healthcare Research and Quality, 2008; Marx & Slonim, 2003). Nurses are perceived by developers as not using software correctly; nurses think engineers and developers cannot build a system that can be used at the bedside. Unfortunately, when gaps, including patient safety, are identified, there is often a tendency to blame *the other*. Instead of coming together to develop language and mutual understanding, nursing and healthcare software professionals often retreat into our own areas of domain knowledge and fail to communicate, so problems remain unresolved (Johnson, 2006).

Despite the limitations of BCMA it is often the least expensive and most reliable system to augment medication administration. All information systems rely upon an inputting device for data. The most common data input device, the keyboard, is also the most prone to errors. "Bar code technology has a distinct advantage over other input devices such as optical scanners, radio frequency detection devices related to the low cost of printing and high first read rate, usually greater than 90%" (morovia.com).

Technological changes require large investment in capital and staff resources. There are huge initial capital investments, such as BCMA product purchases, implementation and training costs, as well as sustainability. For technology such as BCMA to be successful in hospitals, teams involved in evaluating the complex iterative relationship amongst social networks, technology, and users need to be funded and supported during the entire HIT lifecycle (Borycki, Kushniruk, & Brender, 2010; Koppel, Wetterneck, Telles, & Karsh, 2008).

The Mixed Message

When technology impedes patient care, nurses become primary problem solvers and innovators in developing solutions to deliver healthcare to patients (Halbesleben, Savage, Wakefield, & Wakefield, 2010). Despite known technology weaknesses, nurses are encouraged to be problem solvers and are informally rewarded as we care for patients (F. Hughes, 2006; R. Hughes, 2008). Unfortunately, this mixed message puts both patients and nurses at risk in hospitals that use BCMA when administrative controls are the standard to which nurses are held despite the tacit acknowledgment that the HIT system doesn't work well for nurses.

Qualitative inquiry, with an emphasis on delineating multiple perspectives, describing tacit knowledge, and demarcating positions of power and influence, is instrumental in developing personas, user stories, and social processes that guide future HIT development.

Exploring New Healthcare Environments

Kim Martz

Assisted Living Facilities (ALFs) appeared on the scene approximately 30 years ago as an alternative housing environment to nursing homes for healthier older adults still needing some help with the tasks of everyday living. These housing environments have dramatically increased over the past few years, and the reasons for the increase are varied. First, the fastest growing segment of the population are those 85 years and older, and we as a society and as a scholarly community are only beginning to understand the impact on individuals, families, and society as a whole of the consequences of living longer. Along with these current issues, the large baby boomer generation has turned 65, and the "silver tsunami" is coming to the long-term care industry and health care in general. It is estimated that by 2020, 12 million people will need these services (Long-term Care, 2014). Second, families are geographically distant; resources may be an issue of bringing care into the home, which is quite costly. In addition, there is the management and oversight of caregivers in the home with this vulnerable population. If a family member is doing the care, there are issues of caregiver breakdown and the difficult decisions of finding a healthcare facility for the care of his or her loved ones. When choosing "a place for mom," many people have fears about the quality of care in nursing homes and are drawn to the ALF environment as a home-like alternative.

ALFs are marketed as a social model of care rather than a medical model. They provide assistance with daily living in a "home-like" environment as opposed to an institutional setting such as a nursing home. The marketing also includes a philosophy of autonomy and dignity while having physical needs met. With this philosophy of maximizing independence and accommodating residents' changing needs, including promotion of the ability to "age in place" (Ball et al., 2004), one could argue that if you could age in place, you should be able to die in place. However, more than 67% of consumers were uninformed about facility policies on care of the dying, retention, and discharge. This lack of knowledge is evident in that 98% of residents in a national study of ALFs believed they would be able to stay in their ALF for as long as they wished. In fact, as residents' needs for nursing care increase, these needs may not be met by the ALF, and residents must be transferred to another institution at the end of life. When they are transitioned, it is generally to a skilled nursing facility or nursing home, which is the institution they were trying to avoid with a move to an ALF. The transitions are burdensome for families, especially at a time of grief and pending loss. Many residents discharged from ALFs (i.e., 25% to 45%) are transitioned to a nursing home (Kane, Chan, & Kane, 2007), but some are transferred directly to the hospital. The rate of hospitalization for ALF residents is higher than for community-dwelling elderly; while residents and their families support aging and dying in place in their assisted living "home," policies and processes are not available within the facilities to meet end of life care needs (Cartwright, Hickman, Perrin, & Tilden, 2006).

The lack of staffing, especially licensed staff, to manage changing conditions and medications, along with the frailty of the population, may lead to an increase in the hospitalizations from ALF and deaths that occur in hospitals rather than at home, where the majority of people say they want to die (Abarsh, Echteld, Donker, Van den Block, Onwuteaka-Philipsen, & Deliens, 2011). Moreover, what kind of quality of care are these vulnerable older adults receiving if there is minimal staffing? The staffing at some facilities consists of one aide per 20 residents. ALFs are for-profit facilities, and the occupancy rate needs to be 100% in order to be financially successful. If a family decides to move a loved one to an ALF for more care, is the type of care that they need provided? In some states a registered nurse needs to evaluate the patient upon admission and at least every 90 days thereafter in order to see if the ALF can provide the necessary care. However, on admission, if the new residents needs can be met, increasing frailty means increasing needs, and even if these needs cannot be met, it is in the financial interest of the ALF to retain the resident as long as possible. As a result, transfers from the ALF to a hospital occur in crisis situations.

It appears that older adults and their families may be sold a bill of goods. This is a highly profitable industry; however, it does not appear to meet the complex needs of the population as they age and include those who are medically, cognitively, and functionally diverse (Podrazik, 2005). Therefore, is it a housing alternative or is it a health care environment? It appears to be both. The ALFs are trying to bridge these two environments, and paradoxically, therefore, meet the needs of neither as soon as the consequences of aging become complex. The residents who live in ALFs in the United States are largely over 85 years of age with chronic conditions and disabilities (Podrazik, 2005). The National Center for Health Statistics (2012) concluded that the three most common ailments of residents in these communities were: high blood pressure, Alzheimer disease, and heart disease, with approximately 42% suffering from some type of dementia. In this environment the residents are provided some basic health monitoring, medication assistance, incontinence care, special diets, along with physical and occupational therapy. When compared with nursing homes, there are three primary differences: the environment, the licensed staffing, and the payer system. ALFs are mostly private pay, whereas nursing homes have Medicare/Medicaid benefits. However, the staffing requirements are vastly different and vary from state to state and facility to facility. Licensed staffs are not required to be present 24 hours in an ALF, whereas in nursing homes licensed nurses and certified assistance are mandated by the federal government. The state government alone regulates assisted living facilities. ALFs have been under researched thus far, whereas research in skilled nursing facilities (SNF) or nursing hospices (NHs) has made an impact on the quality of care of vulnerable adults in these facilities.

Research in the New Environment of Study

In a review of the literature from 1989 to 2004 in ALF environments, Kane, Chang, and Kane (2007) noted that qualitative studies were prevalent and longitudinal studies were rare. These studies are critical to trying to understand the most salient constructs in ALF. Do we even know yet what to measure in ALF, given the lack of standardization and the variability between facilities? The constructs that have been developed through qualitative studies include: personal autonomy, choice, resident-centered assessment, homelike qualities of the environment, individuality, and aging in place (Kane, Wilson, Spector, 2007).

Since 2004, there have been a few studies focusing on end-of-life care, particularly hospice care, but virtually none on residents who don't choose hospice. Hospice is considered crucial to the ability to age and die in place because of the increase in staffing required for the resident. Even with hospice support, due to medication regulations, residents may need to leave the facility. The resident of ALF has to be able to take his or her own medications, and this may not be possible when he or she is dying and needs to be kept comfortable. In some states families are not permitted to give the medications without a waiver obtained through state regulations. Residents may also need to leave if they develop a pressure ulcer from immobility at the end of their life. In addition, if a resident should develop a multiple resistant staph infection, he or she would need to leave within an hour of diagnosis. End-of-life or dying in place is an underdeveloped area or a "hole" in health-care research. Qualitative studies are needed to understand the processes that residents and families experience during a transition in health care facilities at the end of life. Transitions, or transfers from one health care setting to another, are shown to have burdensome consequences of stress, depression, financial burden, loss of personal possessions, and loss of personhood (Mitty & Flores, 2008; Mollica & Jenkens, 2001).

The Need for Qualitative Inquiry

The ALF environment is conceptually difficult to research. Quantitatively, the settings are not consistent and there is no payer system, such as the Minimum Data Set that exists in the Long Term Care environment, to examine outcomes . Qualitative researchers could investigate problems, such as assisting, to determine what the outcomes of ALFs should be beyond quality of life. Such research involving human activity, taking meaning and perspective into account, as well as healthcare issues, examines the whole context rather than its parts. Qualitative inquiry enables us to study the issues in depth and provides details, including the perspectives of multiple stakeholders, such as the family, the staff, the resident, and the state regulators.

Research that has made a dramatic impact on policy and quality in nursing homes was conducted by Dr. Jeanie Kayser Jones beginning in 1978. Her studies were qualitative studies, including interviews with patients, families, and providers (Kayser-Jones et al., 2003). In addition, she examined the behavioral context of eating and nutritional support using ethnography (Kayser-Jones & Schell, 1997). She also examined dying in a nursing home through ethnography and documented a case study of dying with a Stage IV pressure ulcer (Kayser-Jones, Kris, Lim, Walent, Halifax, & Paul, 2008). Due to her qualitative work and numerous publications, public attention was generated. Subsequently, guidelines and protocols were revised to identify areas she uncovered in her research. The contextually rich, detailed data that she obtained ultimately influenced staffing requirements in nursing homes. This same examination should take place in ALFs.

There is an urgent need to conduct qualitative research on end-of-life care in ALFs and the transitions that occur at this vulnerable time for residents and their families. Qualitative research will uncover the voices of families and residents that may be the basis for in-depth investigations that will influence staffing, regulation, and the quality of care for residents in ALFs in this new environment. It is crucial to build this body of knowledge qualitatively in order to understand the complex and challenging issues of growing older in America and the impact of care environments on this vulnerable population.

Discussion

In this chapter we argue that qualitative research provides an essential role in healthcare research. Our three examples reveal how qualitative inquiry provided the skills and the methods to document slight changes. In the first example, Vann-Warn revealed persons with Parkinson's Disease, as they strove to maintain a sense of self, in the face of increasingly debilitating illnesses. The second example suggests that qualitative research could reveal behaviors that are unofficial, even illegal, yet, ironically, necessary for patient safety. That is, paradoxically, nurses are breaking rules to provide essential medications to patients when the official policies in place were intended to protect patients, rather than cause harm. The third example, by Martz, shows that in a new living situation, assisted living facilities, residents believe they can remain in place for the remainder of their lives. However, as they became increasingly ill, they suddenly find themselves transferred to a nursing home or hospital.

These three examples are highly descriptive. They provide details of processes that may otherwise be unobserved or ignored; yet, each is exceedingly important in the provision of safe care. It is this basic work of recognizing processes and interactions and identifying micro-analytics processes and models of causation that is exceedingly important in healthcare research and cannot be done, at least initially, using quantitative methods.

We are often asked if our qualitative studies should be "followed by quantitative research, to confirm our findings." We are puzzled why such a progression in research methods and logic is necessary, and sometimes even possible. Recall, the reason that we use qualitative methods is that quantitative methods are not available to conduct such research. Sometimes the concepts are not available for the development of measurement tools. Simply because such careful qualitative work has been conducted does not mean that the research is invalid, and there is no reason why it should not be considered an endpoint.

Acknowledgments

This chapter was adapted from a presentation, "Holes in health care: The role of qualitative inquiry" presented at the 9th International Congress of Qualitative Inquiry, at the University of Illinois, Urbana-Champaign, May 15–18, 2013.

Note

1 For example, we are still puzzling over the differential symptoms of heart attacks, first described in 1990 (Johnson & Morse, 1990).

References

Abarsh, E., Echteld, M. Donker, G., Van den Block, L., Onwuteaka-Philipsen, B., & Deliens, L. (2011). Discussing end-of-life issues in the last months of life: A nationwide study among general practitioners. *Journal of Palliative Medicine, 14*(30), 323–330.

Ball, M. M., Perkins, M. M., Whittington, F. J., Connell, B. R., Hollingsworth, C., King, S. V., & Combs, B. L. (2004). Managing decline in assisted living: The key to aging in place. *Journals of Gerontology. Series B, Psychological Sciences and Social Sciences, 59*(4), S202–212.

Bijur, P. E., Latimer, C. T., & Gallagher, E. J. (2003). Validation of a verbally administered numerical rating scale of acute pain for use in the emergency department. *Academic Emergency Medicine, 10*(4), 390–392.

Blumer, H. (1969). *Symbolic interactionism: Perspective and method.* Berkeley: University of California Press.

Borycki, E., Kushniruk, A., & Brender, J. (2010). Theories, models and frameworks for diagnosing technology-induced error. *Studies in Health Technolology Information, 160* (Pt 1), 714–718.

Bowlby, J. (1973). *Separation: Anxiety & anger.* London: Hogarth Press.

Bryant, M. S., Rintala, D. H., Hou, J. G., Rivas, S. P., Fernandez, A. L., Lai, E. C., & Protas, E. J. (2012). The relation of falls to fatigue, depression and daytime sleepiness in Parkinson's disease. *European Neurology, 67*(6), 326–330.

Bury, M. (1982). Chronic illness as biographical disruption. *Sociology of Health & Illness, 4*(2), 167–182.

Cartwright, J. C., Hickman, S., Perrin, N., & Tilden, V. (2006). Symptom experiences of residents dying in assisted living. *Journal of the American Medical Directors Association, 7*(4), 219–223.

Charmaz, K. (1983). Loss of self: A fundamental form of suffering in the chronically ill. *Sociology of Health & Illness, 5*(2), 168–195.

Charmaz, K. (1990). 'Discovering' chronic illness: Using grounded theory. *Social Science & Medicine, 30*(11), 1161–1172.

Charmaz, K. (1991). *Good days and bad days: The self in chronic illness.* New Brunswick, NJ : Rutgers University Press.

Charmaz, K. (1995). The body, identity, and self: Adapting to impairment. *The Sociological Quarterly, 36*(4), 657–680.

Charmaz, K. (1999). Stories of suffering: Subjective tales and research narratives. *Qualitative Health Research, 9*, 362–382.

Charmaz, K. (2002). Stories and silences: Disclosures and self in chronic illness. *Qualitative Inquiry, 8*(3), 302–328.

Corbin, J., & Strauss, A. (1985). Managing chronic illness at home: Three lines of work. *Qualitative Sociology, 8*(3), 224–247.

Corbin, J., & Strauss, A. L. (1988). *Unending work and care: Managing chronic illness at home.* Hoboken, NJ: Jossey-Bass

Dall, T. M., Storm, M. V., Chakrabarti, R., Drogan, O., Keran, C. M., Donofrio, P. D., & Vidic, T. R. (2013). Supply and demand analysis of the current and future U.S. neurology workforce. *Neurology.* Retrieved December 22, 2013, from www.neurology.org/content/early/2013/04/17/WNL.0b013e318294b1cf.short

Dickson, D. W. (2012). Parkinson's disease and Parkinsonism: Neuropathology. *Cold Spring Harbor perspectives in medicine, 2*(8). Retrieved December 22, 2013, from perspectivesinmedicine.cshlp.org/content/2/8/a009258.abstract

Dorsey, E. R., Constantinescu, R., Thompson, J. P., Biglan, K. M., Holloway, R. G., Kieburtz, K., & Tanner, C. M. (2007). Projected number of people with Parkinson disease in the most populous nations, 2005 through 2030. *Neurology, 68*(5), 384–386.

Dorsey, E. R., George, B. P., Leff, B., & Willis, A. W. (2013). The coming crisis: Obtaining care for the growing burden of neurodegenerative conditions. *Neurology, 80*(21), 1989–1996.

Eidelberg, D., & Pourfar, M. (2007). Parkinson's disease. In R. S. Porter & J. L. Kaplan (Eds.), *The Merck manual: Home health handbook.* Whitehouse, NJ: Merck, Sharp, & Dohme.

Farabaugh, A. H., Locascio, J. J., Yap, L., Fava, M., Bitran, S., Sousa, J. L., & Growdon, J. H. (2011). Assessing depression and factors possibly associated with depression during the course of Parkinson's disease. *Annals of Clinical Psychiatry, 23*(3), 171–177.

Harrison, C. (7/16/2013). GRAY MATTERS: Sequestration means service reductions. *Eureka Times-Standard.* Retrieved December 22, 2013, from www.times-standard.com/ci_23668380/gray-matters-sequestration-means-service-reductions

Gitlin, L. N. (2003). Conducting research on home environments: Lessons learned and new directions. *The Gerontologist, 43*(5), 628–637.

Goffman, E. (2009). *Stigma: Notes on the management of spoiled identity.* New York: Simon & Schuster.

Goetz, C. G., Poewe, W., Rascol, O., Sampaio, C., Stebbins, G. T., Counsell, C., & Seidl, L. (2004). Movement Disorder Society Task Force report on the Hoehn and Yahr staging scale: Status and recommendations. *Movement Disorders, 19*(9), 1020–1028.

Goldman, L., & Schafer, A. I. (2012). Approach to medicine, the patient, and the medical profession: Medicine as a learned and humane profession. In L. Goldman & A. I. Schafer (Eds.), *Goldman's Cecil Medicine* (24th ed., Vol. 1, pp. 34–54). New York: Saunders.

Green, L. W., Ottoson, J., Garcia, C., & Hiatt, R. (2009). Diffusion theory and knowledge dissemination, utilization, and integration in public health. *Annual Review of Public Health, 30*, 151–174.

Halbesleben, J. R., Savage, G. T., Wakefield, D. S., & Wakefield, B. J. (2010). Rework and workarounds in nurse medication administration process: Implications for work processes and patient safety. *Health Care Management Review, 35*(2), 124–133.

Halpin, H. A., Morales-Suárez-Varela, M. M., & Martin-Moreno, J. M. (2010). Chronic disease prevention and the new public health. *Public Health Reviews, 32*, 120–154.

Henriksen, K., & United States Agency for Healthcare Research and Quality. (2008). Advances in patient safety: New directions and alternative approaches. *AHRQ publication no 08-0034-1.* Retrieved December 22, 2013, from www.ncbi.nlm.nih.gov/bookshelf/br.fcgi?book=apscollect

Hoehn, M., & Yahr, M. D. (1967). Parkinsonism: Onset, progression, and mortality. *Neurology, 17*(5), 427–442.

Howard, A. F., Balneaves, L. G., Bottorff, J. L., & Rodney, P. (2011). Preserving the self: The process of decision making about hereditary breast cancer and ovarian cancer risk reduction. *Qualitative Health Research, 21*(4), 502–519.

Hughes, F. (2006). Nurses at the forefront of innovation. *International Nursing Review, 53*(2), 94–101.

Hughes, R. G. (2008). Nurses at the "sharp end" of patient care. In R. G. Hughes (Ed.), *Patient safety and quality: An evidence-based handbook for nurses.* (Prepared with support from the Robert Wood Johnson Foundation.) AHRQ Publication No. 08-0043. Rockville, MD: Agency for Healthcare Research and Quality. Retrieved from www.ncbi.nlm.nih.gov/books/NBK2672/

Institute of Medicine. (1999). *To err is human: Building a safer health system.* Washington, D.C.: National Academies Press.

Institute of Medicine. (2006). *Preventing medication errors: Quality chasm series.* Washington, D.C.: National Academies Press.

James, E., & Levine, A. S. (2012). The Inevitability of health reform. *Duquesne Law Review, 50*(2), 235–252

Johnson, C. W. (2006). Why did that happen? Exploring the proliferation of barely usable software in healthcare systems. *Quality & Safety in Health Care, 15*(1), 76–81.

Kane, R. A., Chan, J., & Kane, R. L. (2007). Assisted living literature through May 2004: Taking stock. *The Gerontological Society of America, 47*(Special Issue 3), 125–140.

Kane, R.A., Wilson, K.B., Spector, W. (2007). Developing a research agenda for assisted living. *The Gerontological Society of America, 47*(Special Issue 3), 4–54.

Kayser-Jones, J., & Schell. E. S. (1997). Staffing and the mealtime experience of nursing home on a special care unit. *American Journal of Alzheimer's Disease and Other Dementias, 12*(2): 67–72.

Kayser-Jones, J., Schell, E. S., Porter, C., Barbacaccia, J. C., & Shaw, H. (1999). Factors contributing to dehydration in nursing homes: Inadequate staffing and lack of professional supervision. *Journal of the American Geriatrics Society, 47*(10), 1187–1194.

Kayser-Jones, J., Schell, E., Lyons, W., Kris, A. E., Chan, J., & Beard, R. L. (2003). Factors that influence end-of-life care in nursing homes: The physical environment, inadequate staffing, and lack of supervision. *Gerontologist, 43*(2), 76–84.

Kayser-Jones, J., Kris, A. E., Lim, K. C., Walent, R. J., Halifax, E., & Paul, S. M. (2008). Pressure ulcers among terminally ill nursing home residents. *Research in Gerontological Nursing, 1*(1), 14–24.

Kayser-Jones, J., Beard, R. L., & Sharp, T. (2009). Dying with a stage IV pressure ulcer: An analysis of a nursing home's gross failure to provide competent care. *American Journal of Nursing, 109*(1): 40–48.

Keenan, T. (2010). Home and community preferences of the 45+ population. *Surveys and Statistics,* 1–25. Retrieved December 20, 2013, from www.aarp.org/home-garden/livablecommunities/info-11-2010/home-community-services-10.html

King, K. M., & Jensen, L. (1994). Preserving the self: Women having cardiac surgery. *Heart & Lung, 23*(2), 99–105.

Koppel, R., Wetterneck, T., Telles, J. L., & Karsh, B. T. (2008). Workarounds to barcode medication administration systems: Their occurrences, causes, and threats to patient safety. *Journal of the American Medical Informatics Association, 15*(4), 408–423.

Landsberger, H. A. (1958). *Hawthorne revisited.* Ithaca, NY: Cornell University Press.

Long-term Care (2014). Facts on care in the US. Brown University Alpert Medical School. Retrieved February 9, 2014, from www.ltcfocus.org/2/faq

Lucke, R. (2009). What is dignity? Is it a useful concept? Retrieved December 12, 2013, from open.salon.com/blog/rick_lucke/2009/01/01/what_is_dignityis_it_a_useful_concept

Maddox, R. R., Danello, S., Williams, C. K., & Fields, M. (2008). Intravenous infusion safety initiative: Collaboration, evidence-based best practices, and "smart" technology help avert high-risk adverse drug events and improve patient outcomes. *Technology and Medication Safety, Vol. 4.* Retrieved February 9, 2014, from www.ncbi.nlm.nih.gov/books/NBK43752/

Marx, D. A., & Slonim, A. D. (2003). Assessing patient safety risk before the injury occurs: An introduction to sociotechnical probabilistic risk modelling in health care. *Quality and Safety in Health Care, 12*(2), 33–38.

Mead, G. H. (1934). *Mind, self, and society: From the standpoint of a social sehaviorist.* (C. W. Morris, Ed. reprint ed.). Chicago: University of Chicago Press.

Mills, C. W. (1959). *The sociological imagination.* (T. Gitlin, Ed. 40th anniversary ed.). New York: Oxford University Press.

Mitty, E., & Flores, S. (2008). Aging in place and negotiated risk agreements. *Geriatric Nursing, 29*(2), 94–101.

Mollica, R., & Jenkens R. (2001). *State assisted living practices and options: A guide for state policymakers.* Portland, ME: National Academy for State Health Policy.

Morse, J. M. (2003). Expired research. (Editorial). *Qualitative Health Research, 13*(5), 595–596.

Morse, J. M. (2012). *Qualitative health research: Creating a new discipline.* Walnut Creek, CA: Left Coast Press, Inc.

Morse, J. M., & Johnson, J. (1991). Toward a theory of illness: The illness constellation model. In J. M. Morse & J. Johnson (Eds.), *The illness experience: Dimensions of suffering* (pp. 315–342). Newbury Park, CA: Sage.

Morse, J. M., & O'Brien, B. (1995). Preserving self: From victim, to patient, to disabled person. *Journal of Advanced Nursing, 21*, 886-896.

National Center for Health Statistics. (2012). Data brief. Retrieved December 12, 2013, from www.cdc.gov/nchs/data/databriefs/db91.htm

National Institutes of Health (NIH). (2013, November 26). *Brain research through advancing innovative neurotechnologies (BRAIN) initiative.* Retrieved December 11, 2013, from www.nih.gov/science/brain/.

Nijhof, G. (1995). Parkinson's disease as a problem of shame in public appearance. *Sociology of Health & Illness, 17*(2), 193–205.

Patterson, E. S., Cook, R. I., & Render, M. L. (2002). Improving patient safety by identifying side effects from introducing bar coding in medication administration. *Journal of American Medical Informtics Association. 9*(5), 540–553.

Patterson, E. S., Rogers, M. L., Chapman, R. J., & Render, M. L. (2006). Compliance with intended use of bar code medication administration in acute and long-term care: An observational study. *Human Factors. 48*(1), 15–22.

Perlmutter, J. S. (2009). Assessment of Parkinson disease manifestations. *Current Protocols in Neuroscience.* Retrieved December 21, 2013, from: www.ncbi.nlm.nih.gov/pmc/articles/PMC2897716

Piaget, J., & Cook, M. T. (1952). *The origins of intelligence in children.* Cambridge, MA: Harvard University Press.

Pinder, R. (1992). Coherence and incoherence: Doctors' and patients' perspectives on the diagnosis of Parkinson's disease. *Sociology of Health & Illness, 14*(1), 1–22.

Podrazik, P. M. (2005). The subtext of the AGS assisted living facilities position statement: The frail or failing older adult. *Assisted Living Consult,* September/October, 25. Retrieved December 30, 2013, from www.assistedlivingconsult.com/issues/01-05/ALC1-5_AGS.pdf

Potter, P., Wolf, L., Boxerman, S., Grayson, D., Sledge, J., Dunagan, C., & Evanoff, B. (2005). Understanding the cognitive work of nursing in the acute care environment. *Journal of Nursing Administration, 35*(7–8), 327–335.

Roig, M., Eng, J. J., & Reid, W. D. (2009). Falls in patients with chronic obstructive pulmonary disease: A call for further research. *Respiratory Medicine, 103*(9), 1257–1269.

Schwalbe, M. L. (1983). Language and the self: An expanded view from a symbolic interactionist perspective. *Symbolic Interaction, 6*(2), 291–306.

Senger, A. (2013). Obamacare's impact on seniors: An update. *Health Care.* Issue Brief #4019. Retrieved December 21, 2013, from www.heritage.org/research/reports/2013/08/obamacares-impact-on-seniors-an-update

Shulman, L. M., Taback, R. L., Rabinstein, A. A., & Weiner, W. J. (2002). Non-recognition of depression and other non-motor symptoms in Parkinson's disease. *Parkinsonism & Related Disorders, 8*(3), 193–197.

Strauss, A. L. (Ed.). (1975). *Chronic illness and the quality of life.* St. Louis: C. V. Mosby.

Strauss, A. L., Corbin, J., Fagerhaugh, S., Glaser, B. G., Maines, D., Suczek, B., & Weiner, C. L. (Eds.). (1984). *Chronic illness and the quality of life* (2nd ed.). St. Louis: C. V. Mosby.

United States General Accounting Office. (1999). Assisted living: Quality-of-care and consumer protection issues in four states. Retrieved December 21, 2013, from www.gao.gov/archive/1999/he99027.pdf

Part IV
Beyond

Chapter 12

Performance Ethnography
Decolonizing Research and Pedagogy

Virginie Magnat

What are the implications, for performance ethnography, of the critique of dominant Euro-American research models articulated by Indigenous researchers? The most provocative and productive dimension of performance ethnography is arguably Norman K. Denzin's integration of Indigenous perspectives on research and pedagogy that legitimize embodied knowledge as a counter-hegemonic mode of inquiry. Writing in support of collaborations between Indigenous and non-Indigenous researchers, Denzin hence asserts that "Westerners have much to learn from Indigenous epistemologies and performance theories," and suggests that "the performance turn in Anglo-Saxon discourse can surely benefit from the criticisms and tenets offered by Maori and other Indigenous scholars" (2003, p. 108), thereby charting new directions for interdisciplinary and cross-cultural research.

Yet in the preface to the *Handbook of Critical and Indigenous Methodologies* (2008), Denzin and his co-editors state in a section titled "Limitations" that they were "unable to locate persons who could write chapters on indigenous performance studies" (p. xii). Later in the introduction, Denzin and Yvonna S. Lincoln envision

---

Qualitative Inquiry Outside the Academy edited by Norman K. Denzin and Michael D. Giardina, 235–252. © 2014 Left Coast Press, Inc. All rights reserved.

a performative critical pedagogy grounded in Indigenous perspectives and in Augusto Boal's model of political theatre (p. 7). They advocate what they describe as a "post-colonial, indigenous participatory theater, a form of critical pedagogical theater that draws its inspirations from Boal's major works: *Theatre of the Oppressed* (1974/1979), *The Rainbow of Desire* (1995), and *Legislative Theatre* (1998)" (p. 7). However, a close examination of recent critical reassessments of the Marxist-inflected emancipatory discourses underpinning Boal's relationship to the work of Paulo Freire demonstrates that the seemingly unilateral integration of the Boalian performance paradigm by social scientists is far from unproblematic, especially from an Indigenous perspective.

Revisiting the Relationship between Brecht, Boal, and Freire

The predominance of the Brecht-Boal lineage in the academy can be traced to the polemic that famously opposed European academics who favored Bertolt Brecht to those who defended Konstantin Stanislavsky on the one hand, and Antonin Artaud and Jerzy Grotowski on the other. The absurdity of these academic turf wars was dramatized by Eugène Ionesco in his 1955 play *L'Impromptu de l'Alma*, a mordant satire featuring grotesque renditions of the theorists Roland Barthes and Bernard Dort, two fervent proponents of Brechtian theatre, cast by Ionesco as "*Docteurs en Théâtrologie*" who put on trial the artistic competence of the play's author, whom they publicly accuse of not being Brechtian enough. Originally from Romania, Ionesco was an outspoken critic of fascism and totalitarianism—that is to say, the ideologies of the Nazi and Soviet Communist regimes he indicted in his writing. Ionesco's (1967) provocative critique of Brechtian theatre scrutinizes Brecht's rejection of the magic of theatre that operates through affective participation, and revisits Brecht's assertion that he does not want spectators to identify with the characters of his plays (p. 23). Indeed, Ionesco argues that Brecht wants spectators to participate in his plays by identifying not with the characters he created but with his thinking or ideology, so that the latter becomes endowed with the very magic Brecht claims to repudiate. Ionesco extends this analysis to politically engaged theatre makers by asserting that what they desire is to convince and recruit their audiences, which he equates with violating spectators (p. 23).

Ionesco's recriminations notwithstanding, Brecht clearly remains the undefeated champion of a materialist paradigm that has successfully endured the sea-changes of structuralism, post-structuralism, and post-modernism in the academy. Like Stanislavsky, considered to be the father of realist theatre, Brecht is upheld as the father of political theatre, a perspective whose influence reaches well beyond the field of theatre studies, since the Brechtian theatrical paradigm also prevails across the humanities and social sciences in the form of Boal's *Theatre of the Oppressed*.

The privileging of Boal by proponents of critical pedagogy is, of course, linked to their explicit allegiance to Freire, since Boal's conception of performance is grounded in Freire's pedagogy of the oppressed as well as in Brecht's Marxist approach to theatre. Boal, inspired by Freire, advocates a post-Brechtian theatre in which the separation between audience members and actors dissolves, and where the "spect-actor" can intervene and change the course of events presented by the *Theatre of the Oppressed*, the latter being defined by Boal (1996) as "a rehearsal of revolution" (p. 97). In her examination of competing scholarly assessments of Boal's approach, Helen Nicholson (2005) remarks that "depending on how you look at his work, Augusto Boal is either an inspirational and revolutionary practitioner or a Romantic idealist" (p. 15). She provides the examples of Richard Schechner's and Michael Taussig's diverging perspectives, with the former identifying Boal as a post-modernist who refuses to offer solutions to social problems, and the latter indicting Boal for being a traditional humanist who believes that human nature has the power to transcend cultural differences (p. 116). Nicholson goes on to suggest that it is Boal's relationship to the work of Freire which is most relevant to "those with an interest in applying Boal's theatrical strategies to pedagogical encounters" (pp. 116–117).

From an Indigenous perspective, Boal's relationship to Freire's pedagogy of the oppressed is problematic because of the missionary undertone of its Marxist-inflected emancipatory discourse. In "Theatre as Suture: Grassroots Performance, Decolonization and Healing," Qwo-Li Driskill (2008) articulates a critique of the *Theatre of the Oppressed* methodology within the context of

Indigenous communities—a critique based on seven years of experience as an activist. While acknowledging that the *Theatre of the Oppressed* model benefits from "the radical and transformational possibilities in Freire," Driskill argues that "it also inherits a missionary history and approach in which Freire's work is implicated" (p. 159). Highlighting the alphabetic literacy projects that were key to Freire's activism, Driskill states that "while certainly alphabetic literacy is often an important survival skill for the oppressed, the teaching of literacy is also deeply implicated in colonial and missionary projects" (p. 158). In light of the violent history of Canadian residential schools that severed Aboriginal children from their families and uprooted them from their ancestral culture and native land, Driskill contends that "it makes sense for Native People to be critically wary of Freireian work," and stresses: "Many of the concepts that Freire asserts in regards to pedagogical approaches— community-specific models that differ from the 'banking model' of education, for instance—are already present in many of our traditional pedagogies" (pp. 158–159).

This critique is furthered by C. A. Bowers and Frédérique Apffel-Marglin (2005), editors of *Rethinking Freire: Globalization and the Environmental Crisis*, who state in the introduction that, according to Third World activists who tested the pedagogy of the oppressed in their work with specific communities, Freire's approach is "based on Western assumptions that undermine indigenous knowledge systems" (p. vii). They hence suggest that the emancipatory vision associated with such an approach is grounded in "the same assumptions that underlie the planetary citizenship envisioned by the neoliberals promoting the Western model of global development" (pp. vii–viii). Bowers (2005) later contends that it is urgent to acknowledge that Freire's emancipatory discourse is "based on earlier metaphorical constructions that did not take into account the fact that the fate of humans is dependent on the viability of natural systems" and that the preservation of biodiversity and "the recovery of the environment and community" are dependent on a nuanced understanding of the function and value of traditions (pp. 140, 143).

Questioning Freire's conviction that the individual can and should be freed by critical thinking from the weight of tradition,

Bowers (2005) argues that such a view is linked to conceptions of self-determination that emerged from the Industrial Revolution in Europe (p. 139). He suggests that this kind of individualism isolates members of a society by replacing "wisdom refined over generations of collective experience" with consumer-oriented culture and new technologies upon which everyone becomes increasingly dependent (pp. 140–141). Bowers contrasts intergenerational knowledge, which is community-based, with technology-driven hyperconsumerism that promotes a "world monoculture based on the more environmentally destructive characteristics of the Western mind-set" (p. 145). Having specified that he intends neither to romanticize traditional knowledge nor to discount critical inquiry, he provides the example of an Indigenous community in British Columbia whose elders "spent two years discussing how the adoption of computers would change the basic fabric of their community," suggesting that while they were engaged in critical reflection, this discussion was framed "within a knowledge system that highlighted traditions of moral reciprocity within the community—with 'community' being understood as including other living systems of their bioregion" (p. 189).

Finally, in "Red Pedagogy: The Un-methodology," Sandy Grande (2008) foregrounds the anthropocentric dimension of Marxism and posits that, while "the quest for indigenous sovereignty [is] tied to issues of *land*, Western constructions of democracy are tied to issues of *property*" (p. 243). She points out that what is at stake for revolutionary theorists is the egalitarian distribution of economic power and exchange, and asks: *"How does the 'egalitarian distribution' of colonized lands constitute greater justice for indigenous people?"* (p. 243, emphasis in original). Grande further remarks that although Marx was a critic of capitalism, he shared many of its deep cultural assumptions, such as a secular faith in progress and modernity, and the belief that traditional knowledge, a connection to one's ancestral land, and spirituality based on one's relationship to the natural world were to be dismissed as the worthless relics of a pre-modern era. Moreover, while Marx emphasized human agency by invoking the power of human beings to change their social condition, an anti-deterministic view which has greatly contributed to the development of revolutionary movements and struggles for self-determination among oppressed and colonized peoples, Grande (2008) concurs with Bowers's critique of Freire by stating that Marxism "reinscribes the colonialist logic that conscripts 'nature' to the service of human society" (p. 248).

While it is undeniable that Boal's approach has been as influential in political theatre practice as Freire's has been in radical critical pedagogy, the absence of a discussion of alternative conceptions of performance and the singling out of the Boalian theatrical paradigm by scholars in the humanities and social sciences result in making it a default position which serves as the sole model of critical pedagogical theatre. Although my performance training is Grotowski-based, I was fortunate to meet Boal during a brief but engaging Theatre of Images workshop held at the University of Southern California in 2003, and I was touched by his kindness and generosity, and impressed by his energy and commitment. I am therefore not advocating Grotowski over Boal, but suggesting instead that what Grotowski and his collaborators propose may open up different possibilities for performance research and pedagogy.

Applying Indigenous Research Principles to *Meetings with Remarkable Women*

I will now turn to my embodied research on women artists belonging to a small transnational community of experimental performance practitioners whose work reflects the endurance of Grotowski's legacy. As the first investigation of women's contributions to this community, this project, titled *Meetings with Remarkable Women* and supported by two major grants from the Social Sciences and Humanities Research Council of Canada, provides insight into the teaching and creative research of Grotowski's key women collaborators. The main research outcomes are my monograph, titled *Grotowski, Women, and Contemporary Performance: Meetings with Remarkable Women* (Magnat, 2013) and the companion documentary films I created in close collaboration with these artists, featured on the Routledge Performance Archive.

While my intention was to invite performance studies scholars and theatre practitioners to reassess the significance of Grotowski's legacy for contemporary performance, I also wanted to make my interdisciplinary approach relevant to scholars in the humanities and social sciences whose research on the performative dimension of cultural processes has become increasingly focused on experiential cognition, embodiment, and creativity. My main objective for this book, therefore, was to strike a balance between practice and theory by foregrounding the dialogical relationship between scholarly and artistic modes of knowledge production.

In light of the dominance of the Boalian performance paradigm in the academy, examining recent critiques of Freire's and Boal's respective approaches was instrumental to my research for two main reasons: first, because Marxist-inflected discourse tends to conflate spirituality with false consciousness, hence making it impossible to apprehend the post-theatrical approaches to performance developed by the women involved in my project, since they often cross the boundaries of aesthetic and ritual performance; second, because such a discourse supports the fraught relationship to nature that we have inherited from the Enlightenment. In contrast, the physically-based performance training taught by the women artists involved in my project sustains an interconnection between the organicity of the human body and the organicity of the natural world, so that the relationship to nature fostered thereby constitutes a material and embodied experience of spirituality. Linking the Indigenous critique of Boal to the environmentalist critique of Freire has therefore enabled me to address the limitations of the dominant performance paradigm in qualitative research, and to propose alternatives based on an ecological understanding of performance, in the broader sense of ecology articulated by Indigenous scholars.

Moreover, I needed to overcome a major methodological obstacle, namely, the gap that separates performance scholars from performance *practitioners* within the field of performance studies. This institutionalized separation has been described by Dwight Conquergood (2002) as a counterproductive "academic apartheid" (p. 153) and defined by Shannon Jackson (2004) as an insidious "division of labor" privileging those who think over those who do (p. 111). Such an entrenched practice/theory divide severely undermines research projects whose methodology requires building relationships with artists based on trust, respect, and reciprocity. In *Research Is Ceremony*, Cree scholar Shawn

Wilson (2008) points to a similar disjunction between Western and Indigenous scholars:

> As part of their white privilege, there is no requirement for [dominant system academics] to be able to see other ways of being and doing, or even to recognize that they exist. Oftentimes, then, ideas coming from a different worldview are outside their entire mindset and way of thinking. The ability to bridge this gap becomes important in order to ease the tension that it creates. (p. 44)

While Indigenous research principles are designed by and for Indigenous scholars and activists working within their own communities, Wilson observes: "So much the better if dominant universities and researchers adopt them as well" (p. 59). I have found these principles to be more pertinent to my research process than the methodologies developed by those whom Wilson identifies as "dominant system academics."

Pursuing this project has therefore led me to walk in the footsteps of feminist and Indigenous scholars, and I drew inspiration from the courageous ways in which they position themselves reflexively within their research process, and discuss how their double and often multiple consciousness provides insights into what is at stake in that process. Significantly, Indigenous ethical research principles have guided me throughout the writing process, requiring me to strive for reciprocity, relevance, and accessibility as I developed a range of writing strategies to engage with questions pertaining to positionality, lived experience, and embodied ways of knowing.

Accounting for What Is at Stake

Prior to my meetings with Grotowski's foremost women collaborators, I wondered how working with these artists and learning about their experiences might inform and transform my perspective of and relationship to a type of performance training that had been important to me as a young woman for a number of reasons. What I felt was most valuable about the experience I had with my Paris-based group led by actors who had trained with Ludwik Flaszen and Zygmunt Molik, two key founding members of Grotowski's Laboratory Theatre, were the ways in which this work stretched in a literal and figurative sense the boundaries of what was defined as theatre in my culture. For the creative process activated by this work was intensely engaging: although the training was quite challenging, it provided me with a deep sense of psychophysical fulfillment, a feeling of being fully alive which I had never experienced in my previous theatre training.

Situating my embodied research at the intersection of performance studies, cultural anthropology, and Indigenous epistemologies, I conducted four years of multi-sited fieldwork in Poland, Italy, France, Denmark, and Canada. My bearing witness to the consistency of these women's testimonies and to the vitality of their on-going engagement in creative research compelled me to consider them in light of their accomplishments rather than as the disenfranchised Others of a performance tradition whose legacy appears to remain anxiously guarded by its male inheritors. Consequently, I became increasingly interested in the implications of women's independent creative research beyond dominant notions of artistic merit that pertain to the evaluation of more conventional performance models. The stakes are high for these artists who have taken the risk to commit to their passion and follow their aspirations, drawing energy, courage, and determination from their experience with Grotowski, without letting the latter weigh them down or deter them from moving forward.

Perhaps most significantly, these women have succeeded in maintaining a sense of integrity in their work that is also reflected in their lives, which follow the principles of their creative research through the rejection of social conformism and normative gender roles. Indeed, they resolutely reject any kind of categorization that might limit, constrain, or stultify what they envision as the human creative potential. However, they do not align themselves or identify with post-structuralist feminist theory, so that my project confronts what Luke Eric Lassiter (2005) describes as "the gap between academically-positioned and community-positioned narratives," grounded in concerns about the politics of representation; that is to say, concerns "about who has the right to represent whom and for what purposes, and about whose discourse will be privileged in the ethnographic text" (p. 4). While extremely empowering for women scholars, the feminist critique of essentialist representations of gender is itself a construction informed by a particular way of positioning oneself, which contains its own limitations. It seems impossible, for instance, to argue against biological determinism while simultaneously being engaged in forms of practice-based research that foreground embodied experience and generate alternative conceptions of what constitutes knowledge.

Furthermore, the artists who participated in my project often anchor their creative research in traditional cultural practices that can provide access to embodied experiences of spirituality. In a number of these cultural practices, health, or wellbeing, is experienced as a form of balance between human and non-human sources of life. Such practices have existed around the world for thousands of years, yet their spiritual dimension is something which, when not simply dismissed as a form of false consciousness, is left entirely unexamined by post-structuralist analyses of cultural processes, and I have found in Indigenous research methodologies alternative theoretical frameworks that are inclusive of spirituality.

Embodying the Ecological Dimension of Performance

I argue in my book that the ecosystemic performance paradigm underlying the post-theatrical performance practices developed by women in the Grotowski diaspora points to alternative conceptions of creativity, embodiment, and spirituality that challenge anthropocentric and gendered conceptions of agency. Indeed, these artists envision the body-in-life as a microcosm of the ecosystemic organization of the natural environment and convey through their teaching that it is possible to experience the human organism "as if" it were a natural ecosystem regulated by energy flow and animated by a self-perpetuating and self-restoring form of life with a capacity for open-ended evolution. This is reflected in their creative work by the importance of connection to space/place as well as by the fluidity of the notion of organicity which, for them, encompasses all forms of life, human and non-human. Interestingly, this ecosystemic conception of organicity is supported by the scientific speculation that human life and natural ecosystems share fundamental features, as discussed by environmental biologist Daniel A. Fiscus (2001) in "The Ecosystemic Life Hypothesis."

Cree performer and writer Floyd Favel, who shared with me his experience of working with Rena Mirecka, a founding member of Grotowski's Laboratory Theatre and the eldest woman in my project, suggested during my interview with him that the ultimate purpose of this type of performance training should be to make practitioners feel balanced, in the sense of physical and mental well-being. Within the specific context of his culture and community, Favel highlighted a point of convergence between performance and tradition by relating the function of performance to that of traditional practices and rituals. He suggested that the training transmitted by Mirecka fulfilled a specific need pertaining to the shortcomings of modern living and its negative impact on people's mental and physical health. Favel hence pointed to a lack of balance that also manifests itself in the ecological crisis that may be interpreted as resulting directly from industrial and technological development in service of capitalist productivity. Indigenous scholars observe that destroying the environment is a form of self-destruction, and foreground the interconnectedness of human beings and all other forms of life, a principle which Hawaiian scholar Manulani Aluli Meyer (2008; 2013) argues is fundamental to Indigenous epistemologies. This is echoed by Kenneth J. Gergen (2009), who contends in *Relational Being: Beyond Self and Community* that a sustainable relationship between human beings and the natural world is critical to the survival of all forms of life on earth: "To understand the world in which we live as constituted by independent species, forms, types, or entities is to threaten the well-being of the planet. ... Whatever value we place upon ourselves and others, and whatever hope we may have for the future, depends on the welfare of relationship" (p. 396). This compelling notion of welfare as relational, which Gergen associates with the well-being of the planet, supports an ecosystemic view of our relationship to the environment which has become increasingly informed by Indigenous ecological knowledge.

Linda Tuhiwai Smith (2002) hence states in *Decolonizing Methodologies* that

> indigenous communities have something to offer to the non-indigenous world [such as] indigenous peoples' ideas and beliefs about the origins of the world, their explanations of the environment, often embedded in complicated metaphors and mythic tales [which] are now sought as the basis for thinking more laterally about current theories about the environment, the earth and the universe. (p. 159)

Smith points to the strategic essentialism that characterizes the way in which Indigenous peoples have managed, in spite of colonial epistemic violence, to preserve an embodied knowledge of their identity, which is rooted in the land of their ancestors. She specifies that, although "claiming essential characteristics is as much strategic as anything else, because it has been about claiming human rights and indigenous rights . . . the essence of a person is also discussed in relation to indigenous concepts of spirituality" (p. 74). Indigenous perspectives are thus informed by "arguments of different indigenous peoples based on spiritual relationships to the universe, to the landscape and to stones, rocks, insects and other things, seen and unseen," which, she remarks, "have been difficult arguments for Western systems of knowledge to deal with or accept" (p. 74). She asserts that this place-based conception of identity and the spiritual dimension of its relationship to the natural environment "give a partial indication of the different world views and alternative ways of coming to know, and of being, which still endure within the indigenous world [and which are] critical sites of resistance for indigenous peoples" (p. 72). Honoring Indigenous worldviews that colonial powers attempt to systematically suppress therefore constitutes a fundamental aspect of the healing process fostered by Indigenous research and pedagogy. Performance, which is vital to the embodied transmission of traditional knowledge, sustains cultural and spiritual identity through material practice, thereby significantly contributing to this healing process, as argued by Favel.

Relating Cultural Continuity to Ecosystemic Balance

The women in my project often work with traditional songs as an embodied cultural practice informed by the specificity of place. According to Grotowski, what keeps a song alive is the particular vibratory quality linked to the precision of the song's structure, so that it is necessary to search for the vocal and physical score inscribed within each particular song. When a competent performer actively and attentively embodies a traditional song, it can become a vehicle that reconnects her or him to those who first sang the song. If ancestral embodied knowledge is encoded in traditional songs, and if the power of these songs hinges upon the embodied experience of singing them, then trusting that the body can remember how to sing, as if traces of this ancient knowledge had been preserved in the body memory, can become a way of recovering that knowledge and reclaiming cultural continuity.

Driskill (2008) might be referring to a similar process when writing about learning to sing a Cherokee lullaby:

> As someone who did not grow up speaking my language or any traditional songs and who is currently in the process of reclaiming those traditions—as are many Native people in North America—the process of relearning this lullaby was and is integral to my own decolonial process. The performance context provided me an opportunity to relearn and perform a traditional song, a major act in intergenerational healing and cultural continuance. As I sang this lullaby during rehearsals and performance, I imagined my ancestors witnessing from the corners of the theatre, helping me in the healing and often painful work of suture. (p. 164)

The relationship between performance, embodiment, and cultural continuance expressed here by Driskill points to a creative agency which is intimately linked to lived experience and yet which is not limited to or defined by a single individual perspective.

Indigenous scholars consider embodiment to be key to self-knowledge, and Meyer (2008) affirms that "the body is the *central* space from which knowing is embedded" and stresses that "our body holds truth, our body invigorates knowing, our body helps us become who we are. ... Our thinking body is not separated from our feeling mind. *Our mind is our body. Our body is our mind.* And both connect to the spiritual act of knowledge acquisition" (p. 223, emphasis in original). For the Hawaiian people, cultural continuity vitally depends on performance-based practices such as ritual chanting and dancing, that is to say, trans-generational embodied modes of transmission ensuring the type of spiritual continuity that sustains Hawaiian identity and cultural sovereignty.

While highlighting the specificity of traditional ways of knowing, Meyer contends that Hawaiian epistemology is relevant and valuable beyond the confines of its geographical and cultural boundaries. She posits an Indigenous conception of universality based on the notion that it is specificity that leads to universality. She defines the latter as hinging upon "respect and honoring of

distinctness" and ties it to Hawaiian Elder Halemakua's provocative statement *"We are all indigenous"* (p. 230, emphasis in original).
Fending off potential controversies, Meyer cautions that "to take
this universal idea into race politics strips it of its truth" (p. 231).
The notion of Indigeneity evoked by Halemakua and supported
by Meyer is grounded in a place-specific understanding of universality predicated on the interrelation of land and self, experience
and spirituality, embodiment and knowledge. Meyer, therefore,
proposes to redefine epistemology as necessarily linked to direct
experience and to a "culturally formed sensuality."

In the ecosystemic performance paradigm I have begun to
articulate, the body-voice connection epitomizes the interrelation of embodiment, place, and experiential cognition, since the
vibratory qualities of the voice depend on the resonance of both
body and space, or body and place. Speaking about his research
on ancient vibratory songs, Grotowski (2001) states:

> As one says in a French expression, 'Tu es le fils de quelqu'un'
> [You are someone's son]. You are not a vagabond, you come from
> somewhere, from some country, from some place, from some
> landscape. ... Because he who began to sing the first words was
> someone's son, from somewhere, from some place, so, if you
> refind this, you are someone's son. [If you don't,] you are cut off,
> sterile, barren. (p. 304)

He suggests that these songs may reconnect us not only to
those who first sang them but also to the natural environment in
which these songs were created, for people living in the mountains
had different ways of singing than people living in the valleys, and
traces of these places therefore subsist in the modes of transmission
of traditional songs (p. 304). Meyer also links identity, lineage, and
place when she writes: "You came from a place. You grew in a place
and you had a relationship with that place. ... Land is more than
just a physical place. ... It is the key that turns the doors inward
to reflect on how space shapes us" (p. 219). She goes on to cite
Halemakua, who states: "At one time, we all came from a place
familiar with our evolution and storied with our experiences. At
one time, we all had a rhythmic understanding of time and potent
experiences of harmony in space" (in Meyer, p. 231).

Significantly, Wilson (2008) observes in *Research Is Ceremony*
that, from an Indigenous perspective, "knowledge itself is held

in the relationships and connections formed with the environment that surrounds us" (p. 87). He notes that relationships made with people and relationships made with the environment are equally sacred, and defines knowledge of the environment as the pedagogy of place (p. 87). He remarks that experiencing place as relational and sacred is key "within many Indigenous peoples' spirituality," and concludes that "bringing things together so that they share the same space is what ceremony is all about" (p. 87). For the women in my project, bringing people and things together within a shared space is, to some extent, what defines their creative work, whether that shared space be an enclosed workspace or the open space of our natural environment. Through their ongoing engagement in this kind of creative research, these artists support an alternative approach in which cultural, traditional, and ritual practices significantly contribute to sustaining health, or well-being, experienced as ecosystemic balance between all forms of life.

Coda: Changing the Spirit of Research and Pedagogy

Indigenous conceptions of knowledge, embodiment, experience, and spirituality have important implications for research and pedagogy. Meyer (2008) hence contends that researchers should acknowledge that "objectivity is a subjective idea that cannot possibly describe the all of our experience" (p. 226), and urges them to "expand [their] repertoire of writers and thinkers" in order to overcome "the limitations of predictable research methodologies." She therefore challenges researchers to have the maturity to seek "what most scholars refuse to admit exists: *spirit*" (p. 228, emphasis in original). In her discussion of 'spirit,' Meyer cautions her readers not to confuse the category of spirit with religion, since Hawaiian elders speak of spirit with regard to intelligence (p. 218). Describing 'spirit' as that which gives "a structure of rigor" to research, she specifies that it is "the contemplation part of your work that brings you to insight, steadiness, and interconnection. … It is understanding an unexpected experience that will heighten the clarity of your findings" (p. 229). She states that "knowing is bound to how we develop a *relationship* with it," which leads her to posit that "*knowing is embodied* and in union with cognition," and that *"genuine knowledge must be experienced directly"* (p. 224, emphasis in original). This is also a fundamental aspect of Grotowski's conception of embodiment that his women collaborators continue to uphold in their own creative research and their teaching. By promoting in their work a search for balance between human and non-human life, and by privileging experiential ways of knowing grounded in an ecology of the body-in-life, these artists challenge conventional notions of artistic production and provide alternatives to anthropocentric conceptions of creative agency.

Embodied experience, spirituality, and relationship to the natural world are fundamental to Indigenous conceptions of knowledge. According to Native Canadian, Hawaiian, Maori, and American Indian pedagogy, "the central crisis is spiritual, 'rooted in the increasingly virulent relationship between human beings and the rest of nature'" (Grande, 2008, p. 354). In response to this crisis, Indigenous activists propose a "respectful performance pedagogy [that] works to construct a vision of the person, ecology, and environment" compatible with Indigenous worldviews. Meyer further contends that it is necessary to be changed by one's research in order to change the culture of research, and encourages researchers to reflect on the implications of their work for their own lives, and to ask themselves: "Are the ideas learned by doing research something I *practiced* today? Truly, why do research if it doesn't guide us into enlightened action? Is the vision I hold in my heart something I extend in all directions?" (2013, p. 254, emphasis in original). From such a perspective, research should not be conceived as a competition for knowledge between individuals striving for academic recognition, but as a relational process dependent on mutual trust, collaboration, and healing.

Since the call of Indigenous scholars to change research from within the academy can be perceived as an impossible task, it is helpful to be reminded by Bagele Chilisa (2012) that it is precisely because "all research is appropriation" that the way in which it is conducted always has consequences. She points out that when "benefits accrue to both the communities researched and the researcher," conducting research can be reconfigured as a two-way transformative process which she identifies as "reciprocal appropriation" (p. 22). Learning from each other how to respectfully engage in reciprocal appropriation might thus enable us to envision the research process as part of a larger collective journey. In her book *Kaandossiwin: How We Come to Know,* Kathleen E. Absolon (Minogiizhigokwe) (2011) describes Indigenous ways of searching for knowledge by stating: "We journey, we search, we converse, we gather, we harvest, we make meaning, we do, we create, we transform, and we share what we know. Our Spirit walks with us on these journeys. Our ancestors accompany us" (p. 168). She stresses that "the academy is being pressured to create space for Indigenous forms of knowledge production, and change is occurring," which leads her to contend: "Without a doubt we continue to establish channels to have an impact on making Indigenous ways of knowing, being, and doing a solid method-ological choice within the academy" (p. 167). Working together to create space for such epistemological and methodological pos-sibilities in the academy might therefore result in collaborations between Indigenous and non-Indigenous researchers that can generate alternative conceptions of research and pedagogy, and foster new embodied engagements and experiential solidarities.

References

Absolon (Minogiizhigokwe), K. E. (2011). *Kaandossiwin: How we come to know.* Halifax and Winnipeg, Canada: Fernwood.

Boal, A. (1996). The theatre as discourse. In M. Huxley and N. Witts (Eds.), *The twentieth-century performance reader* (pp. 80–92). London: Routledge.

Bowers, C.A. (2005). How the ideas of Paulo Freire contribute to the cul-tural roots of the ecological crisis. In C.A. Bowers and F. Apffel-Marglin (Eds.), *Rethinking Freire: Globalization and the environmental crisis* (pp. 133–150). Mahwah, NJ: Lawrence Erlbaum.

Bowers, C.A., & Apffel-Marglin, F. (Eds.) (2005). *Rethinking Freire: Globalization and the environmental crisis.* Mahwah, NJ: Lawrence Erlbaum.

Chilisa, B. (2012). *Indigenous research methodologies.* Thousand Oaks, CA: Sage.

Conquergood, D. (2002). Performance studies: Interventions and radical research. *TDR T174 , (Summer),* 145–156.

Denzin, N. K. (2003). *Performance ethnography: Critical pedagogy and the politics of culture.* Thousand Oaks, CA: Sage.

Denzin, N. K., Lincoln, Y.S., & Smith, L. T. (Eds.) (2008). *Handbook of critical and Indigenous methodologies.* Thousand Oaks, CA: Sage.

Driskill, Q. (2008). Theatre as suture: Grassroots performance, decolonization and healing. In R. Hulan & R. Eigenbrod (Eds.), *Aboriginal oral traditions: Theory, practice, ethics* (pp. 155–168). Halifax and Winnipeg, Canada: Fernwood.

Fiscus, D. A. (2001). The ecosystemic life hypothesis I: Introduction and definitions. *Bulletin of the Ecological Society of America, 82*(4), 248–250.

Fiscus, D. A. (2002a). The ecosystemic life hypothesis II: Four connected concepts. *Bulletin of the Ecological Society of America, 83*(1), 94–96.

Fiscus, D. A. (2002b). The ecosystemic life hypothesis III: The hypothesis and its implications. *Bulletin of the Ecological Society of America, 83*(2), 146–149.

Gergen, K. J. (2009). *Relational being: Beyond self and community.* New York: Oxford University Press.

Grande S. (2008). Red pedagogy: The un-methodology. In N. K. Denzin, Y. S. Lincoln, & L. T. Smith (Eds.), *Handbook of critical and Indigenous methodologies* (pp. 233–254). Thousand Oaks, CA : Sage.

Grotowski, J. (2001). Tu es le fils de quelqu'un. In R. Schechner & L. Wolford (Eds.), *The Growtoski sourcebook* (p. 304). New York: Routledge.

Ionesco, E. (1963). *Les chaises; L'impromptu de l'Alma; Tueur sans gages.* Paris: Gallimard.

Ionesco, E. (1967). *Journal en Miettes.* Paris: Gallimard.

Jackson, S. (2004). *Professing performance: Theatre in the academy from philology to performativity.* Cambridge, UK: Cambridge University Press.

Lassiter, L. E. (2005). *The Chicago guide to collaborative ethnography.* Chicago: University of Chicago Press.

Magnat, V. (2013). *Grotowski, women, and contemporary performance: Meetings with remarkable women.* London and New York: Routledge.

Meyer, M. A. (2008). Indigenous and authentic: Hawaiian epistemology and the triangulation of meaning. In N. K. Denzin, Y. S. Lincoln, & L. T. Smith (Eds.), *Handbook of critical and Indigenous methodologies* (pp. 217–232). Thousand Oaks, CA: Sage.

Meyer, M.A. (2013). The context within: My journey into research. In D. M. Mertens, B. Chilisa, & F. Cram (Eds.), *Indigenous pathways in social research.* Walnut Creek, CA: Left Coast Press, Inc.

Nicholson, H. (2005). *Applied drama: Theatre and performance practices.* New York: Palgrave Macmillan.

Smith, L. T. (2002). *Decolonizing methodologies: Research and Indigenous peoples.* London: Zed Books.

Wilson, S. (2008). *Research is ceremony: Indigenous research methods.* Halifax and Winnipeg, Canada: Fernwood.

Chapter 13

(Re)Membering the Grandmothers

Theorizing Poetry to (Re)Think the Purposes of Black Education and Research

Cynthia B. Dillard
(Nana Mansa II of Mpeasem, Ghana)

Introduction

> ...the canvas rejoices
> in the extraordinary nature
> of yourself...
> when it is done
> the world knows
> you are here.
>
> —Marita Golden (1986, *Self Portrait*, p. 138)

The knowledge and presence, the gifts and wisdom of African world women, although too seldom recognized as "scholarly" or important, are fundamental to addressing the historical, cultural, and social needs of our increasingly troubled world today. The need for a (re)telling. The need for a (re)creating. The need for a (re)membering. The need for a (re)visioning. And in this (re)structuring, one thing is very clear: there is a fine line between theory, as explanations or principles guiding thought and action, and poetry. I am suggesting, as Audre Lorde (1984) has before me, that there is not an inherent conflict between theory and poetry. That, by definition,

Qualitative Inquiry Outside the Academy edited by Norman K. Denzin and Michael D. Giardina, 253–267. © 2014 Left Coast Press, Inc. All rights reserved.

they are not ruled by the mind and ruled by the soul respectively, but instead have been framed as such to advance traditionally racist and sexist agendas. Certainly African world women share problems and issues particular to being female with European and other world women. However, fundamental to this discussion is an assumption grounded both in critical race scholarship and endarkened/Black feminist theory, that is, that there are also realities, understandings, and responses which are particularly African and female, common amongst women of African descent throughout the diaspora. And it is that coming together of race and gender—of being African and being female—that I explore here in an effort to illuminate those ways in which educational perspectives, institutions, and the broader society can learn and be informed by our understandings. The power of our biographies and experiences convinces me that poetry is a way to affirm our lives and that it embodies our theory. Considered in this way, African world women's voices might be seen as an impetus for (re)visioning a more just and humane way of educating and engaging in qualitative inquiry.

In this chapter, I am arguing that personal narratives, as both (re)search tools and as "data," are critical in our work as academics and teachers. I'm not suggesting some sort of unsystematic way of searching for "truth" but instead a disciplined attention to the true meaning of "it feels right to me" (Lorde, 1984, p. 38). For as Lorde further suggests: "There is a Black mother within each one of us. [She is] the poet. [She] whispers in our dreams, '*I feel, therefore I can be free*'" (p. 38, emphasis mine).

Poetry and the creative expressions of African world women embody the language to express, to move, to demand, to revolutionize, and to implement that freedom. So it "feels right to me" to name, to speak, to share the works and worlds of my African sisters on the continent and in the diaspora, even at the risk of having these understandings misunderstood or of making folks uncomfortable. For, as Lorde suggests, silence has not protected me as a Black woman in the world, and it will not protect others. For it is only when we name it that we can think upon it. And it is only when it can be thought upon that it can be acted upon.

When I talk about poetry, I lean on Lorde (1984) for a definition. She states that poetry, from an African woman's perspective, is "a revelatory distillation of experience not the sterile word play that White men distorted the word to mean in order to cover a desperate wish for imagination without insight" (p. 37). In this way, for African women throughout the world, poetry is *not* a luxury. *Our poetry is our theory; our poetry is our life.* It's the place where we put our hopes and fears and anger and joy and it's the way of survival and change. It is both an individual way and a collective way, and we tell of this way in our words, our ideas, and our actions, grounded in ways African, whether we are conscious of those ways or not (Dillard, 2012).

Although Black world women have always been important to the structures and relationships within our communities, at the same time, we have too often been rendered invisible and silent by racism and by sexism. Since the onslaught of colonization, slavery, and the intentional and brutal acts of destruction against us, African world women share two common understandings, grounded in this collective history. First, *we understand that we were not meant to survive,* not as full human beings. So in having done so, it is important to (re)cognize that the abilities, talents, and theories (which have served as habits of being and survival) are strong and they are powerful. They need to be heard, so as to inform those seeking to survive in the world today. Secondly, for Black women throughout the world, *we understand the paramount need to define ourselves for ourselves.* For not to do so is to be defined by others for their use and to our demise. It is exactly these two common understandings, garnered through our collective histories and experiences as woman of Africa, that we can, from a critical perspective, very ably see, feel, and ultimately address these destructive forces in contemporary world societies. For women who have stood outside the circle of the world's traditional definition of "acceptable" women know that survival is not an academic skill: it is what some call women's wit or mother wit. And, as Lorde (1984) suggests, the master's tools will never dismantle the master's house. The dismantling—and I would argue the (re)building—of a new house arises from gazing at phenomena in ways different. In this chapter, that gaze is from an African and female perspective. It is intended to unsettle, maybe even make angry. It is intended to turn the lenses around, to examine and challenge, to "dig ourselves up," as Jayne Cortez (1990) has said. It is intended to push us to think in ways that may be revolutionary.

I can (re)member as a young girl growing up in the south end of Seattle. Like most Black children, whether in Africa, South and Central America, or the United States, I learned what it meant to be a Black woman in the company of Black women, as they created what bell hooks (1990) calls 'homeplace.' Homeplace is that place where one comes to be affirmed, to recapture the self-respect and dignity battled daily in a White supremacist society. It's that safe place where we come to restore our pride as African people. In my own experience of homeplace, the language of African women was so rich, poetic, and alive that it always beckoned me. I wanted to talk, to have a space and a voice in this beautiful creation of words and of the world. So I talked, darting in and out of grown folks' conversations, looking for any opportunity to jump in and to be heard. And I (re)member all too vividly when my mother would shoot me one of those glances that let me know I had violated an unspoken rule: I had "talked too much." And as I (re)collect these experiences, I see now that her glances came as a warning to let me know that I had interrupted the conversation that was intended to teach, intended to shape my own understandings and meanings as a Black girl: The story. The telling of stories, a well-documented way of living for African people, is often carried out by African women providing not only a continuity of culture from the ancestors to the descendents, but to ground and (re)vitalize our communities, and to share the responsibility of leadership within our homeplaces. However, often unrecognized is the role of African women throughout the diaspora to also use the story as a tool for critically questioning the values and history of African culture, as well as to explore the impact of the collective past on our current and future generations (Aidoo, 1977). This is the data and analysis that I share here, in honor to those African women everywhere who provided this wisdom. I share these stories in the hope that we can shift the ideology and the stance from in which we do our work to one that ultimately transforms our own educational theory and practice.

I want to share several understandings garnered from African continental and diasporic poets who provide what Aidoo (1977) calls our "black-eyed squint" on matters of education. This black-eyed squint of African women comes through having developed ways of being, living, and surviving in a world intent upon our demise. These habits of survival are the ways African women adjust and adapt to on-going economic, gender, and racial oppression. Although such habits might initially be responses to pain and suffering that help us to lessen anger and bitterness, they often serve as means of self-definition, self control, maybe ways to offer explanation and even hope. Sometimes these habits over time can also serve as outdated responses and unexamined traditions. I am suggesting that simple habits of survival are not enough: in order to be liberated and to critically gaze upon and change oppressive educational systems and mind sets, *conscious* choices must be made as to the pluses and minuses of such habits. As choice is the key to liberation, these diaspora voices, from a black-eyed [female] squint, provide a way to view education and liberation from a different perspective, perhaps a deeper consciousness that encourages our socio-political empowerment, particularly in education. The following are three central calls that are issued and examined through the voices of African world women and their lived poetry.

Three Powerful Calls for Educational Change

Call I: African World Women Say:

"Education and Inquiry Begins with Wholeness."
Are you sure you want to be well?... Just so's you're sure, sweetheart, and ready to be healed cause wholeness is no trifling matter, A lot of weight when you're well ... Release, sweetheart. Give it all up. Forgive everyone everything. Free them. Free self.
—Bambara (1980, pp. 10–18)

Seeking wholeness is the beginning of education, the very fundamental need of any humanity. As Lorde (1984) suggests:

> My fullest concentration of energy is available to me only when I integrate all parts of who I am, openly, allowing power from particular sources of my living to flow back and forth freely through all my different selves, without the restrictions of externally imposed definitions. Only then can I bring myself and my energies as a whole to the service of those struggles which I embrace as part of my living. (pp. 120–121)

Such wholeness begins with self-reflection, in (re)membering our individual and collective histories, as women of Africa, including that which transcends national boundaries and reflects a cultural lineage beyond even familial ancestry (Dillard, 2012; Dillard & Okpalaoka, 2012). Gates (1988) calls this way of being a "self-reflective tradition, reassembling the fragments [of the diaspora] that contain the traces of a coherent system of order" (p. xxiv). Both in the stories we tell and in the telling itself, we attempt to gain a sense of who we are by (re)assembling the fragments of ourselves and our past, rendering the implicit as explicit, and thus creating the dialectic necessary to critically examine and (re)construct our present and future lives. My Ghanaian sister, Abena P. A. Busia (1992), speaks of how moving from our own ignorance of the brilliance of African history and culture can be liberatory, as we (re)assemble the pieces, in her poem *Liberation,* excerpted below:

> *...Ignorance*
> *Shattered us into such fragments...to recover with our own hands*
> *...We wondered how we could hold such treasure.* (p. 869)

The process of (re)assembly and (re)connection is particularly poignant for people and women of African heritage, as the legacy of the slave trade with Africa confronts us daily in the very existence of a diaspora. All of Europe, certainly the Americas, Britain, Holland, France, and even Africa herself can be implicated in this history. Meiling Jin's (1988) poem, *Strangers in a Hostile Landscape,* speaks to the ways in which colonization, coupled with religion, was a connected plot to benefit European and Western imperialism, in the excerpt below:

> *...But essentially, they were intent*
> *On making themselves rich...*
> *And at the same time,*
> *Sung psalms.*
> *Such sweet psalms.* (pp. 123–126)

Even against these plots, Black women have always engaged in a deep watching, seeking, and critical analysis that is the process of coming to wholeness, reconnecting fragments as the process of education and (re)search for freedom. This is our way to critical consciousness, to an expanded, multiple "whole" narrative of our individual and collective histories (and herstories). This is our way to become wholly and fully *ourselves*.

Call II: African World Women Say:

"Memory and History Are Crucial Sites of Resistance."

Gayl Jones (1975), in the book *Corregidora*, bears witness to the abuses of memory and history at the hands of those who were considered more powerful given guns, physical violence, and enslavement and other oppressive means. However, the narrative below is (re)membered by Ursa, the granddaughter of a Brazilian slavemaster:

> Old man Corregidora... They did the fucking and had to bring him the money they made. My grandmama was his daughter, but he was fucking her too. She said when they did away with slavery down there they burned all the slavery papers so it would be like they never had it... My great-grandmama told my grandmama the part she lived through... and my grandmama told my mama what they both lived through and we pass it down like that for generations so we'd never forget. Even though they'd burned everything to play like it didn't never happen. (pp. 10–11)

This narrative speaks to the ways that within White supremacist capitalist patriarchal societies, forgetfulness is encouraged (Dillard, 2012). As bell hooks (1992) states: "When people of color remember ourselves, remember the myriad ways our cultures and communities have been ravaged by white domination, we are often told by white peers that we are 'too bitter,' that we are 'full of hate'. Memory sustains a spirit of resistance" (p. 191). It is that very memory which can and has served as strength and courage for African world women; as Jones (1975, p. 72) speaks again through Ursa's mother: *"They burned all the documents, Ursa, but they didn't burn what they put in our minds."* She goes on to say something that is critical to the work of Black women (re)membering as an act of resistance. That we must not dare to forget these experiences, however traumatic and brutal: we must keep what we need to bear witness to those memories, as they continue to make an impact on today.

It is important to understand that engaging memory is a process of answering questions from both a particular and a collective standpoint. From what political place do you stand, upon whom do you stand, and on behalf of whom do you work? More importantly, who do you place in the center of your politics, of your educational inquiry (Dillard & Okpalaoka, 2012)? As part of an on-going struggle to (re)learn and (re)member my Africanness and my womanness, I choose to love Blackness as a conscious political act. I choose also to stand in memory and history of Black people as a place from which to resist. As bell hooks (1992) writes in the forward of *Black Looks: Race and Representation*:

> I dedicate this book to all of us who love blackness, who dare to create in our daily lives spaces of reconciliation and forgiveness where we let go of past hurt, fear, shame and hold each other close. It is only in the act and practice of loving blackness that we are able to reach out and embrace the world without destructive bitterness and ongoing collective rage. (p. 1)

Even just one line of Maya Angelou's well known poem, *Still I Rise* (1978), further shows us the power which personal and collective history and memory hold as catalysts for changing and shifting one's consciousness and perspective:

> *...Bringing the gifts that my ancestors gave*
> *I am the dream and the hope of the slave*
> *I rise*
> *I rise*
> *I rise.* (pp. 33–37)

You see, the politics and history of racial and sexual domination have necessarily created African women's realities that are distinctly different from European women's realities: from that place has emerged a distinct (albeit diverse) Black women's culture. But all too often, particularly in institutions of higher education, the call is for sameness, for homogeneity of view, regardless of experience and memory. However, collectively, African world women and other allies who vigilantly work to (re)member are empowered when we practice self-reflection and self-love as a revolutionary means of resistance to domination. African world women and other indigenous women of color deeply understand the nature of struggle over memory and interpretations of history and culture. Living in power hungry racist and sexist societies has taught us what it means to see education and inquiry as a spiritual, personal, intellectual, and ultimately social struggle towards freedom. As the practice of resistance, Alice Walker (1979) calls our work "stripping bark from [our] self" (p. 23). But, we also see that the issue of power is central to racist and sexist ideology and actions. Thus, our strength arises from developing the personal and social power that comes from questioning, from acting up, from jumping into conversations in order to learn the lessons vital to transforming structures and systems meant to oppress and to silence. So we raise questions like Sojourner Truth (1981) did in her poem, written in 1852: "Ain't I a woman?" (p. 38). We acknowledge, as Maud Sulter does (1992), that being Black and being female and choosing to embrace and act in the world from that place is inherently a political and powerful act of self and collective affirmation, spoken in this excerpt of her poem, *As a Blackwoman:*

> ...*As a Black woman*
>
> *Every act is a personal act*
>
> *Every act is a political act...*
>
> ...*Holds no empty rhetoric.* (p. 922)

The lack of "empty rhetoric" points to the esteemed and appreciated place in which African world women hold our roots: we hold them in our hearts and in our convictions. The strength of our convictions arises from (re)membering our current place, as African world women to all places before and all places to come. We ultimately define ourselves in order to transform the unjust uses of power against race and gender throughout the world. As Alice Walker (1992) says: "Resistance is the secret of joy" (p. 279). As women of African heritage, we are definitely raising a joyful noise.

Call III: African World Women Say:

"Education and Inquiry Must Serve to Name and to Voice."

Silence protects no one. I would argue, as do many African world women and others, that power is often enacted in words. In naming. In labeling. In describing. Words have been used to abuse African world women from the time in which time began, and certainly through our colonial history and neo-colonial present. What we have come to understand is that what is important *must* be spoken. It must be shared. But what we also understand intimately is that the transformation of silence and submissiveness into language (and ultimately to action) is one of the most dangerous acts that a Black woman can engage in. However, it is also an act of self-revelation, one which African world women have understood since time began, but which has only in recent history begun to be seen as valuable in broader world circles. These voicings, from Black women like Jamaican writer Christine Craig (1992) through her poem, *The Chain*, capture eloquently the ways in which language serves as an oppressive force in silence and a liberating force as African women begin to name our oppressions. The poem begins with Craig's description of how her grandmother and mother, out of necessity, kept their silence through demonstrations of deference and agreement. However, she ends the poem with this line, her clear voice of resistance:

...I no longer care, keeping close my silence
Has been a weight,
A lever pressing out my mind. (p. 555)

The belief in the singular power of our own words to "say the truth," to "right the world" as Sojourner Truth says, is also characteristic of African world women's voicings of resistance, as seen in Iyamide Hazeley's (1988) poem, *When You Have Emptied Our Calabashes*. In this piece, Hazeley speaks of how rebuilding for African women will be done through telling our stories and traditions, through (re)membering. Even these rather truncated lines show the power assigned to this task of (re)membering for Hazeley—and for Black women everywhere:

...To spit in the mouths/of the new born babies
so that they will remember/and be eloquent also
and learn well/the lessons of the past...
so that if you come again...
they will say
we know you. (p. 152)

The belief in the power of words to define one's own reality, according to Marcus (1984), shows us that culture (of which formal education should be a formative element) consists also in passing on the technique of its making. Further, she writes:

"Stories are made to be told, and songs to be sung. In the singing and the telling, they are changed. ... Transformation, rather than permanence, is at the heart of this aesthetic, as it is at the heart of most women's lives" (p. 85). These serve as an echo of Marita Golden's (1986) excerpted poem below, dedicated to two South African world women, Winnie Mandela and Mamphela Ramphela, entitled *A Woman's Place*:

> ...*What are words anyway*
> *But a way to discover*
> *What you can do*
> *What is living*
> *But the deed*
> *Finally done.* (pp. 210–211)

This poem is a reminder that although words and speaking serve as both warning and inspiration for African world women, they are also a deep source of power. And used in coalition and solidarity with others, such naming and voicing can serve as a source of power where truth and transformation might emerge for all.

After the Call, We Need to Respond: Possibilities for Education and Inquiry

Over two decades ago, when I was a young faculty member at Washington State University, I attended a play entitled *Our Young Black Men Are Dying and Nobody Seems to Care*, written by James Chapman. During the question and answer session (after what was a very poignant and heart wrenching experience for most in the audience about how race operates to systematically disenfranchise young Black men), a young White woman stood up to ask a question. However well intentioned she was and however direct the young African American actor's response, both are still on my mind and in my heart.

> White Woman: *"So, what should we do? You know, I'm not Black* (to which there was uncomfortable laughter from the audience) *and I don't know what to do..."*
>
> Black Male Actor: *"I don't know what you should do. I've never been White either. I could tell you what I'd like for you to do. But you're gonna have to look inside to decide what you should do."*

The next day in the campus newspaper there were several articles about the negative way that the Black actor responded to the White woman's "innocent" question. And reflecting on this event makes clear for me why, having shared the call of African world women in this chapter, that dictating a response is so difficult. In short, like the actor, I really can't tell another the nature of his or her response, nor his or her manner or commitment to answering these calls. Those are guided by the spirit, or the essence of a person's heart. What I can say is that structurally, most educational systems and the societies in which they are grounded are in desperate need of change. They are primarily structures and instruments for maintaining disconnectedness versus these Black women's call for and struggle to reclaim lost humanity, a call for wholeness. Such systems perpetuate unquestioned myths and racist and sexist forgetfulness versus truthfulness, balance, and fairness in representations of humanity. Further, our educational systems worldwide (and particularly in the United States) are designed to maintain a culture of silence when there needs to be dialogue and relationship, naming and speech. So the response I choose to enact here to this collective call of Black world women's voices will also be from a Black and female center, my own. What do the voices of African world women tell me my response might be—as a woman, a sister, a teacher of teachers, a (re)searcher, a daughter, a writer, a human being? My hope is that the reader might find inspiration, a catalyst, or some possibilities for herself or himself as well.

In the African performative call and response tradition, I see a central commitment for systems of education and inquiry that responds to the essence of African world women's call, represented in the following possible "collective" response:

We must do all that we can to regain our humanity.

1. African world woman have perspectives and ways of being that must be valued, respected, and known. Through opening spaces in education and in our inquiry to do so, all persons gain personhood and power in the speaking and naming of their own world—and ultimately transform the act of education in the process...

We must do all that we can to regain our humanity.

2. As educational (re)searchers, our pedagogies and inquiry practices must embrace humanity and inclusion, the goal being not to oppress but to open up the dialogue of possibilities, of being the one taught as well as the one who teaches. And as (re)searchers, we must choose methods that, as Audre Lorde says, "feels right to us," even as they may be contrary to those traditionally used by others...

We must do all that we can to regain our humanity.

3. As we work to be fully integrated human beings who are both African and women, we also restore and heal those who seek to oppress. This is ultimately an act of love (Freire, 1970; hooks, 2000), one that is absolutely central to (re)creating education and society. This spirituality is our methodology: I have written of it in previous works (Dillard, 2006, 2012; Dillard & Okpalaoka, 2012)...

We must do all that we can to regain our humanity.

4. In order to stand with/in solidarity with African world women, many of us must undergo a new way of existing: We can't remain the same as we are. We must work together and, working, we will ultimately transform education, practices of inquiry, and the world...

We must do all that we can to regain our humanity.

5. No one liberates herself by her own efforts alone. She is liberated in social contexts and through social contact and interactions with others. We must talk. We must be honest. We must tell the truth as we understand it. We must learn to listen to multiple truths, even if they are not our own or implicate us in the process...

We must do all that we can to regain our humanity.

6. Finally, educational change and transformation of inquiry must start with our own hearts and minds. Memory, history, personal stories, and poetry must be our sites of resistance. For to know my story is to know me. To know the stories of African peoples is to know the very history of humanity, including your own.

Acknowledgments

This paper is a revisited and revised version of an earlier work: Dillard, C. B. (1994). The power of call, the necessity of response: African world feminists' voices as catalysts for educational change and social empowerment. *Initiatives, 56*(3), 9–22.

References

Aidoo, A. A. (1977). *Our sister killjoy (or reflections from a Black-eyed squint).* London: Longman.

Angelou, M. (1978). *And still I rise.* New York: Random House

Angelou, M. (1990). *I shall not be moved.* New York: Bantam Books.

Bambara, T. C. (1980). *The salt eaters.* New York: Vintage Books.

Busia, A. P. A. (1992). Liberation. In M. Busby (Ed.), *Daughters of African: An international anthology of words and writings by women of African descent from ancient Egyptian to the present* (pp. 868–870). New York: Pantheon Books.

Cortez, J. (1990). Personal interview. Pullman, WA.

Craig, C. (1992). The chain. In M. Busby (Ed.), *Daughters of Africa: An international anthology of words and writings by women of African descent from ancient Egyptian to the present* (pp. 554–556). New York: Pantheon Books.

Dillard, C. B. (2006). *On spiritual strivings: Transforming an African American woman's academic life.* Albany: State University of New York Press.

Dillard, C. B. (2012). *Learning to (re)member the things we've learned to forget: Endarkened feminisms, spirituality and the sacred nature of teaching and research.* New York: Peter Lang.

Dillard, C. B., & Okpalaoka, C. L. (2012). The sacred and spiritual nature of endarkened transnational feminist praxis in qualitative research. In N. K. Denzin & Y. S. Lincoln (Eds), *Handbook of qualitative research (4th Edition)* (pp. 147–162). Los Angeles: Sage.

Freire, P. (1970). *Pedagogy of the oppressed.* New York: Continuum.

Gates, H. L. (1988). *The signifying monkey.* New York: Oxford University Press.

Golden, M. (1986). *A woman's place.* New York: Ballantine.

Hazeley, I. (1988). When you have emptied our calabashes. In R. Cobham & M. Collins (Eds.), *Watchers and seekers: Creative writing by Black women.* New York: Peter Bedrick Books.

hooks, b. (1990). *Yearning: Race, gender, and cultural politics.* Boston: South End Press.

hooks, b. (1992). *Black looks: Race and representation.* Boston: South End Press.

hooks, b. (2000). *Feminist theory: From margin to center.* Boston: South End Press.

Jin, M. (1988). Strangers in a hostile landscape. In R. Cobham & M. Collins (Eds.), *Watchers and seekers: Creative writing by Black women* (pp. 123–126). New York: Peter Bedrick Books.

Jones, G. (1975). *Corregidora.* Boston: Beacon Press.

Lorde, A. (1984). *Sister outsider: Essays and speeches.* Freedom, CA: Crossing Press.

Marcus, J. (1984). Still practice, a/wrested alphabet: Towards a Feminist aesthetic. *Tulsa Studies in Women's Literature, 3,* 79–97.

Sulter, M. (1992). As a Blackwoman. In M. Busby (Ed.), *Daughters of Africa: An international anthology of words and writings by women of African descent om the ancient Egyptian to the present* (pp. 922–923). New York: Pantheon Books.

Truth, S. (1981). Ain't I a woman? In E. Stetson (Ed.), *Black sister: Poetry by Black American women, 1746–1980* (pp. 24–25). Bloomington: Indiana University Press.

Walker, A. (1979). *Good night, Willie Lee, I'll see you in the morning.* San Diego, CA: Harcourt Brace Jovanovich.

Walker, A. (1992). *Possessing the secret of joy.* New York: Harcourt Brace Jovanovich.

Chapter 14

Ghosts, Traces, Sediments, and Accomplices in Psychotherapeutic Dialogue with Sue and Gracie

Jane Speedy

Professor Godtrick: Strange that this paper, which is all about mapping the ghosts and residual traces that have been left behind, seeping into the walls of rooms that have held psychotherapeutic conversations, should have been chosen by Norman Denzin and Michael Giardina as a chapter for their forthcoming book. Jane was immensely flattered when she got the e-mail requesting that this paper, which had been accidentally left in the program of a congress that she did not attend in 2013, be included as a chapter of the book that Denzin and Giardina were going to include in the conference packet for the ICQI congress the following year:

Dear Jane,

We hope this message finds you well. We write to invite you to contribute a version of the paper you presented at ICQI, titled "Ghosts, Traces, Sediments, and Accomplices in Psychotherapeutic Dialogue," for publication in our next Congress volume, which as in previous years will be published by Left Coast Press. The volume will be published in May 2014.

The volume is provisionally titled *Qualitative Inquiry Outside the Academy*, and will foreground the politics of taking inquiry

Qualitative Inquiry Outside the Academy edited by Norman K. Denzin and Michael D. Giardina, 268–276. © 2014 Left Coast Press, Inc. All rights reserved.

into the 'outside' world, into the spaces of advocacy, to form coalitions, to engage in debate on how qualitative research can be used to advance the causes of social justice, while addressing racial, ethnic, gender and environmental disparities in education, welfare and healthcare (to name but a few possible directions).

If you are able to contribute, please note the following two points: 1) manuscripts should be no more than 6,000 words in length, inclusive of notes, references, and so forth; and 2) we would need your completed manuscript by no later than November 15, 2013.

> All best wishes,
> Michael & Norman

At first Jane thought she'd better write back to Norman and Michael and confess that she had not attended the 2013 congress and simply decline their invitation, but then the content and form of the paper began to play around in her mind, alongside Mary Weems's (2003) conceptualizations of the imagination-intellect, and eventually she decided that it must have been the strength and siren call of the residual traces of this paper, together with timeliness and prescience, that had led her North American colleagues to issue this invitation for a paper concerned with residual traces, ghosts, and sediments...

Jane: My attic office/therapy room is thick with stories. Every now and then I open my rooflight up wide and let them out, letting in great gulps of air from the surrounding city and folding in snatches of bird song from the park opposite. At a previous stage of my life I had regularly sought the advice of a shamanic healer who had been influenced by Native American traditions. She used to sweep her consulting rooms clean of ghosts, stories, and other sediments by sweeping out the corners of her workspace with smoking clumps of white sage. There are times when I long for such a psychic broom, but I do not possess such a thing and have no equivalent traditions. Thus, I sit and engage in conversation in a space that, over time, harbors traces of many entanglements and stories. The worst accumulations are those stories half-told, or untold, the words awkwardly loitering in the corners, unsaid or unsayable: at best entering my room is like entering a 'sea of stories.'

Sue[1] had been working with me weekly for nearly a year. She did not seem to have any particular goals for this work, which was fine by my lights, but I was getting the disconcerting feeling that I was a routine and permanent fixture in her busy schedule, rather than a co-researcher alongside somebody actively engaged in a healing or learning process.

"I don't know why I still come," Sue had replied, when I had asked her where she saw all this going, and whether she'd like to stop for a while and take a break from seeing me.

"I suppose I come so that I can say that I am seeing a therapist," she conceded. [Not exactly the most enthusiastic vote of confidence that I have ever had in my work!]

"Who do you feel the need to say that to?" I had asked.

¤ *"Well, friends; my parents; myself. Most of all I need to say it to myself."* She'd replied.

¤ "'And is there a 'because' lurking in the background there, that might add something more to that sentence?" I had inquired.

¤ *"Because... if I am seeing a therapist, then... Well, that's my excuse for not being in a relationship still. To all of them—everybody— and to me... It's not because I am no longer desirable or not on the prowl. Perhaps it's an indication that I'm just not ready yet... not ready for an intimate relationship. A loving relationship. Perhaps I'm seeing you instead of finding a new partner?"*

¤ *"I suppose... this is the place for intimacy in my life at the moment."*

¤ *"Perhaps if I had a partner I'd tell her all the things I tell you, well not all of them, but before, when Gracie was alive, sometimes I used to store stuff up, things that happened at work, in life, just little things... store stuff up. Thinking to myself, even when things were happening, right at the time they were happening: 'Gracie'd love all this. I'll tell Gracie about this, tonight'. Now I don't think:*

¤ *'coo Jane'd love this' in the same way,*

¤ *but it's those kind of things I tell you about. The little snatches of life events that make a difference, that stay with me. The stuff that stays in the back of my mind. I report on them here. Instead of taking them home to pick over with Gracie. I miss her. Those are the times I really miss her, but that's normal isn't it?"*

[Sue regularly asked if her thoughts, feelings and behaviors since her partner Grace had died were 'normal.']

¤ "I think so," I had replied. "What makes you ask?"

¤ *"Oh there I go again. Just wondering how long it'll be before I stop missing her," she said.*

¤ "What makes you think you'll stop missing her? I still miss my brother and he died 23 years ago." I said, "These conversations with you often evoke his memory for me."

¤ *"Are therapists supposed to say things like that? It's supposed to be me who's a bit screwy, not you."*

¤ "What's screwy about that? I don't think either of us is especially screwy—anyway according to popular mythology all shrinks are barking mad, not their clients."

¤ *"Good point. Although I am quite barking you know. I often feel as though Gracie is here with us in this room. I've talked about her so often in your attic, it feels as though this is where she lives for now. Perhaps one day I'll leave her here with you and walk away, but for the moment I just keep coming. Gracie, too, I keep coming for her, in memory of her. Just so I don't forget her, you know... It was Gracie who'd heard about you, your kind of therapy work, not me. I came to see you originally when Gracie was ill, I came here to please her really, to do something for me, to be seen by Gracie to be coming to see you. I suppose I think on some level she can still see me coming up that path every couple of weeks or so and... that's partly why I come. Do you believe in ghosts? Do you believe she's listening in?"*

¤ "No I don't personally believe in ghosts, not literally, not literal incarnations of people, but I do believe that those of us who are living carry with us traces and memories of the people we knew that have died. I think we keep people alive in and for our own minds. I expect that there are all sorts of traces from the stories that you and other people have told me in this room. Occasionally, I open up the velux windows and let them out, but I'm sure that there are lots of traces of Gracie and others lingering in here. I'll keep those memories safe for you if you want to leave them here, but it feels to me as if you want to keep them quite close to you for the moment."

"Well I've found a letter she wrote to me just before she died, here it is, it was in her watercolor box in the study, I don't know why she left it in there… I might not have found it for years, if ever. I don't paint, I was packing up all her art things to give to her niece. Perhaps that's why. Perhaps it was a sort of a random roulette act to put it in there… I've been carrying this letter around with me. Listen; you're in it."

Dear Sue,

I expect by the time you find this I'll be long since gone and you'll be packing all my stuff up to go to charity shops and the needy poor. Don't keep anything you won't use yourself, sling it all out and start again—you always were such a hoarder, but this is no time for hoarding—be ruthless!!

This stuff is only stuff, not 'my' stuff, I don't know whether it ever was my stuff really , but it isn't any more. So chuck all the clutter and the stories and memories that go with it. The ones that want to keep with you will stay. And the ones I want to take with me I have already taken.

By the time you read this letter I'll be well dead,

love and hugs, Gracie.

(long silence)

Freud: *Du liebe Gott. Was machen sie hier? Unglaublich!!*

Sue *(looking around disconcerted): Who was that?*

Jane (deadpan): Sigmund Freud, Founding Father of psychoanalysis.

Sue: *Crikey, Isn't he dead? Where the hell did he come from?*

Jane: I think he came out of that book on the shelves behind your head. You can't see it, but I can, so I think it came right out of that book, the Penguin *Freud Reader* (2006), through my mind's eye and straight out into cluttering up our space.

Freud *(furious—in a Viennese accent): Cluttering? Cluttering? I am certainly not the one cluttering this space! Why I've never witnessed a therapist who behaved like this. What is this, a television chat show? It is you who are doing the cluttering. Cluttering with this poor woman's mind!!*

Jane: That's a tad anachronistic isn't it, Professor Freud? You made quite a lot of pertinent criticisms of the cinema in your day, even refused to write for Hollywood as I recall, and I can imagine your hostile critique of the TV chat show as a genre—but you died in 1939, long before the advent of the chat show.

Sue: Hang on, what's going on? This is my therapy session, and I'm not sitting here paying for you to go on some chat show rampage with a dead German geezer when it's me you should be attending to!

Freud: German geezer? Who is she calling 'some German geezer?' I'm Austrian, goddammit!!

Jane: It's through my attention to you that he's got here in the first place, I'm afraid.

Freud: Haroomph!

Sue: Bad-tempered old bugger isn't he?

Professor Godtrick: And so the conversation between Jane and Sue went on—with Freud interrupting Jane's attention to her client from the bookshelves and Gracie interjecting via letters and memories, both were 'submerged into the lives' of the speakers:

> The storytelling that thrives for a long time—is itself a form of communication, as it were. It does not aim to convey the pure "in itself" or gist of a thing, like information or a report. It submerges the thing into the life of the storyteller, in order to bring it out of him again. Thus, traces of the storyteller cling to the story the way the handprints of the potter cling to a clay vessel. (Benjamin, 1936/1968, p. 92)

Thus the layering of different realities (agential, magical and critical) and inquiring voices (human, ghostly and writerly/narrational) continued as an integral aspect of the dialogue.

> To think about mapping spectral traces is to look at places where there might be difficult or unacknowledged pasts and social histories that continue to structure present day relations and ideas about home and place. Those historical layers and emotional layers may not be directly visible, but they are continuing to structure present-day relations. (Krinke, 2012)

Thus unacknowledged voices in the memories and histories of therapists and their clients, together with the accumulated residual traces of others and the agencies of objects that have previously inhabited places of therapeutic dialogue, make for cacophonous conversational spaces, full of sedimented trauma and bereavement and populated with ghost voices. These traces create openings, allow for slippages and displace meanings within the ongoing surface conversations. As in conceptualisations of a/r/tography, this sense of "loss, shift and rupture creates presence through absence and becomes tactile, felt and seen" (Springgay et al., 2005, p. 898).

Jane: We are accumulating an entangled range of voices in this room: on the surface of the conversation there is a dialogue between you and me, but this includes interjections that are available to both of us from both Gracie and Freud, and then in my mind's eye, there's another layer that includes both the voice of my brother Chris and the voices of deceased friends, parents, partners, colleagues, and other members of the families of other clients who have sat where you are sitting now…

Sue: And in the back of my head are the voices of my dead comrades from the struggle in South Africa, some of whom died too young and too quickly to have much of a take on even the events in their own live: they always crop up at times like this to shout others down and demand to be heard, but I thought you didn't believe in ghosts?

Jane: Well, as I said, I suspect that the memories and traces of people we have known that have died *do* haunt us, and inhabit our landscapes and dreamscapes alongside us. Michael White (2007), one of the founders of narrative therapy, departed radically from established psychological understandings of mourning and bereavement by maintaining that we needed to 'learn to say hello again' to people who had died. What do you think?

Sue: Well I think I never stopped saying hello to Gracie.

Professor Godtrick: We are reaching out here, to the unacknowledged inhabitants of what Mazzei (2007) would describe as the 'inhabited silence' or perhaps, I would prefer, 'the spaces that we fail to inhabit' in qualitative research texts. To quote Grace McCleen (2013, p. 371), we are reaching beneath the surface of the texts for the sounds that are submerged beneath it : "a current flowing covertly along the riverbed, along the sea floor; a pattern so subtle it might be missed completely, yet nonetheless shaped the movements above." The question is, am I 'in' this text, or hovering just outside it, offering a commentary? This god trick is hard to do, but you are all so used to it, it's easy just to slip it past you in a journal like this, isn't it?

▶ ▶ ▶

Gracie: I can't see the point of you myself; I thought you were narrating at first, but Jane seems to be doing that for herself, and anyway, you haven't got anything to say for yourself, you just keep quoting other people as if that gives you some kind of authority, which frankly it doesn't.

Freud (haughtily): Well you don't even exist; you are merely a projection of your partner's longings.

Jane: Hey, hey, no need for this unravelling of what was turning into quite a decent paper. Don't speak to people like that, Professor Freud, not in my therapy space, anyway. What kind of therapist *are* you? Don't answer that, it was rhetorical—and in any case you are only another projection yourself—this time of my of my longing for a deeply skilled colleague to be working alongside me... I could do with some really good supervision with this client, but not from a Freudian, it's just coincidental that yours was the face staring out at us from the bookshelves...

Freud: I don't believe in coincidence, but I do believe in timeliness and prescience...

▶ ▶ ▶

Michael Giardina: Whaddya think, boss, shall we include it?

Norman Denzin: Well, she's fundamentally crazy, but she writes well.

Michael Giardina: Is she layering the account too much? I mean, there's the bottom-line realist tale of the dialogue in a therapy session, intercalating overlaid voices from past experience and literature; then there's another layer of the therapy practitioner becoming a researcher and transposing that conversation into a performance for a conference, which also includes allusions to Donna Haraway's (1988) 'god trick'— presumably the writer signalling an affinity with feminist research methods, or at the least, situated knowledges. Then there's a top layer of the correspondence with us and of the writing for this book—she's even included this conversation between the two of us, but she doesn't state whether this is a 'real' or an' imagined' tale. In fact the whole paper appears to segue back and forth between different realities and between different conceptualizations of time, space, and place throughout. Are we 'ourselves' here or symbolic equivalents?

Norman Denzin: Just as I said. Fundamentally crazy. Let's print it.

Note

1 The names of all 'clients,' as well as identifying characteristics and details of case material, have been changed. The stories and people are not taken from case notes of actual therapeutic encounters, but from what Irvin Yalom (1991) described as "symbolic equivalents." The stories and personalities described in this chapter are composed from the accumulated documents and experiences of 28 years in therapeutic practice rather than one singular experience.

References

Benjamin, W. (1936/1968). The storyteller: Reflections on Nikolai Leskóv. In H. Arendt (Ed.), H. Zohn (Trans.), *Illuminations* (pp. 83–109). New York: Harcourt, Brace & World.

Freud, S. (2006). In A. Phillips (Ed.), *The Penguin Freud reader*. London: Penguin Modern Classics.

Haraway, D. (1988) Situated knowledges: The science question in feminism and the privilege of partial perspective. *Feminist Studies, 14* (3), 575–599.

Krinke, R. (2012). A conversation with the mapping spectral traces collaborative. *ias.umn.edu/2012/11/28/mapping-spectral-traces-conversation/* (accessed, September 16, 2013).

McCleen, G. (2013). *The professor of poetry*. London: Sceptre

Mazzei, L. (2007). *Inhabited silence in qualitative research*. New York: Peter Lang.

Springgay, S., Irwin, R., & Wilson Kind, S. (2005). A/r/tography as living inquiry through art and text. *Qualitative Inquiry, 11*, 897–906.

Weems, M. (2003). *Public education and the imagination-intellect: I speak from the wound in my mouth*. New York: Peter Lang

White, M. (2007). *Maps of narrative practice*. New York: W. W. Norton.

Yalom, I. (1991). *Love's executioner and other tales of psychotherapy*. Harmondsworth, UK: Penguin.

Chapter 15

Stampedagogy

Brian Rusted

1. Affect at the Art Auction

I am eating beef-on-a-bun. Well, a diminutive metonym for beef-on-a-bun, the commissary's compromise of elegance and convenience. I add too much horseradish and feel the need to revise what I know about heat. It is not intellectual knowledge. It starts at the back of my throat, enters my sinus, and then vaporizes my eyes: you know the route. The selection of bite-sized food adds a gala quality to the Calgary Stampede's annual Western Art Auction. The Quick Draw (an event where artists complete a painting in under an hour) has ended, and their pieces are being auctioned off to the three or four hundred guests who have paid to watch artists work, mingle, and then bid on the other 100 or more lots in the main auction. Over the next few hours, a half million dollars of art will sell.

A small group approaches me on their way out of the ballroom. The auctioneer's voice singing music into money clings to them as the door closes. The group represents the city's arts community: educators, members of artist-run centers, gallery personnel, curators, cultural activists. They are touring various activities

Qualitative Inquiry Outside the Academy edited by Norman K. Denzin and Michael D. Giardina, 277–292. © 2014 Left Coast Press, Inc. All rights reserved.

278 ● *Brian Rusted*

with members of the Calgary Stampede's "public art committee" in an effort to build community partnerships and increase recognition of the Stampede in the development of a civic arts policy.

One member of the group, an arts educator and gallery director from a postsecondary institution, I have not met. I am introduced as someone who teaches a university course on and volunteers with the Calgary Stampede (as if placing these epithets in one sentence is contradictory, ungrammatical). That hint of incompatibility may explain why the gallery director tells me without pausing for breath that *everything* the group has just been shown amounts to so much "sentimental hogwash" and that the last thing he would ever think of doing is "sending a student to see this stuff. Or god-forbid, participate!" I recognize the multiple layers of affect here: naming the base, bodily appeal of western art to the least critical of emotions; dismissing all things representational incumbent on that naming; classifying the commercial appeal, diminishing the commodification of those representations; and my being drawn into the heat of this judgemental encounter. We are both educators. This should be a teachable moment.

I know the group has to move on to the next event on its itinerary, but I try speed debate to engage him in dialogue:

Relativism: this is a socially distinct art world with its own aesthetics and practices. No.

Critical irony: think how generative the concept of kitsch was for Clement Greenburg or camp for Sontag? No.

Postmodernism: what happened to all that talk in the 80s about the collapse of distinctions between high and low culture? No.

Even, somewhat desperately, relational aesthetics: isn't this also an art that constitutes its own social network? No, the last rebuff, and the group moves on.

This is not an unfamiliar encounter, although the intensity is. And I am not exaggerating. The reaction—felt, visceral, affecting—offers no point of entry, no space for conversation, no dialogue. As an ethnographer, I am in no doubt as to the rigidity of categories, the impenetrability of border. Such a rejection renders the complex social practices and experiences of artists, subjects, and patrons lifeless, inert, and leaves me momentarily wondering whether my time has been wasted being involved with teaching a course on the Calgary Stampede for the last decade. Am I complicit in the sentimental, the commodification of hegemonic representations? Is critique at the level of representation the only valid position for an academic to occupy when engaging western art? Does a large scale, cultural performance like the Calgary Stampede offer nothing to teach except the complete absence of oppositional critique? Is such teaching merely, or, more properly, a performance of complicity? Or, perhaps, again desperately, in the words of Fiona Probyn-Rapsey, is "this capacity of complicity…to unsettle" an aspect of its "political agency" (2007, p. 79)? Is such judgemental affect a response to being unsettled? Can it be part of a pedagogy, a stampedagogy?

I'm over the horseradish.

2. "We're a Jolly Bunch of Cowboys…"

Although the brand of the Calgary Stampede may be widely recognized, there are a number of features about its formation that are less well known. As a regional, cultural institution, it is a volunteer-run, non-profit with roots that go back to 19th century agricultural exhibitions (MacEwan, 1950). Although what have come to be known as rodeo events such as steer roping were introduced to the agricultural exhibition as early as 1894 (Wetherell & Kmet, 1990, p. 332), it was the appearance of the Miller 101 Ranch Show during Calgary's 1908 Dominion Exhibition (Gray, 1985, p. 26) where the agricultural exhibition was first cross-bred with the Wild West show. Following the inaugural Stampede in 1912, Charlie Russell wrote to general manager Guy Weadick to comment on this hybrid: "Ive seen som good wild west showes but I wouldint call what you pulled off a show, it was the real thing an a whole lot of it" (Taliaferro, 1996, p. 189; formatting original). The debate about the authenticity of the Stampede's connection to western heritage continues into the present (Turner, 2012).

By 1912, the open range style of ranching had ended and was even then the subject of nostalgia (Kelly, 1913). Although this economic model of cattle raising and grazing lasted a little longer on the Canadian prairies, it was recognized as finished by 1906. Vaudeville entertainer and trick roper Guy Weadick returned to Calgary following his appearance with the Miller 101 Ranch Show in 1908 and during the first decade of his management of the Calgary Stampede, formalized its program and worked to represent and celebrate indigenous and settler cultures of the West (Livingstone, 1996). Through his efforts, local First Nations signatories of Treaty 7 began the longest continuous participation of any group in the Stampede (Dempsey, 2008). While their display "village" has consistently been located at the margins of the Stampede's festival space, their participation began at a time when they were discouraged from wearing traditional dress, and policy required them to stay on reserves. Some 1800 led the first Stampede parade.

This chapter does not offer a close or closed "reading" of the Calgary Stampede or its visual culture, although the event and organization continue to be a demonstrative and much contested force in shaping a sense of place and heritage for those in the region. It is an exploration of the performance of complicity from the standpoint of experiences derived from diverse and incompatible roles: as curator of an exhibition that charted the Stampede's century long involvement with (western) art (Rusted, 2012); as an active volunteer with the Stampede; and from teaching an undergraduate Canadian Studies course on "The Culture of the Calgary Stampede" that continues with the cautious support of the Stampede's board of directors. Despite my research interests at the intersections of visual culture and performance (Rusted, 2006), writing about the Stampede does not make for a neat "study" or research project: there are too many intertwined connections to determine where one aspect of participation stops and another begins. The Calgary Stampede has unraveled any unified identity as a researcher I might (ever) have had, and muddled it irreparably with those of participant, teacher, volunteer, curator, shareholder, pundit, critic, spokesperson. I have been encouraged in this community service while being denounced for my romantic involvement. This chapter attempts to trouble my performance of the Stampede as a way to begin a conversation about what and how the Stampede teaches; to engage what Dewsbury describes as the "imperceptibles" lost when treating visual culture and performance solely as representation (Dewsbury, 2003, p. 1907); and to discern possibilities for a sensory, embodied pedagogy, occasioned or shaped by unsettling affect.

3. Calgary Stampede as Site

American Studies scholar John Dorst subtitled his study of Chadd's Ford, Pennsylvania, as "an ethnographic dilemma" because he recognized that the prolific self-representations that characterize late capitalism render the ethnographer superfluous (Dorst, 1989). Writing on the cusp of postmodernism, he queried the authority of ethnographic representations by wondering about the ethnographer's role when the community being studied was already represented in what he called a "perpetual flow of auto-ethnographic practice" (p. 4). While his sense of the auto-ethnographic (as vernacular, subject generated self-representations under late capitalism) has been displaced by its subsequent methodological usage (that uses researcher experience as the basis of cultural understanding), the dilemma is no less relevant. His response was to treat Chadd's Ford as a "Site," one produced by and reflected in its flow of self-representations. The revised or revived role of the ethnographer, then, is as reader of those auto-ethnographic texts.

Although I have no interest in retrieving the textual analysis of culture, it is important to note that the Calgary Stampede is deeply invested in the proliferation of self-representations. It holds copyright on two of the more prominent books ever published on it (Gray, 1985; Dixon & Read, 2005).[1] In recent years, its archival holdings have been digitized and placed online: a century of posters, rodeo programs; lists of parade floats, account books, and so forth. The centennial of 2012 accelerated the production of these auto-ethnographic texts: the local newspaper, the *Calgary Herald*, produced ten special weekend editions about the Stampede, retelling its history a decade at a time; every opportunity to repeat founding legends was taken, and the Stampede produced a special

Las Vegas *Cavalia*-style musical that placed the Stampede at the center of the settling of the Canadian West, replete with a cast of generous and cooperative First Nations peoples, who embraced the ranchers, farmers, and entertainers without question or hesitation (Potkins, 2012).

Such auto-ethnographic texts that reflect and produce the Site of the Stampede are part of its own broader investment in pedagogy. As an agricultural society, its mandate was to educate agricultural and livestock producers about best practices. While the last 100 year has seen a shift in focus from producers to consumers, the Stampede is still involved in pedagogies of food production, but now in an uneasy balance between industrial food producers (Pork Producers Association, Alberta Beef, etc.), that erase any sense of place by standardizing products, and the emphasis their own their food concessions claim on locally sourced bison, pork, tomatoes, etc. (Van Rosendaal, 2008).

I participate in this proliferation of "auto-ethnographic" texts as a volunteer for the Barn Tour committee by contributing revisions to the guidebook used for those touring the public through the livestock barns. For me it is an opportunity to connect the contemporary, spectator-focused event with the earlier governmentalist agendas that readied the prairies for immigrant settlement, created a sense of healthy regional competitiveness, and mixed with emergent nationhood. The great Dominion Exhibition of 1908 is the start of the built environment for the Stampede and a pinnacle of colonial thinking. In charting the successive waves of settler culture, ranches, livestock companies, and livestock breed associations, it is possible to see the outlines of center-margin economics, the Site as a bread basket for the centers of capital in eastern Canada and England.

The barns are dark and cool on summer days, fresh with the scent of sawdust and the noises of heavy horses, llamas, cattle, stock dogs, sheep, and such. The families I tour listen with feigned patience as I try to bring to life the pedagogies of agriculture, animal classification, and technology that shaped the plains we stand on. They want to pet an animal. Heavy horses are best, hooves as big as your chest, the Shires and the Percherons bend down like aliens entering our atmosphere as the newly fledged earthlings reach up for that comforting gust of warm breath, the curious, delicate nudge from hair covered nostrils.

They want to pet an animal, and then they want to tell a story about their grandparents' farm, about how cows have the right of way in the streets at home in India, how their sister had a pony but the family moved off the farm too soon for the rest of the siblings to share. Not quite counter-pedagogy, their "everyday memory talk" (Kuhn, 2007, p. 286) is one way of connecting with the Site. I tread lightly with the pedagogical text, going just far enough into the barn's embrace for their stories to begin.

4. Showing Seeing

I don't know anything about capitalism. I don't know anything, but every Tuesday and Friday morning of my summer holidays I spend with Mr. P. to try at least to understand the economics of beef. He's a cattle buyer and works those mornings at local auction markets buying for one of the large, American-owned meat packing plants. What he pays on the floor of the auction market seems to be the starting point of a value chain that concludes with the price of a Styrofoam tray of meat in the supermarket, or the promotional price of a Whopper at Burger King. At least I imagine it is that simple: like I said, I don't know anything about capitalism. Mr. P. has been in the business for 40 years. His daughters have been rodeo royalty, and are accomplished horsewomen, public speakers, and ranchers in their own right. When the cattle enter the sale ring—whether an old bull or a selection of heifers—he has less than 10 seconds to decide if he is going to bid and if so, how much. He'll turn to me and say, "That one has been standing in the pen all night with no water or hay," just as the auctioneer says, "Hey, hey overnight stand on 'em boys". This is a good thing to know: "You can tell what you are buying," Mr P. says, "You can see the bone and muscle better." Or, "See the hitch in that one's get-along? He was probably kicked by another bull: no point bidding because the meat'll be bruised and have to be cut out. A 'dark cutter' they call it in the bone room."

The whole time he is bidding and talking with me, he is also on the phone with the packing plant. They are telling him what contracts have come in from wholesalers: if a supermarket chain wants to buy hamburger at so-much-a-pound, Mr. P. has to calculate how much meat the carcass will yield, what it will cost to ship to the plant, and whether there is still profit in it. He snaps his palm shut like a clam shell to indicate his bid to the auctioneer. The auctioneer jokes at my expense: he knows me from the Stampede's Western Art Auction: "Quit buying art, have you, and going to buy some real cattle? You got the world expert right next to you!"

I still don't know anything about capitalism, but Mr. P. has shown me something about how he sees. He understands cattle the way a figure painter or a sculptor understands anatomy: when the cow walks into the sale ring, he sees skeleton, muscle, organ, pathology. He spent decades working the line at the processing plant: he knows how cattle come apart and he can tell now if they are put together well. He is not seeing a representation of a cow.

However auto-ethnographic the visual culture of the Calgary Stampede, it does not produce or reflect a Site that is a simple representation of the West. And as W. J. T. Mitchell says, it is "reductive" to think of "images as all powerful forces and to engage in a kind of iconoclastic critique which imagines that the destruction or exposure of false images amounts to a political victory" (2002, p. 175). I want students to engage with the sensory particularity of pictures, the networks of social relations that gave rise to them, the way they circulate and accrue meanings and uses over time. I want them to look with the skill of someone who could work in the bone room. I start with showing students their own seeing: a slideshow quiz of western art. I show sequences of images, all from the history of Stampede's exhibitionary practices. I pose a series of questions about the images:

Which are made by artists of native ancestry?

Which are made by artists with academic training, which self-taught?

Which are more or the most contemporary?

Which are based on historical research?

There are right answers, but that is not the point. They aren't bidding on art or cattle. When students compare their answers to information that contextualizes the pieces, their habits of looking may be unsettled, how they've shaped what they see. They might look at cattle, but they don't know what they should be seeing if they do not step beyond seeing only a representation. They also learn something about the social character of convention. The art exhibited at the Stampede is what Lynes or Bourdieu would call middle-brow (Lynes, 1954), constructed out of warm, polished, and familiar conventions, nesting somewhere between "plagiarism and parody" (Bourdieu, 1984, p. 128). While the students almost always find the art boring and unrelenting, something they imagine their grandparents might have liked, they also begin to recognize another dimension of these visual practices: the work is not about originality. The redundancy of subjects, poses, and styles are theatrical attempts at living up to the expectation of genre. *The Importance of Being Ernest* performed yet again. They begin to sense how others' seeing is shaped by the scripts they are trying to re-present and re-inhabit through the bodily practices of making images.

I take my students in small groups to the Stampede's Western Art Show: a 100,000 square feet of paintings and sculptures featuring cowboys, horses, mountain landscapes, and First Nations subjects. The Stampede doubled the square footage of the art show, which must be a sign of something. I want students to meet artists, have a sense of how they talk about their own work, and take some time to look at actual paintings and sculptures instead of the dematerialized reproductions they are more used to seeing on the multiple screens that facilitate their information lives, and so much of their education. The artists are there for the 10 days of the Stampede to speak with patrons and showcase what in many instances is their annual output of creative work.

Michelle Grant identifies as an equine artist. More than anything else, she paints horses: ponies, heavy horses, Arabs, chuckwagon thoroughbreds, in the pasture, in harness, in races, where ever and how ever she can find them. She has been internationally recognized for the quality of her work, and the

Canadian Mint commissioned her to design coins commemorating the Stampede. There is a large painting of an Arabian stallion on the back wall of her sales salon. Moving left to right across the canvas, the horse's mane signifies motion as it spills upwards and off the top edge of the canvas. The students huddle around the painting, feigning interest in the animal, but beginning to admire the crisp discipline of its realism. When she begins to speak about the work, I can sense how it unsettles them. She makes no mention of the horse, the subject, the flesh and hair creature that must absolutely have been before her, palpably present, for her to make such a painting. She begins instead by talking about the size and texture of the brushes she used, the way they hold paint and allow her certain gestures on the canvas, the way she mixed the paints, the ways she moved lines across the canvas to suggest the kind of energy that had drawn the students initially. She concludes by talking about the importance of a single brush stroke, a dab of red paint in the very corner of what we read denotatively as the horse's eye. "This," she says "is what pulls your eye across the canvas and creates whatever sense of energy you feel the painting has." The title, worthy of James McNeill Whistler is, *Grey Eye Shadow*. In a few moments, she has translated the illusionistic space of the canvas into a gestural map of her technically masterful bodily practices that guide and shape our bodily practices of viewing. As we leave, the image of the horse has disappeared, replaced with a sensory, embodied account of its making. Pigment is now a trace of gesture, a residue of her skill in performing energy.

Doug Levitt is waiting for us when we reach his booth. There is one painting of his I want the students to encounter, *Spirit of 1912*. At first glance it appears to be a painterly attempt at recreating a tintype image of a somewhat weary First Nations man, wrapped ineffectively in the ubiquitous, much contested Hudson's Bay blanket. It is reminiscent of the Library of Congress image of Sitting Bull posed in a commercial photographer's studio.[2] Aside from the historical patina of the piece, Levitt has done something unusual for an artist working with this subject matter in this genre: he has made the piece life size, and more significantly, he has displayed at floor level rather than suspending it higher up on the wall of his booth. The effect he wanted was to have the man in the painting confront the viewer across time. This seems to be a distinctly different approach than the more totemic approaches to First Nations subjects common to western art shows like this.

Before I turn the students loose for the afternoon to make their own discoveries, we visit Don Oelze. Don is one of the younger artists in the show but has already established his career in both Canada and the United States. With occasional forays into rodeo, his primary subjects are First Nations groups, full costumes, epic poses, with an ethnographic ambition to illustrate everything from daily chores to war parties. The majority of students find the work tedious, something (they tell me later) they imagine finding on a calendar they would never consider buying. Oddly, it is the First Nations students who find the work appealing. Not because of its pretense to historical or cultural accuracy, or the heroic and romantic poses. They like these paintings because the subjects are frequently shown with evidence of settler technology and artifacts (parasols, telescopes, etc.). They admire the ingenuity of those depicted in the paintings to turn these technologies against White society. Oelze is amused by the interpretation, but it was not something he consciously considered, and it is more consistent with the ethnographic gaze common in *National Geographic* where the sophistication of white European technology is enhanced when placed in the hands of less technologically advanced societies (Lutz & Collins, 1993).

5. Calgary Stampede as Pedagogical Place

Sarah Pink has suggested that ethnographers create "ethnographic places." These are not the spatial locations where fieldwork occurs, but the discursive places they craft when communicating research (Pink, 2009, p. 42). A classroom is like such an ethnographic place, or more properly a pedagogical place, a shared fiction crafted by students and teachers alike in communicating ideas, research, and their unsettled sense of complicity with the social world.[3]

As Elyse Pineau says, students and teachers effectively have been schooled to forget "their bodies when they enter the classroom in order that they might give themselves more fully to the life of the mind" (2002, p. 45). Returning the body to the classroom—or even returning the classroom to bodily sites like the Stampede—acknowledges that students live in their bodies, know through their bodies, and that being in such sites requires them "to struggle bodily with the course content" (p. 52), or, as Paul Edwards says, to question "through the medium of their own bodies the very limits of textual authority" (2006, p. 148). That struggle is manifest when students are unsettled by the complex social practices they enact on a daily basis.

In her history of small town rodeos in western Canada, Mary Ellen Kelm takes up Mary Louise Pratt's notion of the contact zone to describe the "extraneous, surprising, subverting strands" (2011, p. 8) of the experience of rodeo, its development, and its organization at the community level. For Pratt, a contact zone is a site "where cultures meet, clash and grapple with each other, often in contexts of highly asymmetrical relations of power" (1991, p. 34). For Kelm, small town rodeos are sites of that clash and grapple, certainly between indigenous and settler cultures, but also of other immigrant ethnicities, of gender, and of class. Her work is an effort to recover the "multiple perspectives" lost when one views such cultural performances solely as expressions or constructions of dominant values (2011, p. 9). Rodeos are also sites of dissent, sites where new identities are negotiated, sites that accommodate diverse needs and uses. If, as Kelm says, rodeos "historicized whiteness and justified a status quo," they were also sites where First Nations participants and contestants could challenge "the place that they held in small-town rodeos ... and provide alternate versions of Western Canada's history from within the arena" (p. 176). This view of small town cultural performances has carried forward into the present Calgary Stampede, where, Kelm continues:

> the improvisational coexisted with the staged, where hybridity rubbed shoulders with racial and gendered segmentation, and where colonial power infused events, but did not overdetermine how people would behave or indeed how they would ascribe meaning to what they saw or experienced. (pp. 8–9)

Often, the first lecture in the course on the Calgary Stampede takes place at its Indian Village[4] along the southern edge of the

Calgary Stampede grounds. Students meet teepee "owners," learn something of the history of the Village and the Treaty 7 communities that populate it for 10 days each July. They are then toured through the Village by members of these communities who act as interpreters. It does not take long for discussions to move beyond teepee construction or pemmican recipes to discussions on tax benefits, health care, educational or housing standards, or careers with the Canadian military. The students come away from a few hours in that contact zone, that pedagogical place, with an affective sense of "what it means to live with history" (Probyn-Rapsey, 2007, p. 65). They may not have shared or produced the history of settler colonialism, but they recognize their relational complicity in the contemporary experiences of those who live under it. As Probyn-Rapsey says, "Complicity connects us to others, ideas, structures, and not least of all that which we might hope to keep at a distance through critique, through the distance of time, and through apology" (p. 69).

6. Bull Sale

On the west side of the old Agriculture Building on the Stampede grounds is a mural that commemorates the "Seed Grain and Hay Exposition" that was a feature of the original Calgary Exhibition through the 1880s and 1890s. Painted by Stan Phelps in 1998, the mural dates from a period when the organization commissioned public art to represent and preserve a history of the exhibition displaced by the city's explosive population growth, and the turn away from a producer focused mandate. The mural depicts the buildings erected to support the 1908 Dominion Exhibition and frames an office window in the side of the building. I wonder sometimes if it would be possible to look out from that window and see the West as an artist does, not as a sentimental representation or a nostalgic text that commodifies a distorted past, not as an object to be distanced by critique, but as a site produced by bodies connected and affected by complicity with the histories they live.

Notes

1 Many of the early publications on the Calgary Stampede, such as Kennedy (1965), have been digitized and are also available online from the Calgary Stampede's archives: www.ucalgary.ca/stampede/node/15

2 Taken by David Barry of the Dakota Territory, the photo was copyrighted in June, 1885, and a print of it is in the Library of Congress's high demand collection, LC-YSZ62 111147 (www.loc.gov/pictures/item/94506170/).

3 I have developed this notion of a pedagogical place more generally in an earlier article (Rusted, 2011). Passages of this section have been adapted from that original article.

4 According to the Calgary Stampede's *Trail Guide* for volunteers, when asked by visitors if the name "Indian Village" is appropriate, volunteers are to respond, "Although changing the name of Indian Village has been discussed with the tribes, they have made the decision to keep this historic name" because for them, it "does not have a negative connotation" (2012, p. 24).

References

Bourdieu, P. (1984). The market of symbolic goods. In R. Johnson (Ed.), *The field of cultural production: Essays on art and literature*. New York: Columbia University Press.

Calgary Stampede. (2012). *Trail guide 2012*. Calgary: Volunteer Services.

Dempsey, H. (2008). The Indians and the Stampede. In M. Foran (Ed.), *Icon, brand, myth: The Calgary Stampede*. Athabasca, Alberta: AU Press.

Dewsbury, J. (2003). Witnessing space: 'knowledge without contemplation.' *Environment and Planning A, 35*, 1907–1932.

Dixon, J., & Read, T. (2005). *Celebrating the Calgary Exhibition and Stampede: The story of the greatest outdoor show on Earth*. Victoria, British Columbia: Heritage House.

Dorst, J. (1989). *The written suburb: An American site, an ethnographic dilemma*. Philadelphia: University of Pennsylvania Press.

Edwards, P. (2006). Performance of and beyond literature. In S. Madison & J. Hamera (Eds.), *The Sage handbook of performance studies* (pp. 143–150). Thousand Oaks, CA: Sage.

Gray, J. H. (1985). *A brand of its own: The 100 year history of the Calgary Exhibition and Stampede*. Saskatoon, *Saskatchewan*: Western Producer Prairie Books.

Heamon, E. A. (1999). *The inglorious arts of peace: Exhibitions in Canadian society during the nineteenth century*. Toronto: University of Toronto Press.

Kelly, L. V. (1913). *The range men: The story of the ranchers and Indians of Alberta*. Toronto: Wm. Briggs.

Kelm, M. (2011). *A Wilder West: Rodeo in Western Canada*. Vancouver: University of British Columbia Press.

Kennedy, F. (1965). *Calgary Stampede: The authentic story of the Calgary Exhibition and Stampede 1912–1964*. Vancouver: West Vancouver Enterprises.

Kuhn, A. (2007). Photography and cultural memory: A methodological exploration. *Visual Studies, 22*(3), 283–292.

Livingstone, D. (1996). *Cowboy spirit: Guy Weadick and the Calgary Stampede*. Vancouver: Greystone Books.

Lutz, C., & Collins, J. (1993). *Reading National Geographic*. Chicago: University of Chicago Press.

Lynes, R. (1954). *The tastemakers*. New York: Harper.

MacEwan, G. (1950). *Agriculture on parade: The Story of the fairs and exhibitions of Western Canada*. Toronto: Thomas Nelson.

Mitchell, W. J. T. (2002). Showing seeing: A critique of visual culture. *Journal of Visual Culture, 1*, 165–181.

Pineau, E. L. (2002). Critical performance pedagogy: Fleshing out the politics of liberatory education. In N. Stucky & C. Winner (Eds.), *Teaching performance studies* (pp. 41–54). Carbondale: Southern Illinois University Press.

Pink, S. (2009). *Doing sensory ethnography*. London: Sage.

Potkins, M. (2012). Ambitious Stampede production to recall history of the horse in southern Alberta. *Calgary Herald*, June 28. Retrieved December 30, 2013, from www.calgaryherald.com/sports/mbitious+Stampede+production+recall+history+horse+southern+Alberta/6628414/story.html

Pratt, M. L. (1991). Arts of the contact zone. *Profession*, 33–40.

Probyn-Rapsey, F. (2007). Complicity, critique, and methodology. *Ariel, 38*(2–3), 65–82.

Rusted, B. (2006). Performing visual discourse: Cowboy art and institutional practice. *Text and Performance Quarterly, 26*, 115–137.

Rusted, B. (2011). Embodied learning and pedagogical places. In G. Melnyk & C. Sutherland (Eds.), *The art of university teaching*. Calgary, Alberta: Detselig Enterprises.

Rusted, B. (2012). The century of art at the Calgary Stampede. *Alberta History*, Summer, 80–87.

Taliaferro, J. (1996). *Charles M. Russell: The life and legend of an American cowboy artist*. New York: Little Brown and Company.

Turner, C. (2012). Calgary reconsidered. *The Walrus*, June. Retrieved December 29, 2013, from thewalrus.ca/calgary-reconsidered/2/?ref=2012.06-society-calgary-reconsidered&galleryPage

Van Rosendaal, J. (2008). Where's the Alberta beef? *FFWD Fast Forward Weekly*, July 3. Retrieved from www.ffwdweekly.com/article/life-style/food/wheres-alberta-beef/

Weadick, G. (1966). Origin of the Calgary Stampede. *Alberta Historical Review, 14*(4), 20–24.

Wetherell, I., & Kmet, D. G. (1990). *Useful pleasures: The shaping of leisure in Alberta 1896–1945*. Regina: Alberta Culture and Canadian Plains Research Center

Chapter 16

A Marxist Methodology for Critical Collaborative Inquiry

Mirka Koro-Ljungberg and Fred Boateng

Introduction

This chapter has been written as a pamphlet to promote types of literary engagement different from what some journal readers might expect. We hope it will be more accessible than traditional scientific text and will engage and inspire readers to consider the role of collaboration in their scholarship, especially outside academia, and how collaborations are shaped by intentions and ideologies. We use the pamphlet-style texts and images for engagement and provocation purposes. As such, beyond this introductory section we will not use any references but will provide them in the form of a reading list. If you would like a copy of the chapter in APA style, please contact the first author.

Our use of the pamphlet format was inspired by various activists, nationalists, and critical theorists who have used pamphlets to distribute information, poetry, and creative literature; state opinions; reach argumentative opponents; and share policy briefs through far-reaching yet economical ways (see, e.g., *Red Chalk* [www.ieps.org.uk/redchalk.php] published by Hill, Cole, McLaren, & Rikowski). More specifically, the origin of pamphlets

Qualitative Inquiry Outside the Academy edited by Norman K. Denzin and Michael D. Giardina, 293–324. © 2014 Left Coast Press, Inc. All rights reserved.

goes back to Western and Oriental political systems. For example, in the United States pamphlets were used in the fight for independence. Thomas Paine's (1831) *Common Sense* was a literary tool that accelerated the revolutionary fervor of Americans against British rule (Hoffman, 2006; Rakove, 1979). Hunter (2012) described how the Chinese and Russians used newspapers, postcards, stamps, reports, and other printed materials as avenues for political communication or to document the history of societies, organizations, and personalities. Sometimes pamphlets were also used for mass education and to shape public sentiments against foreign powers. Pamphlets were also used in 18th-century France under the Ancien Régime as an instrument of attack by antimonarchists (Darnton, 1995). Specifically in education, pamphlets criticized the control of education by the church and the accessibility of an elite education to only the aristocrats and nobility in French society.

Many pamphlets include images. Pink (2001) and Rose (2007) noted the increased importance of visuals in modern and postmodern societies: "Modern forms of understanding the world depend on a scopic regime that equates seeing with knowledge" (Rose, 2007, p. 3), whereas in a postmodern world people interact more and more with completely constructed visual experiences. Thus, visual materials can serve as effective tools to break free from grand narratives by questioning the connections between seeing and knowing. It was also impossible for us to think about pamphlets and the role of ideology in collaborative inquiry and educational research without visual imagery. Thus we use images to (1) illustrate how ideologies filter into education discourses and (2) show historical visual extensions that exemplify differing degrees of totalizing ideologies in education contexts. The text that accompanies the images represents only one possible reading of the image and visual objects embedded in it.

Finally, our purpose in writing a pamphlet is to promote dialogue and engagement with those, both inside and outside academia, who are interested in methodological concepts and practice of critical collaborative inquiry. Even though we situate our arguments in the context of Marxism, dialectics, and education, we acknowledge that our adaptive and modified uses of dialectics are not "pure" in the sense of totalizing or potentially disempowering discourses, and that is our intentional choice. Instead, we hope that ideas presented in this chapter can be used across disciplines and perspectives. We take a position, but we do not argue that our position necessarily needs to be the reader's position. We do not claim that Marxist dialectics are the only meaningful way to engage in collaborative inquiry, but we want to inspire scholars to read and use Marx to shape their methodologies and research engagements. Dialectics, in this chapter, is used to describe a method of argument and analysis that attempts to 'resolve' and address contradictions in opposing views, conflicting social and material forces, and different relations of production and power (see Kain, 1980, 1982; Marx & Engels, 1967; Ollman, 2006).

Similar to Magnus and Cullenberg (2006), we see Marx or Marxism as plural nouns, and Marxism is always historically situated. Instead of considering Marxism as singular, rigid designator, we view Marxism(s) as historically situated traditions, histories, and scholarship inspired by Marx and Engels and often focusing on diverse aspects of political economy, dialectical conflicts, political history, and analysis of material conditions (see also Audi, 1995; Macey, 2000).

According to Derrida (2006), Marx is always with us, whether we believe in Marxism or not, since our culture always carries a form of Marxist heritage and history; Marx haunts each and all of us who live within a political and economical system. Haunting and pervasive forces of the past work; theorizing, history, and dialogue shape our presence and absences. The memories of Marxist ideology, dialectics, imagined conversations with Marx or Engels, conversations with ourself about Marx talking back to us; these specters stay with us. "They are always there, specters, even if they do not exist, even if they are no longer, even if they are not yet" (Derrida, 2006, p. 221). In this pamphlet we encourage readers to live with the ghost of Marxism, have spectral conversations about dialectics, and enter into simultaneous space of absence and presence; to rethink 'there' and what is being excluded. The more Marxism and Marxist dialects are said to be dead, the more they may still be with us.

Acknowledgment

An earlier version of this chapter will be published in the journal, *Teachers and Teaching: Theory and Practice.*

References

Audi, R. (Ed.). (1995). *The Cambridge dictionary of philosophy.* Cambridge, UK: Cambridge University Press.

Darnton, R. (1995). *The forbidden best-sellers of pre-revolutionary France.* New York: W. W. Norton.

Derrida, J. (2006). *Specters of Marx* (P. Kamuf, Trans.). New York: Routledge.

Hoffman, D. C. (2006). Paine and prejudice: Rhetorical leadership through perceptual framing in Common Sense. *Rhetoric and Public Affairs, 9*(3), 373–410.

Hunter, E. (2012). *Chinese pamphlet digitization project,* Retrieved on September 15, 2013, from ecollections.crl.edu/cdm4/index_hunters. php?CISOROOT=/hunters

Kain, P. (1980). Marx's dialectic method. *History & Theory, 19*(3), 294–312.

Kain, P. (1982). Marx, Engels, and dialectics. *Studies in Soviet Thought, 23*(4), 271–283.

Macey, D. (2000). *The penguin dictionary of critical theory.* London: Penguin Books.

Magnus, B., & Cullenberg, S. (2006). Editors' introduction. In J. Derrida (Ed.), *Specters of Marx* (pp. viii–xii). New York: Routledge.

Marx, K., & Engels, F. (1967). *Capital: A critique of political economy.* New York: International.

Ollman, B. (2006). Why dialectics? Why now? *Synthesis/Regeneration, 40.* Retrieved February 5, 2014, from www.greens.org/s-r/40/40-19.html

Paine, T. (1831). *Common sense.* London: J. Watson.

Pink, S. (2001). *Doing visual ethnography.* London: Sage.

Rakove, J. N. (1979). *The beginnings of national politics: An interpretive history of the Continental Congress.* New York: Knopf.

Rose, G. (2007). *Visual methodologies.* London: Sage.

Call for Marxist Methodology for Critical Collaborative Inquiry

Addressed to
Qualitative Researchers and Critical Researchers
On the Following Subjects:

Part I
Ideologies Infiltrating Methodology and Education

Part II
Dialectics Serving Critical Collaborative Inquiry

Part I
Ideologies Infiltrating Methodology and Education

Ideologies and other value systems that guide people's thinking are not neutral. Every educational and policy decision is based on specific views, purposes, aims, and hidden agendas, and is guided by different values and cultural beliefs about the nature of knowledge. Often these purposes and agendas are guided by production and capital (human and material). The end products of policy-oriented research produce recommendations for actions and change, and policy-oriented research is always responsive and interactive. Thus, an interactive or dialectic relationship between researchers and participants, teachers and policymakers, is based on immediacy; it is purposeful and aims to promote sustainable change.

Are you aware of the different material effects ideology has on your life? Ideology is a fairly coherent set of values and beliefs about the way the social, economic, and political systems should be organized and operated, and recommendations about how these values and beliefs should be put into effect. Ideologies also provide an analysis of the current situation, a vision of the ideal society, and a plan for bringing that society closer to that ideal. Problems arise when ideologies are not talked about but are assumed, when recurring ideological battles result in the emergence of dominant cultural ideologies, and when methodological dogmas are taken as truths.

Sadly, education, too, is used as a dogma. It is used for economical stratification and to divide society into two hierarchical groups: the rich, powerful, upper-class and the powerless poor. Ideology works pedagogically to produce or reproduce social inequalities, and schools and education systems play a pivotal role in inculcating the dominant ideology and entrenching domination. Instead of liberating children, public education reproduces inequalities among children from different backgrounds by creating and re-creating socioeconomic hierarchical relationships and perpetuating social stratification. Some argue that education in the United States promotes choice, equity, quality, and efficiency, but at the same time, production and economical investment is seen as the main asset and product of an effective education system. The training of a compliant and uncritical workforce is considered one of the biggest aims of current educational policy.

(Ideology of colonization): Education as an ideological metaphor for contextual reality and/or as a conduit for totalizing ideology.
Source: Creative Commons

The fierce-looking, patriotically dressed teacher points a cane at four scared children who are inscribed with four territories: Philippines, Hawaii, Cuba, and Puerto Rico (holy grails of territories for the American government). Other children who appear to have the trust of the teacher are comfortably reading, and a Native American student is separated from the other children. Following the example of England, the blackboard informs us of the right of America to rule the territories, regardless of consent. The man represents the American government, and the cane stands for authority/legitimacy. The children stand for the states that were part of the Union. The secluded Native American symbolizes dispossessed Native Americans who were victims of America's territorial expansion (Manifest Destiny).

Policy and methodology are also directly linked with institution-alized positions and frameworks of dominance. We know that, similar to policy research, approaches and methodologies are not neutral or separate from ideologies and philosophies. We also know that during the current times of epistemological and ideological dispersion, epistemological and theoretical aware-ness are increasingly important. Epistemologies and ideologies guide methodological choices, and epistemological diversity is essential to the construction and use of education research and research training. Thus, awareness of one's ideological position and how it potentially builds on and contradicts other positions can be a meaningful point of ethical reflection. Theories and ideologies cannot be divorced from research practices. Instead, closer alignment between methodology and ideology not only strengthens research but can also help scholars and practitio-ners make informed decisions throughout different collaborative research activities.

An increasing number of qualitative researchers engage in collaborative activities. For example, some scholars have developed a transformative model to represent how learning occurs in a collaborative writing partnership in adult educa-tion, and others have propounded the idea of the "interpretive zone" to describe how collaborative interpretation of research unfolds. The interpretive zone's importance lies in its critical location for future methodological inquiry and examination of the dynamics of group research. Sometimes different forms of collaboration are theoretically uninformed and institution-ally driven, and other times collaboration is used as a proxy for diversification of labor or a means to reduce labor costs and increase the profitability of research investments. At the same time, collaborative qualitative research can become a powerful tool to impact policy, promote change, and transform normative notions of reality. In these productively collaborative projects, research designs are often emergent and iterative rather than linear and mechanical. Similarly, data analysis is not conceptualized as an individual discovery but as a collaboratively constructed activity aimed at changing existing practices. Consequently, findings are not represented as an individual product but as part of an ongoing conversation with the public and those served by research.

Instead of seeing collaboration as a productive force aimed at facilitating transformation, collaboration could be considered a normative practice and activity reflective of institutional expectations. When collaboration is viewed as imperative, the ideologies guiding collaboration are accompanied by the positive valuation of the maximal sharing and access of scholarly resources. In this view, scholars have a responsibility toward their discipline and relevant communities (both academic and local) to share information, data, and the results of research in a form (or range of forms) that is accessible to both scholarly and nonscholarly audiences. The high likelihood of collaborative projects rests on research that is longitudinal and more expensive, and that requires multiple disciplines to answer research questions. The ethical context is also important. A primary motivator for collaboration is egalitarianism: consultatively establishing protocols and equally valuing and recognizing the intellectual contributions of all project members.

From another perspective, collaborative inquiry is essential when a solo researcher may not be able to obtain research funding and may be at a competitive disadvantage on the job market. Collaboration as a Trojan horse reflects current neoliberal emphasis on cost-cutting to avoid wasting scarce resources. Collaboration is carried out in the name of advancing scientific knowledge and is needed, for example, to mine "big" data. While there is absolutely no a priori disadvantage to such collaboration, some of the skepticism from social scientists is likely rooted in the suspicion that humanism will be tainted either by economic ideologies or by association with commercial enterprises.

Furthermore, collaboration in social sciences can be seen as an ethical responsibility. For example, the work of the American Anthropological Association's El Dorado Task Force emphasized that collaborative research models should include not only research combined with advocacy but also collaborative research, where all parties work together toward a mutually beneficial research program. Furthermore, collaborative ethnography and collaboration between researchers and study participants are powerful ways to use anthropology to serve humankind more directly and rapidly. Collaborative ethnography may include research practices that use participants as readers and editors, enlist focus groups to solicit responses and participants' reactions to the research process, employ editorial boards and consultant teams, organize community forums, and implement coproduced or cowritten texts. Similarly, in public ethnography, research questions, study sites, and methods are relevant to the public and people's everyday activities.

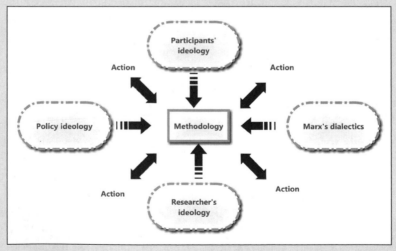

Figure 1: Complex relationship between ideologies and methodology in collaborative inquiry

Making ideology and methodology more evident and relevant is a more challenging task in a collaborative inquiry (see Figure 1) compared with many individually directed research projects. Ideology and methodology often become plural, or at least have various layers and components, and the actions following or preceding ideology and methodology are numerous. Sometimes ideologies and methodologies are hidden, unspoken, and not communicable. Even though many ideologies and methodologies might exist, collaborative projects form coalitions. For example, in a feminist collaborative community, there might be a plethora of standpoints, contexts, and positions, but collaborators can still drift into effective and powerful issue-based coalitions between the standpoints.

In addition, questioning and addressing policy implications can become even more critical when scholars collect data from multiple sources, design collaborative projects that move toward a shared goal, or analyze data in conjunction with theories of emancipation and empowerment. More radical, transformative, and collaborative qualitative research is needed that occurs at points of tension and builds on multiple sites and transformative methodologies. This collaboration should interrogate political discourses, structures, and material environments, and this transformative collaborative research is likely to build on numerous locations, differential consciousness of participants and collaborators, and various epistemologies.

Think about the paucity of methodologically meticulous projects where different research phases (from discovery to activism) come together in one project or in a series of projects. In the approach we advocate here, scholars are grounded in research practice, which brings together tools and concepts from Marx, dialectics, critical theory, and emancipatory discourses conceptually, methodologically, longitudinally, and collaboratively. Theory and practice connect in a new space where ideology shapes abstractions and abstractions shape activities. It is time to research, theorize, and study collaboratively.

(Ideology of liberalism): Success and failure.

Source: Creative Commons

The text in this image can be translated from top left to bottom right as "Success," "Liberal people should try all their efforts to build a liberal world," and "Failure." This image shows the dichotomy of success and failure. Education leads to success and happiness. In the first half of the image, there is a smiling graduate and a pupil being awarded by a man. Under Mao's era, peasants and downtrodden people accessed education for the first time. Education for all meant all would be liberated to contribute to the progress of society. A lack of education meant deprivation, which is indicated by the second half of the image.

Part 11
Dialectics Serving Critical Collaborative Inquiry

Dialectical theory of knowledge as conceptualized by Marx, following Hegel, is based on the reciprocal transformation of subject and object. Marx's dialectical method analyzes concrete circumstances and classifications by breaking social worlds into different units of abstraction. For Marx, abstractions are not things but processes. Each process of abstraction serves as a subordinate part of other processes that form clusters of relations. For example, capital is a relation in that it links means of production to labor, value, and commodity. These classifications and reconstructions of social worlds enable transformation and the translation of theory into social and political action. Dialectic method allows researchers to look back from the present not to study historical developments per se but rather the development of categories and relationships.

Dialectics can also be seen as a "method" (for us, this refers to an inquiry, ways to process modes of life) that attempts to resolve or address contradictions in opposing views or ideas by understanding the relations. Dialectics is a heuristic orientation toward contradictions and relations. Since contradictions are interrelational yet different (sometimes viewed as isolated) aspects of the same phenomenon, contradictions form an internal conflict. The analysis of contradictions acknowledges that all things have inherent negatives and positives, are dying but simultaneously developing.

Dialectical method is also a historical inquiry into how those in power use ideology to make oppression, inequity, and injustice appear natural and historical. Dialectical method begins with abstract categories and then moves toward concrete categories, ultimately forming advocacy-in-action. Not only does the praxis of labor or industry transform the object, but also consciousness is a form of praxis that dialectically transforms and constitutes the object. Marx begins his analysis with simple categories like value, labor, worker (i.e., teacher, student, achievement, responsibility) and works out the relationships between the concepts in modern society, such as measuring workers' value in labor (teachers are responsible for the production of student achievement). Marx was interested in how wealth is produced, distributed, and exchanged among different classes. After he identified patterns in interactions between different processes and relations, he considered preconditions. The examination of relationships enables researchers to understand the concrete, such as prices, profit, and rate of profit (accountability movement, inequity, or teachers' lack of pedagogical independence).

In his later work, including *The German Ideology*, Marx slightly redefined his method and described three parallel processes: historical generation of the actual concrete; historical rise and development of categories that represent the actual concrete; and methodological ordering, prioritizing, and establishing interconnections of categories. Marx's understandings of the actual concrete are interpretations situated within particular paradigms. By considering the earlier development of the actual concrete, one can understand one's own ideas and science.

The analysis of categories and their relationships that can create oppression and inequity can also be useful tools for collaborative inquiry in educational contexts (see Figure 2). Similar to the public engagement projects in the United Kingdom, our framework also builds on dialogical interplay between community groups and researchers. We use examples from education and how teachers, administrators, community members, and activists could work together against inequitable and unfair educational conditions created, for example, by differential education funding. This research framework might also be best carried out in settings in which participants from different contexts form a core research team that collectively contributes to the project. Diverse representation of various stakeholders (i.e., teachers, children, administrators, community members, policymakers, and university collaborators, among others) could enable deeper investigation of different modes of life that are affected by local educational histories and current educational conditions. Any individual or collective workload and research responsibilities could also vary across stages. For example, teachers from one school could be responsible for discovering teachers' collective voices, whereas university or community partners could contribute more to the interruption and transformation phase of the research. Alternatively, teaching teams could collect data, and school-level teams could analyze findings and create policy recommendations. Ownership within the collaboration needs to be negotiated.

Next, we discuss in more detail the dialectical process for critical collaborative inquiry that can enable deeper understanding of relations between collective experiences, political structures, and material environments. This process begins from a position of undifferentiated unity in which teachers, researchers, and other collaborators work toward the same goals in undivided ways. However, since circumstances, categories, and relationships are only assumed—not necessarily historically situated, thoroughly analyzed, or reflected upon—the perceived unity is undifferentiated. Through analysis, engagement, and dialogue, collaborators begin to notice contradictions and opposing views. The analysis or contradictions can lead to methodological and conceptual ordering that helps collaborators create differentiated unity—unity that is singular and ethical (instead of totalizing), holistic and communal even with irresolvable differences, contradictions, and points of singularity.

The proposed series of encounters with diverse stakeholders can enable researchers to get to know the phenomenon under investigation or the "mode of life" at a deeper level and from a range of perspectives. Four proposed study phases (see Figure 2) allow researchers to build shared commitment and collective responsibility for equity and change. The collaborators carry the main findings from one study phase to another. In other words, findings and insights gained from earlier phases are used as information or discussion points during the subsequent phases. For example, the findings from Phase 1 could shape research questions, conversation topics, and discussion agendas during Phase 2.

(Ideology of communalism): Education as a conduit for the propagation of the state values of collectivity.

Source: Creative Commons

This image shows children belonging to the Young Pioneers. They hold products of innovation and breakthroughs benefitting the state, demonstrating the utility of the talents of children regardless of background. Additionally, family was perceived to be the agency of the bourgeoisie, nurturing children to satisfy individual objectives. The image emphasizes the preeminence of the collective goal of the state to use ideological schools like the Young Pioneers to inculcate and indoctrinate the values of collectivity of the state to children.

Each phase of the collaboration supports and builds on one shared research agenda, but each stage could also include a set of separate yet conceptually and/or materially linked studies. Additionally, each phase has unique goals and purposes that support the shared research agenda of the collaborative team. By *goals*, we mean specific aims and reasons for engaging in proposed tasks and exchanges.

More specifically, Marx's dialectical interpretation of abstract (categories) and concrete (circumstance) refers to the incomplete, lopsided, or homogeneous way of perceiving things (abstract) compared to the synthesis of different perspectives of which each one is abstract in sense making (concrete). For example, in the process of collective meaning-making, if teachers come out with a single method of inquiry, that would fall within abstract categories because it will be seen as totalizing. However, if they come up with many perspectives of inquiry or a multifaceted single inquiry, they achieve the concrete. Collaborators interact with their abstracts, and the end process thereof is the concrete—the synthesized meaning-making of abstracts. For the relationship between abstracts, collaborators' ideas are scrutinized through dialogue. The ideas that emanate out of collaborators' sense making and dialogue are not totalizing, but they may reflect the blend of dialogical interrelated ideologies. Dialectics is a theory of emergence, development, and resolution of contradictions. It is not about transforming one quality or perspective into another, but it is a commitment to ongoing analysis and reflection on emerging contradictions, new qualities, and new concentrations. Research is its own site of production.

During the first phase of the proposed methodological framework, collective experiences, beliefs, and values are studied. The purpose of this phase is not only to document existing perceptions, experiences, and "realities" but also to examine other teachers' and collaborators' investments into a particular line of inquiry, as well as their commitment to specific changes in practice and policy. The first stage involves the study of collectivity of experiences, beliefs, and values as

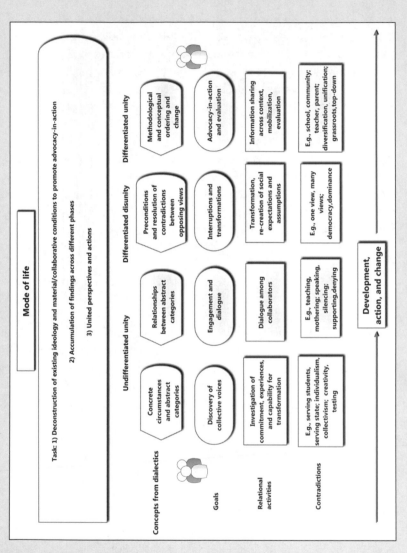

Figure 2: Dialectical process for critical collaborative inquiry

viewed by the participants; whereas, in the second stage, individual views, beliefs, and values are scrutinized in light of other views, beliefs, values.

For example, it could be beneficial to negotiate with other teachers and community members on how the proposed research can impact practice and how collaboration can promote desired policy changes. Researchers ask what kinds of changes are expected or realistic and what it would take to activate change in particular communities in terms of resources, material, and social capital. In this phase, the goal of interactions and data collection is to discover and identify concrete circumstances and abstract categories that shape everyday practices. Following, we share examples of current or recent projects that have some elements of the proposed framework. These examples are meant to serve as stimuli and an indication that this work is not new but already exists in different contexts.

Example 1: MetLife Fellows from Teachers Network Leadership Institute have played a major role in improving economics and student achievement nationwide, especially in New York City schools. They work closely with various campaigns and organizations to provide more equitable educational opportunities for students throughout the nation. More specifically, "Making the Case!" was created to ensure that teachers' voices inform and shape policy making. MetLife Fellows, who were also fulltime classroom teachers, composed 19 cases based on their action research projects to better understand the connections between practice, policy, and student achievement. Collectively, these cases were intended to help policymakers understand firsthand how policy impacts classroom practices. The teacher authors used cases to illustrate their best practices; practice creative problem solving, analysis, and ways of thinking; selfreflect; and, finally, engage policymakers.

Example 2: Many teacher-voice groups work under the assumption that participation in policy discussions also affords teachers prospective leadership opportunities. In this regard, school districts experimenting with career ladders for teachers often collaborate with the teacher-voice organizations to increase opportunities for professional development. Officials of the District of Columbia Public Schools, or DCPS, have added teacher-voice organization opportunities, such as the Hope Street Group National Teacher Fellowship, the Teach Plus Teaching Policy Fellowship, and the U.S. Department of Education's Teaching Ambassador Fellowship, to their list of leadership training experiences in DCPS's career-ladder program for teachers known as the Leadership Initiative For Teachers, or LIFT.

Example 3: In the 2010–2011 school year, Education 4 Excellence (a New York-based teacher-voice organization) teachers authored their first policy papers centered on topics of teacher evaluation and seniority-based lay-offs. Facing budget cuts, at the same time New York City was wrestling with the prospect of retrenching thousands of teachers. E4E teachers met with New York City Mayor Michael Bloomberg and members of the state legislature to present their ideas for how to alleviate the impact of quality-blind layoffs, or when teachers are laid off regardless of their performance in the classroom. Those ideas were adopted by lawmakers and became Senate Bill 3501, which was passed by the state senate. The E4E proposal suggested three levels for teacher layoffs: chronic absenteeism, teachers with multiple unsatisfactory evaluations, and teachers who were in the absent-teacher reserve pool for more than six months.

The second phase of the framework builds on the findings from the first. At this time teachers and other collaborators are encouraged to form working groups, establish informal discussion groups, and participate in formal focus-group interviews to discuss issues raised in the previous study phase. In these groups, participants interact with other teachers, stakeholders, and community members outside their immediate school context. The goal is to begin to question assumed collective meanings and knowledge and to plan, identify action steps, and begin a critical dialogue among involved parties. Scholarship focuses on the relations of forces and modes of life, not individuals. These forces and forms change the state of history by acting, creating, and submerging classes and groups.

Ideally, discussions on relations and forces are decontextualized as little as possible, and different sections of dialogue and various social modes of life, rather than a single word or independent sentence, serve as the analysis unit. Investigation focuses on the consciousness of individuals only in relation to their material conditions and modes of existence. Yet individuals cannot be forced to give away their real life content since this surrendering will make them incapable of defining themselves in a dialectical process with social and material forces.

Example: The National Writing Project (NWP) works in partnership with institutions, organizations, and communities to develop and sustain leadership for educational improvement. It is a network of teacher consultants and university sites that connect with learning communities and teachers from different disciplines and grade levels. Professional development is viewed as one of the main vehicles for school reform, and NWP trains teacher leaders to facilitate change in local communities. NWP emphasizes the importance of dialogue and multiple cultural and experiential ways of knowing. Furthermore, NWP offers an infrastructure for improvement, providing direct services and generating educational capital through shared knowledge, leadership, and partnership.

NIÑOS SANDINISTAS

Toño, Delia y Rodolfo pertenecen a la Asociación de Niños Sandinistas (ANS).
Los niños sandinistas usan un pañuelo.
Participan en las tareas de la Revolución y son muy estudiosos.

(Ideology of patriotism): Education as an ideological tool for serving national interests.

Source: Creative Commons

The text in Spanish translates, "Sandinista Children: Toño, Delia and Rodolfo belong to the Association of Sandinista Children (ANS). The Sandinista children wear Sandinista-colored neckerchiefs around their necks. They participate in the works of the Revolution and are very studious." This image illustrates the connection between the Nicaraguan revolution in the 1980s and the importance of educating children to stimulate desired practices, behaviors, and political beliefs. The Sandinista, a Marxist-oriented political part, ruled Nicaragua from 1979 to 1990. The Sandinista-orientated curriculum was to instill the virtues of patriotism and to uphold collective interests to the detriment of individual interests, among others. The three children together illustrate the benefit of collectivity as children of different classes unite and do well in school. At the time textbooks were inundated with Sandinista nationalistic role models and children were imbued with nationalist

*fervor. Education was believed to achieve egalitarianism and gal-
vanize students together to satiate national interests.*

The third phase of the proposed framework attempts to facilitate
transformation and alleviate assumptions based on findings from
previous phases. It is guided by participants' collective vision
for a better future and their transformation of social expectations. One example of current work that has re-created social
expectations and changed the ways scholars and communities
think about environmental sciences is Corburn's *Street Science*
(2005). According to Corburn, street science is a combination of science, political inquiry, and community action. In his
project, he drew examples from community case studies to
illustrate various health concerns, hybridizing professional and
local discourses and disrupting "traditional" forms of science
by exemplifying how science on the streets of Brooklyn takes
place. He also reconnected and reconceptualized public health
and urban planning in the context of social justice.

Critical scholars embrace and value research practices
that simultaneously produce change and demonstrate historical situatedness. This connection to historical situatedness is a
fruitful beginning for the analysis of differentiated disunity and
preconditions that have shaped the development of the concrete as described by Marx. Furthermore, group discussions
are not arranged to collect data per se but to stimulate questioning and transformation through differences. During the
third phase, the core research team could conduct individual
discussions with key informants, arrange discussion groups,
and observe existing practices and events. Instead of generating collective meanings and knowledge as intended in the
previous phase, now the epistemological focus shifts toward
re-creation, questioning, and challenging dominant views,
structures, and positions. Through shared activities, collaborators begin to notice considerable differences in perspectives
and situational forces affecting individuals' lives.

*Example 1: Scholars have also emphasized the importance
of critical reflection and how this reflection, collaboration,*

315

communicative elaboration, and exchange can create openings for "unthought." For example, some scholar-activists have put the philosophy of difference to work (e.g., using ideas from Derrida, Foucault, and Deleuze) in their knowledge exchange research project (e.g., El Sistema) to create social change through music. Researchers used Derrida's aporetic notions of knowledge to describe various encounters with participants and communities when attending Learning Space meetings. Researchers met with different community members and stakeholders to assemble perspectives and understandings that ultimately highlighted competing obligations and tensions between researchers and policy partners.

Example 2: Through unique and bipartisan events, Hope Street Group, a national nonpartisan organization, convenes diverse networks of leaders to focus on developing bold, evidence-based solutions and identifying and quickly adapting the structural changes needed. These policy teams work on the Hope Street Group platform, a private online workspace that allows participants from all over the country to engage in meaningful conversations about reform.

The last phase of the proposed framework documents various efforts that promote activism and advocacy to mobilize communities, organizations, and individuals. Collaborators must see themselves as united individuals with a shared goal. Only through unity can individuals bring material and social forces under human control and man's potential be achieved. Self-activity and reflexivity is tied to various forms of social ownership. Ideas, processes, and actions are communal, not individual; a new mode of life is being established. At this point collaborators would reflect on the previous phases and accomplishments and evaluate the progress of their advocacy and policy work. For example, during the previous phase, researchers analyzed different preconditions of the concrete and examined resolutions of contractions and opposing views, whereas now collaborators order and prioritize circumstances and practices. They engage in methodological ordering, prioritize certain needs and actions, and establish particular interconnections of categories.

Collaborators can conduct site visits and observe key informants' interactions with stakeholders and policymakers. It can be informative to document and record hearings and collect relevant drafts of policies, bills, and lobbyist letters. Writing policy memos, articles, opinion pieces, newsletters, and blogs is also an effective way to distribute findings and promote ongoing dialogue.

Example: The Civil Rights Project (CRP), founded at Harvard University in 1996 to provide intellectual capital to academics, policymakers, and civil rights advocates (see civilrightsproject. ucla.edu/about-us/mission-statement), was created to serve as a multidisciplinary research and policy think-tank and consensus-building clearinghouse that follows scholarly standards. It is committed to building a network of legal and social science scholars across the nation, including collaborations with different advocacy organizations, policymakers, and journalists. CRP's initial focus on education reform now also includes connections between ideas and actions to promote racial and ethnic equity. CRP has initiated national conferences and roundtables, commissioned hundreds of new research and policy studies, and contributed extensively to the literature on desegregation, diversity, and other equity problems facing U.S. schools. CRP directors and staff have also testified and assisted policymakers at the state and national levels, and their research has impacted legislation, litigations, and hearings.

A Call to *A*ction

Scholars need to stop engaging in research activities for research's sake only. Research needs to serve the public, citizens, students, parents, teachers, and so on. Social science research should be a collaborative effort and a form of "public science." It is time to consider how to increase methodological attentiveness and the potential of collaborative inquiry that builds on collective yet contradictory stories, abstract and material life experiences, and that are located in the intersection of theory and practice. The proposed methodological framework offers one way to increase possibilities for collaborative dialogical inquiry to facilitate sustainable change that builds on stakeholders' involvement and community partners' shared commitment. At the same time, it is important to keep in mind that the framework is a tool to be adapted and modified. Methodological modifications and adaptations are likely to take place when this framework is applied to qualitative studies in different contexts and with different study and research aims.

We did not use Marx's work and theories to confuse, mislead, or divorce readers' attention from methodology and practice. Rather, Marx's dialectic is used to build conceptual connections to the existing critical scholarship. A framework that builds from Marx's dialectic method can enable scholars to build trustworthy and long-term relationships with participating communities while at the same time taking into account historical contexts, concrete circumstances, lived experiences, and distribution of social goods and funds of knowledge. This framework also shifts the inquiry from hierarchical and inflexible research models toward collaborative and practice-based research that is open to methodological modifications and conceptual revisions.

We see qualitative inquiry as a public inquiry that calls for collective action and consciousness raising. Material and historical conditions shape individuals, and more importantly, from Marx's perspective, they form collective experiences and modes of life. The line between researcher and activist, individual and community, becomes blurred, and different roles and knowledge interrelate and overlap. Since many activists share the goals of communication and emancipation, they are unsurprisingly drawn into qualitative research. Researchers' various positions cannot be separated from one another, and ethical questions associated with critical collaborative inquiry—such as standards, expectations, and values—call for ongoing reflection.

Although reading in terms of dialogue and desire is laudable, reading in questioning, countering, and oppositional modes is also beneficial. As a part of ongoing reflection, scholars and collaborators can practice reading "against the text." Reading against a text can be seen as a way to uncover hidden ideological and political connections within a text. We encourage you, our readers, to read against this text. This could alert you to stay sensitive to how the text supports or challenges political assumptions and beliefs. Subjective responses resulting from reading against the text can assist you in unmasking meaning, which fosters involvement and investment. Ask critical questions about yourself and your orientation!

Another way of understanding hidden political and ideological patterns is offered by Fairclough in his work on discourse. The first way to increase understanding includes a description in which ideological lexical choices, classification schemes, etc. are detailed. The second relates to the interpretation readers attach to the described text. And the third approach creates an explanation that involves making explicit power relations, ideologies, and discourse. Throughout all these discursive readings, understanding texts is dependent on the active process of weaving together or connecting things into meaningful patterns. These patterns include understandings of temporal or spatial contexts and zeitgeist and considerations of how to mold specific texts' production and reception.

The hierarchy and intensity of different social and economic forces are hard to control and predict. However, critical collaborative inquiry aims to build social and material capital that can be sustainable long term, especially when communities are involved in research early on (project planning, analysis, dissemination, and locating sustainable and community-based resources). We need to put ideologies in the forefront, showing how they filter research decisions and how histories and realities are being developed dynamically over time. However, at the same time, collaborative inquiries can be less totalizing since every new collaborative team, set of intersubjectivities, and historical conditions create new formations with different dynamics. Systems produce ideologies, and collaborators form those systems, including more or less even distribution of material and social capital. Information sharing, skill building, education, and critical awareness can all contribute to more evenly distributed capital of all sorts.

In this chapter we propose that through transparent ideology, united yet differentiated forces and perspectives, participant involvement and emancipation (in terms of research activities), and the use of cultural artifacts and images, scholars can write texts that are accessible and could serve as inspiring examples of collaboration. Advocacy is about creating a space that can tackle social forces such as capital, production, race, and age in more critical yet productive ways. Advocacy is thus a confluence for the scrutiny of social forces. Dialectics teaches us the art of asking questions that do not generate forced consensus but can lead to action. Dialecticism is an exposition to contradictory views and a platform for the settlement/resolution of such views. Reasoning through dialogue enables collective consensus to be a platform for well-informed transformation and change underpinned by participation and sense making. The methodological framework (involving paradoxical and possibly absent processes characterized by undifferentiated disunity, differentiated unity, undifferentiated unity) seeks to herald the input and participation of teachers in their practice as a link to policy, with an objective to transform current practices and policies. The asking of questions, negotiations, organization of research methods, etc. are prerequisite to eliciting the participatory, dialogical, transformational input and output of teachers and their collaborators. However, our questions, negotiations, writings, and practices are shaped by the specters of other thoughts, writers, texts, theories, and ghosts of anticipated readers. Just imagine the ghosts of teachers in researchers and spirits of researchers in teachers. What changes and what becomes possible?

Reading List

Agostinone-Wilson, F. (2013). *Dialectical research methods in the classical Marxist tradition*. New York: Peter Lang.

Allan, J., Moran, N., Duffy, C., & Loening, G. (2010). Knowledge exchange with Sistema Scotland. *Journal of Education Policy, 25*(3), 335–347.

American Anthropological Association. (2002). *El Dorado Task Force papers.* Washington, D.C.: Author.

Barrett, R., &. Meaghan, D. (2006). Postsecondary education and the ideology of capitalist production. *The Innovation Journal: The Public Sector Innovation Journal, 11*(3), Article 10.

Baez, B., & Boyles, D. (2009). *The politics of inquiry: Education research and the "culture of science."* Albany: State University of New York Press.

Blau, J., & Smith, K. (Eds.). (2006). *Public sociology reader.* Lanham, MD: Rowman & Littlefield.

Burawoy, M. (2005). For public sociology. *American Sociological Review, 70*, 4–28.

Carr, W. (2006). Philosophy, methodology and action research. *Journal of Philosophy of Education, 40*(4), 421–435.

Carr, W., & Kemmis, S. (1986). *Becoming critical: Education, knowledge, and action research*. London: Falmer Press.

Carter, S., & Little, M. (2007). Justifying knowledge, justifying method, taking action: Epistemologies, methodologies, and methods in qualitative research. *Qualitative Health Research, 17*(10), 1316–1328.

Civil Rights Project. (n.d.). Retrieved May 16, 2011, from civilrightsproject.ucla.edu/about-us/mission-statement

Cohen, G. A. (1974). Marx's dialectic of labor. *Philosophy & Public Affairs, 3*(3), 235–261.

Corburn, J. (2005). *Street science: Community knowledge and environmental health justice*. Cambridge, MA: MIT Press.

Creswell, J. (2002). *Educational research: Planning, conducting, and evaluating quantitative and qualitative research*. Upper Saddle River, NJ: Merrill Prentice Hall.

Crotty, M. (1998). *The foundations of social research.* London: Sage.

Darnton, R. (1995). *The forbidden best-sellers of pre-revolutionary France.* New York: W. W. Norton.

Denzin, N., & Giardina, M. (2012). Introduction: Qualitative inquiry and the politics of advocacy. In N. Denzin & M. Giardina (Eds.), *Qualitative inquiry and the politics of advocacy* (pp. 9–37). Walnut Creek, CA: Left Coast Press, Inc.

Derrida, J. (2006). *Specters of Marx* (P. Kamuf, Trans.). New York: Routledge.

DeLyser, D., Herbert, S., Aitken, S., Crang, M., & McDowell, L. (2010). *Handbook of qualitative geography*. London: Sage.

Dupré, L. (1977). Idealism and materialism in Marx's dialectic. *The Review of Metaphysics, 30*(4), 649–685.

Dwyer, A. M. (2006). Ethics and practicalities of cooperative field-work and analysis. In G. Jost, N. Himmelmann, & U. Mosel (Eds.), *Fundamentals of language documentation: A handbook* (pp. 31–65). Berlin: Mouton de Gruyter.

Dwyer, A. M. (2012). Competing ideologies of collaborative research, KU Scholarworks, University of Kansas. Retrieved on September, 15, 2013, from kuscholarworks.ku.edu/dspace/bitstream/1808/10600/1/Dwyer2013_IdeologiesOfCollaboration.pdf

Engels, F., & Marx, K. (1967). *Capital: A critique of political economy.* New York: International.

Fairclough, N. (2001). *Language and power* (2nd edition). London: Longman.

Franks, M. (2002). Feminisms and cross-ideological feminist social research: Standpoint, situatedness, and positionality—Developing cross-ideological feminist research. *Journal of International Women Studies, 3*(2), Article 3.

Fonow, M., & Cook, J. (2005). Feminist methodology: New applications in the academy and public policy. *Signs: Journal of Women in Culture and Society, 30*(4), 2211–2236.

Gans, H. (2010). Public ethnography: Ethnography as public sociology. *Qualitative Sociology, 33*(1), 97–104.

Greco, N. (1992). Reading and writing against the text. *Language Arts Journal of Michigan, 8*(1), Article 4.

Haug, W. F. (2005). Dialectics. *Historical Materialism, 13*(1), 241–265.

Heck, R. H. (2004). *Studying educational and social policy: Theoretical concepts and research methods.* New York: Routledge.

Hoffman, D. C. (2006). Paine and prejudice: Rhetorical leadership through perceptual framing in Common Sense. *Rhetoric and Public Affairs, 9*(3), 373–410.

Howell, K. (2013). *An introduction to the philosophy of methodology.* Los Angeles: Sage.

Hunter, E. (2012). *Chinese pamphlet digitization project.* Retrieved on September 15, 2013, from ecollections.crl.edu/cdm4/index_hunters.php?CISOROOT=/hunters

Iannaccone, L. (1977). Three views of change in educational politics. In J. D. Scribner (Ed.), *The politics of education.* Chicago: National Society for the Study of Education.

Iannaccone, L. (1988). From equity to excellence: Political context and dynamics. In W. L. Boyd & C. T. Kershner (Eds.), *The politics of excellence and choice in education* (pp. 49–65). New York: Falmer.

Issak, A. (1987). *Politics.* Glenview, IL: Scott Foresman.

Ilyenkov, L. V. (2008). *From the history of Soviet philosophy.* Moscow: Sergey Mareev, Kul'turnaia revoliutsiia.

Jackson, A., & Mazzei, L. (2012). *Thinking with theory in qualitative research: Viewing data across multiple perspectives.* London: Routledge.

Kain, P. (1980). Marx's dialectic method. *History & Theory, 19*(3), 294–312.

Kain, P. (1982). Marx, Engels, and dialectics. *Studies in Soviet Thought, 23*(4), 271–283.

Karabel, J., & Halsey, A. H. (1977). *Power and ideology in education*, Oxford, UK: Oxford University Press.

Koro-Ljungberg, M., Yendol-Hoppey, D., Smith, J. J., & Hayes, S. B. (2009). Epistemological awareness, instantiation of methods, and uninformed methodological ambiguity in qualitative research projects. *Educational Researcher, 38*(9), 687–699.

Lassiter, L. (2005). Collaborative ethnography and public anthropology. *Current Anthropology, 46*(1), 83–106.

Lather, P. (2004). This is your father's paradigm: Government intrusion and the case of qualitative research in education. *Qualitative Inquiry, 10*(1), 15–34.

Lather, P. (2006). Paradigm proliferation as a good thing to think with: Teaching research in education as a wild profusion. *International Journal of Qualitative Studies in Education, 19*(1), 35–57.

Lather, P. (2007). *Getting lost: Feminist efforts toward a double(d) science.* Albany: State University of New York Press.

Lordly, D., Maclellan, D., Gingras, J., & Brady, J. (2012). A team-based approach to qualitative inquiry: The collaborative retreat. *Canadian Journal of Dietetic Practice and Research, 73*(2), 91–97.

Macey, D. (2000). *The Penguin dictionary of critical theory.* London: Penguin.

Magnus, B., & Cullenberg, S. (2006). Editors' introduction. In J. Derrida (Ed.), *Specters of Marx* (pp. viii–xii). New York: Routledge.

Making the case! New York: Teachers Network Leadership Institute.

Marx, K., Engels, F., Arthur, C. J., & Marx, K. (1970). *The German ideology: With selections from parts two and three, together with Marx's "Introduction to a critique of political economy."* New York: International.

Meek, M. (1992). Literacy: Rediscovering reading. In K. Kimberely, M. Meek, & J. Miller (Eds), *New readings. Contributions to an understanding of literacy.* London: A & C, Black.

National Writing Project. (n.d.) Retrieved May 16, 2011, from www.nwp.org/cs/public/print/doc/about.csp

Nisbet, J. (1997). Policy-oriented research. In J. Keeves (Ed.), *Educational research, methodology, and measurement: An international handbook* (2nd ed., pp. 211–217). New York: Pergamon.

Ollman, B. (2006). Why dialectics? Why now? *Synthesis/Regeneration, 40*. Retrieved February 5, 2014, from www.greens.org/s-r/40/40-19.html

Paine, T. (1831). *Common sense.* London: J. Watson

Pallas, A. (2001). Preparing education doctoral students for epistemological diversity. *Educational Researcher, 30*(5), 6–11.

Penfield, S., Serratos, A., Tucker, B., Flores, A., Harper, G., Hill, J., & Vasquez. N. (2008). Community collaborations: Best practices for North American Indigenous language documentation. *International Journal of the Sociology of Language 191*, 187–202.

Pennington, K. (2013). *New organizations, new voices: The landscape of today's teachers shaping policy.* Center for American Progress, June 2013.

Pink, S. (2001). *Doing visual ethnography*. London: Sage.

Rakove, J. N. (1979). *The beginnings of national politics: An interpretive history of the Continental Congress*. New York: Alfred A. Knopf.

Rice, K. (2006). Ethical issues in linguistic fieldwork: An overview. *Journal of Academic Ethics, 4*, 123–155.

Rose, G. (2007). *Visual methodologies*. London: Sage.

Sandoval, C. (2000). *Methodology of the oppressed*. Minneapolis: University of Minnesota Press.

Sax, B. C. (1984). Marx' dialectic of identity: The interlocking languages of the individual and structures in "The German Ideology." *Studies in Soviet Thought, 27*(4), 289–318.

Schostak, J., & Schostak, J. (2008). *Radical research: Designing, developing and writing research to make a difference*. London: Routledge.

Stenhouse, L. (1983). *Authority, education, and emancipation*. London: Heinemann Educational Books.

Stenhouse, L. (2001). The relevance of practice to theory. *Theory into Practice, XXII*(3), 211–215.

St. Pierre, E. (2002). "Science" rejects post-modernism. *Educational Researcher, 31*(8), 25–27.

St. Pierre, E. (2006). Scientifically based research in education: Epistemology and ethics. *Adult Education Quarterly, 56*(4), 239–266.

Swartz, A. L., & Triscari, J. S. (2011). A model of transformative collaboration. *Adult Education Quarterly, 61*(4), 324–340

Teachers Network. (n.d.). Retrieved May 16, 2011, from teachersnetwork.org/TNLI/

Teachers Network. (1991). *Teachers' vision of the future of education: A challenge to the nation*. New York: Author.

Torres, C. A., & Antikainen, A. (Eds.). (2003). *The international handbook on the sociology of education: An international assessment of new research and theory*. Lanham, MD: Rowman & Littlefield.

van der Riet, M. (2008). Participatory research and the philosophy of social science: Beyond the moral imperative. *Qualitative Inquiry, 14*(4), 546–565.

Villaverde, L. (2008). *Feminist theories and education*. New York: Peter Lang.

Watermeyer, R. (2011). Challenges for university engagement in the UK: Towards a public Academe? *Higher Education Quarterly, 65*(4), 386–410.

Wasser. J. D., & Bresler, L. (1996). Working in the interpretive zone: Conceptualizing collaboration in qualitative research teams. *Educational Researcher, 25* (5), 5–15

West, A. (1994). Reading against the text: Developing critical literacy. *Changing English: Studies in Culture and Education, 1*(1), 82–101.

Wineburg, S. (2001). *Historical thinking and other unnatural acts: Charting the future of teaching the past*. Philadelphia: Temple University Press.

Index

About the Authors

Editors

Norman K. Denzin is Distinguished Professor of Communications, College of Communications Scholar, and Research Professor of Communications, Sociology, and the Humanities at the University of Illinois, Urbana-Champaign. One of the world's foremost authorities on qualitative research and cultural criticism, Denzin is the author or editor of more than two dozen books, including *The Qualitative Manifesto, Performance Ethnography, Reading Race, Interpretive Ethnography, Images of Postmodern Society, The Recovering Alcoholic, The Alcoholic Self,* and *Flags in the Window.* Most recently, he has completed a trilogy on the American West, *Searching for Yellowstone, Custer on Canvas,* and *Indians on Display* (Left Coast). He is the editor of the landmark *Handbook of Qualitative Research* (4 editions, Sage, with Yvonna S. Lincoln), and coeditor of the *Handbook of Critical & Indigenous Methodologies* (2008, Sage, with Yvonna S. Lincoln and Linda Tuhiwai Smith). With Michael D. Giardina, he is coeditor of *Contesting Empire/Globalizing Dissent: Cultural Studies after 9/11* (Paradigm, 2006), and this series of books on qualitative inquiry published by Left Coast Press, Inc. He is also the editor of the journal, *Qualitative Inquiry* (with Yvonna S. Lincoln), founding editor of *Cultural Studies ↔ Critical Methodologies* and *International Review of Qualitative Research,* editor of *Studies in Symbolic Interaction,* and *Cultural Critique* series editor for Peter Lang Publishing. He is the founding president of the International Association for Qualitative Inquiry and director of the International Congress of Qualitative Inquiry.

Michael D. Giardina is an associate professor in the College of Education at Florida State University, where he also serves as the associate director of the FSU Center for Physical Cultural

Studies. He is the author or editor of a dozen books, including, most recently, *Sport, Spectacle, and NASCAR Nation: Consumption and the Cultural Politics of Neoliberalism* (PalgraveMacmillan, 2011, with Joshua I. Newman), which received the 2012 Outstanding Book award from the North American Society for the Sociology of Sport (NASSS) and was named as a 2012 *CHOICE* Outstanding Academic Title; and *Sporting Pedagogies: Performing Culture & Identity in the Global Arena* (Peter Lang, 2005), which received the 2006 NASSS Outstanding Book award. In addition to a series of books edited with Norman K. Denzin on qualitative inquiry and interpretive research, he is the editor of *Youth Culture & Sport: Identity, Power, and Politics* (Routledge, 2007, with Michele K. Donnelly) and *Globalizing Cultural Studies: Methodological Interventions in Theory, Method, and Policy* (Peter Lang, 2007, with Cameron McCarthy, Aisha Durham, Laura Engel, Alice Filmer, and Miguel Malagreca). His work has appeared in scholarly journals such as *Qualitative Inquiry*; *Cultural Studies ↔ Critical Methodologies*; *American Behavioral Scientist*; *Policy Futures in Education*; and *Journal of Sport & Social Issues*. He is associate editor of the *Sociology of Sport Journal*, special issue editor of *Cultural Studies ↔ Critical Methodologies*, and the associate director of the International Congress of Qualitative Inquiry.

Contributors

Russell Bishop is Foundation Professor for Māori Education in the School of Education at the University of Waikato, Hamilton, New Zealand. He is also a qualified and experienced secondary school teacher. Prior to his present appointment he was a senior lecturer in Māori Education in the Education Department at the University of Otago and interim director for Otago University's Teacher Education program. His research experience in the area of collaborative storying as Kaupapa Māori has given rise to national and international publishing, including the books, *Collaborative Research Stories: Whakawhanaungatanga* (Dunmore Press, 1996); *Culture Counts: Changing Power Relationships in Classrooms* (Zed Books, 2003); *Pathologising Practices: The Impact of Deficit Thinking on Education* (Peter Lang, 2004), *Culture Speaks: Cultural Relationships and Classroom Learning* (Huia, 2007); and *Scaling Up Education Reform* (NZCER Press, 2012).

Fred Boateng is a doctoral fellow in the School of Human Development and Organizational Studies at the University of Florida. He is the author of *An Examination of the State's Role in Ghana's Higher Education System: Status Quo Ante, Status Quo* (Lambert, 2011).

César A. Cisneros Puebla is a professor in the Department of Sociology at Autonomous Metropolitan University-Iztapalapa, Mexico. He consults in the field of qualitative computing and research within South America and abroad, and has conducted research projects supported by the U.S. Centers for Disease Control and Prevention. He has been a visiting professor at the International Institute for Qualitative Methodology, University of Alberta, Canada, and in the CAQDAS Networking Project at the University of Surrey, United Kingdom.

Christine Daum is a PhD candidate in Rehabilitation Science at the University of Alberta, Canada. She holds a Bachelor of Science in Occupational Therapy and a Master of Science in Health Promotion. Through her clinical work in long-term care and community-based rehabilitation settings, Christine generated an interest in the transactions between social and physical environments, participation, and health. Her research and teaching interests also include healthy aging, occupational science, community based participatory research, and qualitative methods. Christine's PhD project explores how inner-city neighborhoods shape older women's everyday activities.

Cynthia B. Dillard is the Mary Frances Early Professor of Teacher Education at the University of Georgia. Her major research interests include critical multicultural education, spirituality in teaching and learning, epistemological concerns in research, and African/African American feminist studies. Most recently, her research has focused on Ghana, West Africa, where she established a preschool and was enstooled as Nana Mansa II, Queen Mother of Development, in the village of Mpeasem, Ghana. She is the author of *On Spiritual Strivings: Transforming an African American Woman's Life* (State University of New York Press, 2007); *Learning to (Re)member the Things We've Learned to Forget: Endarkened Feminisms, Spirituality, and the Sacred Nature* *of Research & Teaching* (Peter Lang, 2012); and *Engaging Culture, Race, and Spirituality: New Visions* (with Chinwe L. Ezueh Okpalaoka [Peter Lang, 2013]).

Uwe Flick is professor for qualitative social and educational research at the Free University of Berlin. Before that he worked at the Alice Salomon University in Berlin in the field of health services research, which is still his major area of research, with a focus on vulnerability and service utilization. He is author or editor of numerous textbooks and handbooks, most of which have been translated into several languages in Europe, Latin America, and Asia. His books include *An Introduction to Qualitative Research* (5th Ed. 2014, Sage), *The SAGE Handbook of Qualitative Data Analysis* (Sage, 2014), *Introducing Research Methodology: A Beginners' Guide to Doing a Research Project* (Sage, 2011), and the *Qualitative Research Kit* (Sage, 2007, 8 Volumes).

Henry A. Giroux holds the Global TV Network chair professorship at McMaster University in the English and Cultural Studies Department. His most recent books include: *America's Education Deficit and the War on Youth: Reform Beyond Electoral Politics* (Monthly Review Press, 2013); *Youth in Revolt: Reclaiming a Democratic Future* (Paradigm, 2013); *The Twilight of the Social: Resurgent Politics in an Age of Disposability* (Paradigm, 2012); *On Critical Pedagogy* (Continuum, 2011); and *Zombie Politics and Culture in the Age of Casino Capitalism* (Peter Lang, 2010).

Mirka Koro-Ljungberg is a professor of Qualitative Research and associate director of the School of Human Development and Organizational Studies in Education at the University of Florida. She is the author of *Naming the Multiple: Segments of Scientific Giftedness* (University of Helsinki Press, 2001) and *Reconceptualizing Qualitative Research: Doing and Thinking Methodologies without Methodologies* (Sage, forthcoming). Her work has appeared in journals such as *Qualitative Inquiry, Qualitative Research, Cultural Studies ↔ Critical Methodologies, Field Methods*, and *International Review of Qualitative Research*.

Margaret Kovach is an associate professor of Educational Foundations at the University of Saskatchewan, Canada. She is the author of *Indigenous Methodologies: Characteristics, Conversations,* *and Contexts* (University of Toronto Press, 2009). Her work has appeared in such journals as *Canadian Review of Social Policy*, *Canadian Journal of Native Education*, and *First People Child & Family Review*.

Lory J. Maddox is senior clinical consultant, Intermountain Healthcare, and a PhD student in the College of Nursing at the University of Utah.

Virginie Magnat is an associate professor in Creative and Critical Studies, and program coordinator for Interdisciplinary Performance, Faculty of Creative and Critical Studies, at the University of British Columbia, Okanagan. Her work sits at the intersection of performance studies, cultural anthropology, experimental ethnography, and Indigenous epistemologies and methodologies. She is the author most recently of *Grotowski, Women, and Contemporary Performance: Meetings with Remarkable Women* (Routledge, 2013), the first examination of women's foremost contributions to Jerzy Grotowski's cross-cultural investigation of performance.

Kim Martz is an assistant professor, School of Nursing, at Boise State University. She has participated in research projects dealing with end of life issues and vulnerable populations, such as with the Idaho End of Life Coalition and with Somali Bantu refugees.

Maria Mayan is an associate professor, Faculty of Extension at the University of Alberta, Canada, and has studied, written about, and conducted qualitative research since the early 1990s. She is an engaged scholar who situates her work at the intersection of government, not-for-profit, disadvantaged, and clinician communities. She focuses on how we can work together on complex health and social issues using qualitative research in rigorous yet creative ways. She joined the Community-University Partnership for the Study of Children, Youth, and Families as assistant director of Women's and Children's Health with the mandate of building qualitative research and community based research capacity for health researchers. One of her most valued activities is joining with colleagues and graduate students to use both conventional and unconventional qualitative methods to explore intriguing and pressing health research issues.

Donna M. Mertens is a professor in the Department of Educational Foundations and Research at Gallaudet University. She is the author most recently of Program Evaluation Theory and Practice: A Comprehensive Guide (with Amy T. Wilson, Guilford, 2012); *Transformative Research and Evaluation* (Guilford, 2008); *Research and Evaluation in Education and Psychology: Integrating Diversity with Quantitative, Qualitative, and Mixed Methods* (2nd ed., Sage, 2005), and editor of the Handbook of Social Research Ethics (with Pauline Ginsburg, Sage, 2008). She is also widely published in journals such as the *Journal of Mixed Methods Research, American Journal of Evaluation, American Annals of the Deaf,* and *Educational Evaluation and Policy Analysis.*

Janice Morse is the Ida May "Dotty" Barnes, RN, & D. Keith Barnes, M.D., Presidential Endowed Chair and professor of Nursing in the College of Nursing at the University of Utah, and professor emeritus at the University of Alberta, Canada, and the Pennsylvania State University. From 1997 to 2007 she was the founding director and scientific director of the International Institute for Qualitative Methodology, University of Alberta, founding editor of the *International Journal of Qualitative Methods,* and editor for the Qual Press monograph series. She presently serves as the founding editor of *Qualitative Health Research,* and is the editor for the monograph series *Developing Qualitative Inquiry* and *Qualitative Essentials* (Left Coast). Her research programs are in the areas of suffering and comforting, preventing patient falls (she is the author of the Morse Fall Scale, used internationally to triage the fall-prone patient), and developing qualitative methods. Morse was an inaugural inductee into the Sigma Theta Tau International Nurse Researcher Hall of Fame, was recipient of the Episteme Award (Sigma Theta Tau), received the Lifetime Achievement Award from the International Congress of Qualitative Inquiry, and has been awarded honorary doctorates from the University of Newcastle (Australia) and Athabasca University (Canada). She is the author of 460 articles and book chapters and 19 books on qualitative research methods, suffering, comforting, and patient falls.

Bekisizwe S. Ndimande is assistant professor of Interdisciplinary Learning and Teaching in the College of Education & Human Development at the University of Texas at San Antonio. His research interest includes the politics of curriculum, examining the policies and practices in post-apartheid desegregated public schools, and the implications of school "choice" for marginalized communities in South Africa.

Laurel Richardson is professor emeritus of Sociology at the Ohio State University. She specializes in qualitative methodology, gender, symbolic interactionism, the sociology of knowledge and arts-based research. She served as co-editor of the Feminist Frontiers series and has authored numerous books, including Cooley Award-winner *Fields of Play* (Rutgers, 1997), *Writing Strategies* (Sage, 1990), *The New Other Woman* (Free Press, 1987), *Travels with Ernest* (AltaMira, 2004), *After a Fall* (Left Coast, 2013), and *Last Writes* (Left Coast, 2007).

Gundula Röhnsch works at the Alice Salomon University in Berlin, Germany, in a project focusing on service utilization of Russian speaking migrants with alcohol and drug problems in Germany. Before that she worked in a number of research projects focusing on chronic illness of homeless adolescents and sleeping problems in nursing homes.

Brian Rusted is a professor of Communication and Culture at the University of Calgary, Canada. He specializes in cultural performance, visual and material culture, and the use of visual media in qualitative research. He is the founding co-editor of the journal *Culture and Organization*, and sits on editorial boards for *Text and Performance Quarterly*, *Visual Studies*, and *Visual Communication Quarterly*. He is past chair of the Visual Communication Division of the National Communication Association, former Coordinator of the Calgary Stampede's Western Art Show, and past chair of the Calgary Stampede's annual Western Art Auction.

Jane Speedy is emeritus professor in the Graduate School of Education at the University of Bristol, United Kingdom, where she is also coordinator of CeNTraL, the Centre for Narratives and Transformative Learning. She is the author most recently of *Narrative Inquiry and Psychotherapy* (PalgraveMacmillan, 2008).

C. Darius Stonebanks is a professor in the School of Education at Bishop's University, Canada. He is the author of *James Bay Cree*

336 • About the Authors

and Higher Education: Issues of Culture and Identity Shock, and co-editor of *Teaching Against Islamophobia* and the award-winning *Muslim Voices in Schools*. He is the coordinator of Praxis Malawi, for which Spring 2014 will mark the sixth consecutive year he has organized experiential learning projects for Bishop's and McGill University undergraduate and graduate students in the rural region of Kasungu, Malawi, connecting social justice theory to practice.

Beth Blue Swadener is professor of Justice and Social Inquiry and associate director of the School of Social Transformation at Arizona State University. Her research focuses on internationally comparative social policy, especially in sub-Saharan Africa; impacts of neoliberal policy on local communities; and children's rights and voices. She is author or editor of ten books, including *Reconceptualizing the Early Childhood Curriculum* (Teachers College Press, 1992); *Children and Families "At Promise"* (SUNY Press, 1995); *Decolonizing Research in Cross-Cultural Context, Power and Voice in Research with Children* (SUNY Press, 2011), and *Children's Rights and Education* (Peter Lang, 2013). She serves as associate editor of the *American Educational Research Journal*.

Terrie Vann-Ward is a visiting professor at Chamberlain University and a PhD candidate in the College of Nursing at the University of Utah.